Biggleswade
and the Great War
Our Own Flesh and Blood

Kenneth Wood

First published 2009

The History Press
The Mill, Brimscombe Port
Stroud, Gloucestershire, GL5 2QG
www.thehistorypress.co.uk

© Kenneth Wood, 2009

The right of Kenneth Wood to be identified as the Author
of this work has been asserted in accordance with the
Copyrights, Designs and Patents Act 1988.

All rights reserved. No part of this book may be reprinted
or reproduced or utilised in any form or by any electronic,
mechanical or other means, now known or hereafter invented,
including photocopying and recording, or in any information
storage or retrieval system, without the permission in writing
from the Publishers.

British Library Cataloguing in Publication Data.
A catalogue record for this book is available from the British Library.

ISBN 978 0 7524 4966 1

Typesetting and origination by The History Press
Printed in Great Britain

Contents

	Acknowledgements	4
	Foreword	5
	Glossary	6
	Introduction	9
1.	1914 A Call to Arms – Biggleswade Goes to War	11
2.	1915 A Widening Conflict	38
3.	1916 Enter the Citizens' Armies	56
4.	1917 Soldiering on – Arras, Passchendaele, Gaza and Cambrai	78
5.	1918 From Defeat to Victory	116
	Epilogue	138
	Appendix 1	149
	Appendix 2	149
	Appendix 3	150
	Appendix 4	154
	Appendix 5	157
	Appendix 6	157
	Index	158

Acknowledgements

I started this book with the intention of completing it over a period of about two years. That was a serious underestimation on my part and, as it took longer to write than the Great War lasted. Now that it is complete I must thank the following: Great uncle Harry; Private W.H. Wood, 5203, 12th Battalion, Northumberland Fusiliers killed on 22 September on the Somme aged nineteen, and who started me on this quest; James Stewart, editor of the *Biggleswade Chronicle*, for his permission to use extracts and photographs from editions of the *Chronicle* from the period of the Great War; Steve Fuller and his excellent website on the Bedfordshire Regiment in the Great War – if only I had discovered it earlier I would have been saved hours of work! Martin Edwards and the Roll of Honour website – a labour of love. It has been a privilege to be able to add to the Biggleswade section; the Commonwealth War Graves Commission website – the starting place for anyone seeking details of relatives who died in the Great War; Ashley Atkinson and Graham Crust, who have accompanied me on many trips to the Western Front – both have been kind enough to bear with me in the quest to locate the graves of the men featured in the book and take photographs as we criss-crossed Northern France and Belgium. Their knowledge and support were invaluable, as was their company as we enjoyed a well-deserved meal and glass of wine at our hotels at the end of those long days on the Somme, at Ypres, Arras, Vimy, Neuve Chapelle, Festubert and Loos. Ashley kindly provided me with photographs from Gallipoli; The staff and students of Stratton Upper School who accompanied me on so many trips to the battlefields, and proved to be such excellent ambassadors for their school, town and country. I apologise if I have infected them with my passion for the Great War! Professor Gary Sheffield of Birmingham University's Centre for First World War Studies for his help, advice and support, especially in directing me towards the History Press, the book's publishers; Biggleswade Historical Society, especially Mike and Jean Strange for their help with the map of Biggleswade and the location of the adresses of families who lost men in the Great War; Billy Doey for his work in scanning photographs, improving their quality and then putting them on disc for me; Mark Thody for his help in creating the maps used; Jane Hunter for proof reading the first edition, Victoria Lincoln and Richard Delahuntey for their publishing advice, my dear wife Shirley, who has supported me throughout, and whose forgiveness I must ask for all of the nights that I disappeared upstairs to our study to write this book.

As the book progressed I felt that I grew to know the men that I was writing about. I came to understand them and to appreciate their bravery, their fortitude, their resilience, their love of their families and country, and their strength in the face of such adversity. I hope that they would feel my work does their effort and sacrifice justice. Of the men on the memorial two have eluded me: Private F.B. Potton of the West Kent Regiment and Operator M.W. Denny. I can find no trace of Private Potton other than that he was killed in action during either 1915 or 1916. Operator M.W. Denny has proved equally difficult to track down. If I were to hazard a guess then I would say that he was probably a trainee signaller who met an unfortunate end during his training, sometime during 1916 or 1917. There was a shop in Biggleswade owned by F.M. Denny that specialised in 'reliable footwear at reasonable cost', and when the War Memorial was dedicated in 1921 there were flowers from the Denny family. Perhaps Operator Denny was a relative.

Foreword

The research undertaken for this book is not to be underestimated. It is clearly the result of many hundreds of hours of dedicated, painstaking and meticulous study and investigation. As such, it is of immense value, not only to those whose interests lie in Biggleswade, but also to general researchers of the military and social implications of the Great War.

We are most fortunate that Kenneth resides in our midst and chose to write about this town and not one of the many other towns that were similarly affected by this terrible event in our history.

We are also fortunate that Kenneth has not just researched for his personal use but has decided to share the information he amassed. It is now accessible for all to read, to enjoy, be enriched by and be deeply moved by. This book shall certainly be a most welcome addition to the archives of Biggleswade.

Mike Strange
Hon. Archivist, Biggleswade History Society

Glossary

All arms attack – by 1918 the BEF had become tactically adept in employing artillery, infantry, aircraft and tanks together to devastating effect. This was a war-winning development.

Artillery barrages – the main weapon used by both sides on the Western Front. Artillery bombardments were a common feature of most sections of the front where the BEF served. The early morning and evening bombardments were known as 'morning and evening hate'.

Attrition – the policy of wearing down the enemy, and the side with the most surviving would win. The term comes from the French word 'usure', meaning to wear down. The German Army employed the tactic at Verdun in 1916, but today it is often associated with battles such as the Somme and Passchendaele.

Bantams – the term used for men who had been originally rejected for being too small and for having too small a chest measurement. By 1915 these men were now needed and special Bantam Battalions were formed. Their height was between 5' 1" and 5' 4".

Battery – an artillery unit with six guns

BEF – the British Expeditionary Force. This is the official name given to the British and Imperial armies that fought on the Western Front.

Blighty – slang term for Britain used by serving soldiers.

Blighty One – a wound that would see soldiers returning to Britain for treatment.

Bombers – the name by which grenade throwers were known during the First World War. The main grenade used by the BEF was the Mills bomb. Platoons had their specialist bombers whose job it was to bomb their way through enemy trenches to secure them.

Box barrage – a concentrated artillery bombardment that was used to protect troops after they had captured enemy trenches. It also prevented German troops from counter-attacking.

Bully – bully beef was the standard ration for British troops. It was similar to corned beef.

Casualty Clearing Station – an area for treating soldiers behind the front lines. Doctors and nurses worked tirelessly to try to save soldiers' lives.

Communication trench – a confined trench that zigzagged its way to and from the front line. These trenches frequently became very congested as troops moved up and down from the front. Changeovers often took hours. The congestion increased following attacks as wounded men were brought back by stretcher bearers through communication trenches.

GLOSSARY

Conscientious objectors – men who, on the basis of religious or moral principles, refused to bear arms or participate in military service during the war. Many served as stretcher bearers in the most dangerous of situations, however.

Conscription – The Military Service Act of 27 January 1916 brought compulsory enrolment to Britain. At first it applied only to single men aged between eighteen and forty-one. This was extended by 1918 to all men, both single and married, aged eighteen to fifty-one.

Counter-battery work – the tactic of seeking and destroying enemy artillery, used to great effect during the Battle of Amiens in August 1918 when British guns destroyed almost every German gun emplacement.

Creeping barrage – a wall of exploding shells that advancing soldiers followed. This gave them protection as they crossed No Man's Land.

Derby Scheme – the final recruitment drive before conscription was introduced. Eligible men were invited to commit themselves to joining up as required. By doing so they could choose the regiment they wished to serve with. These men wore a special armband to show their commitment, which gave them some protection from being given 'white feathers'.

Dog tags – these were identification labels worn by soldiers. During the First World War these were made of leather or a cardboard-type substance. Soldiers wore two – one red and one green. The red one was collected from dead soldiers, whilst the green one was left on the body. Popular belief was that the red symbolised the blood of the dead, and that the green symbolised the earth in which the body would be buried.

Enfilade fire – machine gun or rifle fire from the flanks along a trench or a line of troops. This is one reason why trench lines were not dug in straight lines, for an enemy breaking into the trench would have been able to set up and fire machine guns along the whole length of the trench. Instead, they were dug in a zigzag fashion with bays and traverses

Kitchener's New Armies – the name given to the men who responded to Lord Kitchener's call for volunteers in 1914.

Lewis gun – a light, portable machine gun used by the BEF to good effect.

Mines – underground tunnels were dug under the enemy trenches and then a huge amount of explosive, usually ammonal, was placed there ready to be exploded at the start of an attack. Often fighting ranged underground as both German and British tunnellers sought to destroy each other's work. The mine at Lochnagar on the Somme left a crater 90ft deep and 300ft across. The noise of the explosion was said to be heard back in Britain.

Minenwerfer – German trench mortar.

Mortars – trench mortars and Stokes Mortars were used by the BEF to propel bombs into enemy trenches.

No Man's Land – area between the two front lines, varying in distance from a few yards to hundreds of yards.

Parapet – front of a trench that faced the enemy

Push – the term used to describe a large-scale attack on enemy positions. The Somme was referred to as the 'Big Push'.

Race to the sea 1914 – following the German retreat after the Battle of the Marne, both sides tried to outflank each other moving northwards. This is referred to as the 'race to the sea'.

GLOSSARY

Redoubt – a defensive stronghold contained within the trench system that was heavily fortified. The Germans built many of these, including the Schwaben Redoubt, on the Somme. The BEF would try to incorporate them within the defenses they constructed to oppose the German Spring Offensive of 1918.

Respirator – a gas mask.

Runner – a soldier who carried messages from the front line back to HQ, and then returned with the response. A very dangerous job with high casualty rates.

Salient – A military position, such as that at Ypres, that projects forward towards the enemy. These were very dangerous, for soldiers within a salient could be fired upon from the front and from two sides.

Sandbags – coarse sacks that were filled with soil and then used in the building of defences. Soldiers used spare sandbags to carry food and kit, as pillows and even to collect body parts of their comrades blown to pieces by shelling.

Shell shock – psychological trauma caused by extended exposure to enemy shelling.

Shrapnel – metal from exploding shells that varied in size, from small steel balls to parts of shell casing that could be quite large. Before the introduction of steel helmets fatalities from shrapnel shells were frequent.

Stand-to – daily routine at dawn and nightfall, when soldiers in the front line were required to man the fire-step of their trench in case of an enemy attack. These times were when enemy attacks were most likely to occur.

Suicide club – term used by men in the Machine Gun Corps to describe the dangerous nature of their work

Territorial Army – a force that was set up in 1907 with the intention of being used to defend Britain in the event of attack. The men received fifteen days' training per year together with drilling, and they numbered about 250,000 on the eve of war. They were initially referred to as 'Weekend or Saturday night soldiers' but they certainly proved their worth, seeing service overseas from late 1914 right through to the Armistice.

Tommy – slang for the British soldier, derived from Tommy Atkins, a term used as far back as the Battle of Waterloo and the Duke of Wellington.

Top brass – high-ranking officers in the British Army.

Trench raids – sorties made across No Man's Land to capture enemy soldiers for interrogation. These raids were seen as important by High Command as they kept aggression to the fore, and guarded against the 'live and let live' attitude developing.

Vickers machine gun – a heavy machine gun with a huge killing capacity. From 1916 machine gun barrages were used to support attacks.

War diary – name for the official record of a battalion. Such diaries gave details of movement, attacks and, sometimes, details of soldiers. Usually, however, this meant officers, but some diaries give details of men awarded medals, those involved in trench raids and those mentioned in dispatches. For anyone wishing to research they are an excellent source.

Whizz bang – term widely used by British soldiers for small-calibre German shells. The name comes from the sound these shells made in the air followed by the explosion.

Yeomanry – mounted territorials.

Introduction

The Great War – the words still hold a fascination even as we approach the ninety-fourth anniversary of its start and the ninetieth of its ending. Logically it should be assumed that this would not be the case and that these four years, four months and two days of bitter and prolonged fighting would have been consigned to history in the way that all previous wars had been. Yet this is not so and interest remains high, as can be seen in the increasing number of visitors to the battlefields of the Western Front and the ever-growing number of books published on the subject.

Each year I lead parties of students and adults to the Somme and Ypres, and over the last seven years that I have had the privilege of doing so, the number of coaches at Lochnagar Crater, the Thiepval Memorial to the Missing, the Ulster Tower, Delville Wood and Newfoundland Park on the Somme has visibly increased. At Menin Gate in Ypres the number of those present at the Last Post ceremony has grown similarly, and there are now high-tech visitor centres at Thiepval and Tyn Cot.

Amazon.co.uk lists over 7,000 books that are available on the Great War and at least one British university has a department that specialises in the study of the First World War.

If I were to speculate about the reasons for this then a number of possibilities immediately spring to mind:

- This was the first war of which we have significant surviving film footage
- The sheer number of casualties, not least for the UK alone
- Virtually every village and town has a war memorial dedicated to the memory of those who fought and did not return
- The 'Blackadder' effect and the continued popularity of the war poets of the Great War
- The work of revisionist historians who seek to give a more balanced view of the Great War and counter the work of those who consider the war to have been futile. Their work is controversial to some but it encourages healthy debate
- The fact that we have experienced a huge growth in the idea of family history with greater access to records via the development of the internet as a tool for research

INTRODUCTION

I am, to use Richard Holmes' words, 'haunted' by the Western Front. It is a consuming passion that was sparked off at an early age by the stories in my family of the death of great uncle Harry, a volunteer for Kitchener's New Armies who lost his life on the Somme. As a young boy I can remember looking at his Victory Medal and wondering if his was the body of the 'Unknown Soldier' buried at Westminster Abbey. As I have grown older the need to find out more about him and what happened to him has become something of a personal crusade, as well as wanting to pay him the respect that his sacrifice merits. My research showed me how accessible historical sources can be, revealed the wealth of information that is out there that can be uncovered, and culminated with my discovery of where he is buried and visits to his grave in France.

The work that I carried out looking at local newspapers from the period, together with investigation of regimental war diaries for the war, was experience that I felt that I could draw upon and employ in a bigger project – not just for one person but also for the town where I had taught since 1991.

The following pages are my humble attempt to tell the story of the Great War through the eyes of those who fought, those who died, those who survived and those who remained behind.

This is the story of Biggleswade and the Great War.

Kenneth Wood
Eaton Socon

The author explaining the Lochnagar Crater on the Somme to students from Stratton School.

ONE

1914

A Call to Arms – Biggleswade Goes to War

The second of August 1914 was a typical Sunday in Biggleswade but the expectation of a bank holiday to follow on the Monday must have been an attractive alternative to the prospect of work for many. This would especially have been the case as the Biggleswade Liberal Club and Association were about to hold their ninth annual fete and sports meeting in what would be the aptly named Mr. Kitchiner's Meadow off Hitchin Street. However events were moving quickly on the continent and by the end of the day the possibility of war in Europe increased significantly. On 2 August Germany's issue of an ultimatum to Belgium to allow the passage of its troops through their country was to have severe repercussions. The British response was quick and on the following day the Cabinet delivered its own ultimatum to Germany. Prime Minister Asquith announced in the House of Commons:

> We have repeated the request made last week to the German Government that they should give us the same assurance in regard to Belgian neutrality that was given to us and Belgium by France last week. We have asked that it should be given before midnight.

The initial reaction to the events of Sarajevo over a month earlier had been one of outrage throughout Europe but the move towards war did not seem immediate and it was almost as if the major powers were moving in slow motion. Many did not expect that the assassination of Franz Ferdinand would lead to a general European war but slow motion turned to a jog and then a sprint as ultimatum followed ultimatum. As the crisis developed the people of Britain would have been acutely aware of where events appeared to be leading with all of the popular national newspapers reporting the developments that were taking place in Vienna, Belgrade, Berlin, Paris and Moscow. The expectation of war was easy to see, and the desire to put the German upstart in his place was welcomed by a considerable majority of the people of Britain. Reaction in the popular press supported the British Government's position to the main, with only the *Daily Herald* taking an anti-war stance. Fuelled by the popular press, many felt strongly that the guarantee of Belgian neutrality was an important issue and it was felt that we, as a nation, could not stand aside.

Poster advertising the 9th Liberal Fête on August Bank Holiday 1914.

The clock was counting down and the British ultimatum would expire at 11 p.m. BST on 3 August.

The Bank Holiday began with fine weather but ominously, dark clouds began to gather as one of the largest crowds there had been for the Liberal Fête congregated in Mr Kitchiner's Meadow. Perhaps those clouds were mirroring the events taking place in London, Berlin and Brussels. Showers around 1 p.m. did not detract from the entertainment with a variety of flat, hurdle and cycle races taking place which had attracted healthy numbers of competitors. Many of the prizes were in cash and the competitors came from as far afield as Bedford, Higham Ferrers, Hitchin and Elstow. At 4 p.m. the heavens opened and many of the crowd who were dressed for a summer's day were soaked. The tug-of-war was the most popular event and it attracted a first prize of £3 that was won by a Langford team led by Tom Piper, with second prize of 30 shillings (s) going to another Langford team led by Joe Brown. Following prize giving at about 6 p.m. the local MP for the mid-Bedfords area, Mr Arthur Black, gave a speech outlining England's position with regard to the crisis in Europe – five hours later Britain's ultimatum to Germany expired. No response was made and Britain found itself involved in a major European war for the first time for almost 100 years – Biggleswade was about to go to war.

The newspapers that arrived in the town on 4 and 5 August did not have the front-page headlines that we are used to today. Rather the front page and often the next three would contain advertisements, private notices, extraordinary remedies and even lost pets columns. By the time you reached the fourth page you would be confronted with home and European news, and, as today, the last pages would be dedicated to sport. With no media in the sense that we know it via television or radio, the daily newspaper was the most important source of information for the common man as sales of over 1 million per day for a paper such as the *Daily Mirror* indicate. The publications of the Tuesday and the Wednesday of the first week of August 1914 supported the government's decision and the headline of the *Daily Express* on 5 August summed up feeling well with a familiar phrase: 'England expects that every man will do his duty'.

The British Regular Army in 1914 numbered around 156,000 men, with a further 78,400 stationed in India. The soldiers of that army were all volunteers who had signed on for a twelve-year stint that saw seven or eight years with 'the colours', as active service was known and a further four to five years in reserve. In addition to this there was the Territorial Army that had been established by the Haldane Reform in 1907. These men received fifteen days training per year together with drilling and they numbered about 250,000 on the eve of war. Men from Biggleswade fell into the Serving, Reservist and Territorial categories and by Tuesday evening both the post office and the police station in the town would display the following notices:

CENTRAL MOBILISATION ARMY RESERVE
REGULAR AND SPECIAL RESERVES

His Majesty the King has been graciously pleased to direct by proclamation the Army Reserve be called up on permanent service. All Regular Reservists are required to report themselves at once at their place of joining, in accordance with the instructions on their identity certificates for the purpose of joining the Army.

All Special Reservists are required to report themselves on such date at such place as they may be directed to attend for the purpose of joining the Army. If they have not received any such directions or if they have changed their address since last attendance at drill or training, they will report themselves at once by letter to the Adjutant of their Unit or depot. The necessary instructions as to their joining will then be given.

TERRITORIAL FORCE

His Majesty the King, having been graciously pleased to order by proclamation that directions be given by the Army Council for embodying the Territorial Force, all men belonging to the said force are required to report themselves immediately at their Headquarters.

Telegrams soon began to be delivered, calling the reservists to the colours and the sound of the doorknocker became all too familiar in an age when up to five postal deliveries a day were the norm.

Then, as now, Biggleswade's local newspaper was the *Biggleswade Chronicle* and, also as now, it hit the news-stands on Friday. The edition of 7 August had the usual mixture of local news of pigeon racing, weddings and obituaries but ominously had labelled one column 'The War'. Here it was confirmed that the town was moving towards its own mobilisation and reported that both the Reservists and the Territorials, in accordance with the instructions above, had already departed from Biggleswade. Virtually every train that left the town's railway station carried Reservists leaving to join the 'colours'; mainly the 'Bedfords', and they were soon to be joined by the Territorials. There was a noticeable difference in the mood of the men who were departing to that of the women they were leaving behind as the *Chronicle* of 7 August reported: 'The men all went off in fairly good spirits, but with the women-folk it was a different story, and as in the past women had to weep.'

'D' Company of the 5th Bedfordshire Territorials were mobilised and the 130 men who had been called up on the morning of Wednesday 5 August had their kit inspected by noon and were parading on the Market Square at teatime before they left by train for Bedford. Both the local yeomanry, who were mounted territorials, and militia were the next to depart with the train station and local buses being very busy indeed. The yeomanry would have been in quite some shape before their departure, for, in the three days that they were awaiting orders to leave, their officers had them parading and drilling every two hours!

In line with every town and city in England, years of planning were being put into action in Biggleswade. The War Office had been preparing for the eventuality of war since the Moroccan crisis of 1911 and had produced the *War Book*. By this trains were to be taken over, railway timetables were restructured, workhorses were commissioned and the mobilisation of reservists was all to be in place. The *War Book* also detailed such matters as counter-espionage, trade with enemy states, censorship, and the guarding of key points. The War Office commissioners quickly arrived in Biggleswade and by the second week of the start of hostilities the Market Square in the town resembled a horse fair, as scores of animals were brought in for inspection, and, provided they met the standard, for purchase. These animals would be used for both haulage work and as mounts for officers. The commissioners were certainly thorough in their work and there were a number of rejections.

The destination of these horses, together with that of the departing men was something of a secret for the air was rife with the fear of spies. Undeniably the country was gripped by 'spy mania' and extravagant reports of spies and spying were the order of the day. In just the surrounding areas around Biggleswade wild rumours circulated and local newspapers were full of weird and wonderful stories.

In Dunstable three motorcyclists found themselves questioned for an hour to explain their presence in the town, whilst two German waiters who were trying to get from Liverpool to the port of London were arrested in Clapham. These men had actually reached London but had missed their boat and were returning to their jobs in Liverpool when they fell foul of the authorities in Bedfordshire. They would spend the rest of the war as prisoners.

From nearby Luton a well-known local entertainer, Mr Edgar Wayne, was arrested as a spy in Dover as he returned from holiday in Europe. He spent an uncomfortable hour explaining why he had been abroad before his story was believed. Not to be outdone Bedford was awash with spy stories as the *Chronicle* of the first week of September reported the following stories that it credited to the *Bedford Daily Circular*.

THE SPY SCARE
WILD RUMOURS IN BEDFORD

> Many wild rumours of dastardly outrages perpetrated or attempted by alleged enemies in Bedford have been scattered broadcast in the town during the past few days, and all of them, upon investigation, have proved to be groundless. The German spy, who it was stated, had been caught in an attempt to blow up the gasometer at Queen's Park turned out to be a commercial traveller making his usual call at the offices.
>
> According to another rumour, a Territorial had been poisoned by a drugged cigarette, and £100 reward had been offered by the military authorities for information. Several reports have been circulated of attempts to poison the horses' water in different parts of the town, and each day there are fresh stories of the arrest of spies. The latest is to the effect that a spy was found in the officers' quarters in a Bedford hotel. All the rumours are unfounded.

If Bedfordshire was full of rumours then nearby Cambridgeshire actually saw fear and uncertainty manifest themselves, with anti German riots in Peterborough on 7 and 8 August. In the England of 1914 the presence of German shops was quite common and many Germans made their living in the country, as either shopkeepers or as workers within the hospitality and catering industry. The targets for the riots in Peterborough were two German pork butchers' shops, and later a public house. On the Friday evening a large crowd had gathered in front of the first of the shops in the Westgate area of the town and they then proceeded to pelt the shop windows with bricks, bottles and stones until every one was broken. The crowd then moved on, carrying out the same treatment to the second German shop that they passed en route, and they then wrecked the first shop owner's house. By now the authorities were starting to worry and the chief constable and the mayor agreed to take action. At first the Riot Act was read by the mayor and this was backed up with the use of 100 men of the Northants Imperial Yeomanry, who were stationed in the town, to move the crowd away. By about midnight peace had returned to the streets of Peterborough but it would not last. The following morning saw an attempt to sell off the perishable meats from the shops but another crowd quickly gathered. Pork pies and small joints of meat were seized and were used as footballs whilst strings of sausages literally went flying. The sale was soon abandoned.

Still there was more to come and, even though fifty extra constables were sworn in to add to the police presence, trouble would break out around 11.15 p.m. when the Salmon and Compasses public house was stoned. The landlord of the pub was rumoured to have spoken with derision about the local Territorial force and the crowd obviously were not in the mood to tolerate such criticism. The authorities again reacted but not with any real success, for the fire brigade, who were called to turn their hoses on the crowd, found themselves on the receiving end when the rioters gained control of the fire hoses and turned them on both the firemen and the police. It was not until 2 a.m. that the police were able to contain the troublemakers and a dozen arrests followed.

Recruitment poster from August 1914, used in Biggleswade.

In comparison Biggleswade remained quiet but busy, and the response to Kitchener's call for volunteers was the focus. Advertisements appeared in the *Chronicle* using the soon to be familiar call of 'Your country needs you'.

Readers were advised that Sergeant Yarrell of the Rising Sun could give information and that they could enlist at the drill hall. The response was quick and twenty-three men came forward at once. Two of these would be rejected, as would be George Smith of Sun Street, an experienced soldier who said: 'I should love one more go ... I could cook for the chaps if I couldn't do anything else.' George did indeed have an impressive pedigree and he had experience of fighting in trenches – at Sebastopol in the Crimean War! In 1914 he was almost eighty, and as well as Sebastopol George had fought during the Indian Mutiny of 1857-58. Pressing his claim to be allowed to enlist he had said 'During the Siege of Sebastopol they sent over some real old men to fight under the two year's enlistment regulation'. Even his membership of the National Service League did not help and much to his regret he was turned down.

Equally disappointed would be Captain Hunter of nearby Flitwick, who had offered his services to the Admiralty. He was eighty-one, had also fought in the Crimea and had been the first man to enter Sebastopol after it fell in 1855. He stressed that he had seen heaps of fighting and that he was the proud possessor of eight medals. He was to be as disappointed as George Smith.

Others were to be more successful and Sergeant Yarrell was to find himself a busy man, for the second week of recruiting saw another 111 men come forward, with recruits from Sandy and Potton also heeding the call.

The recruitment drive, spearheaded by the famous Kitchener poster, was amply aided and abetted by the increasing number of stories appearing in both the national and local press, describing the brutal nature of the German armies as they progressed through Belgium. Some of these stories were exaggeration but they were tempered by real atrocities that did wonders for enlistment and world criticism of the German military.

Both the national press and the *Chronicle* ran numerous stories of German brutality in Belgium. The following reports are taken from the *Chronicle* of Friday 28 August:

MEN BOUND AND SHOT

At Linsmeau, where a German officer was killed during the fighting, terrible vengeance was taken on the village, although none of the civilian population took part in the hostilities. Two farms and six outlying buildings were destroyed by gunfire and burnt. The Germans then gathered all the male inhabitants together and divided them into three groups. Those in one group were bound and eleven of them placed in a ditch, where they were afterwards found dead — their skulls fractured by the butts of German rifles.

SLICED AND BURNT ALIVE

Farmer Jef Dierick, of Neerhenpem, bears witness to the following acts of cruelty committed by German cavalry at Orsmael and Neerhenpem on August 10th, 11th, and 12th.

An old man of the latter village had his arm sliced in three longitudinal cuts; he was then hung head downwards and burnt alive. Young girls have been raped and little children outraged, and at Orsmael several inhabitants suffered mutilation too horrible to describe.

A Belgian soldier belonging to a battalion of cyclist engineers who had been wounded and made prisoner was hung, whilst another who was tending his comrade was bound to a telegraph pole on the same Trond road and shot.

TWO TRUSSED, SHOT AND HACKED

On Monday August 10th, at Orsmael, the Germans picked up Commandant Knapen, very seriously wounded, trussed him up against a tree, and shot him. Finally they hacked his corpse with swords.

In different places, notably at Hollogue-sur-Geer, Barchan Pontiffe Haelen, Zelek, German troops have fired on doctors, ambulance bearers, ambulances and ambulance wagons carrying the Red Cross, and they have fired upon the White Flag.

SHOOTING OF A MAYOR

> At Aersschot on August 18th, in one single street, the first six male inhabitants who crossed their threshold were seized and shot at once, under the very eyes of their wives and children. On the next day the Germans returned. They compelled the inhabitants to leave their house, and marched them to a place 200 yards from the town. There, without more ado, M. Thielemans, the Burgomaster, his fifteen-year-old son, the clerk to the Legal Judicial Board, and ten prominent citizens were shot. The Germans then set fire to the town and destroyed it.
>
> Further German atrocities are continuously being brought to notice and may be the subject of official and expert inquiry by the authorities.
>
> In publishing the above statement, the only comment the Press Bureau can offer is that these atrocities appear to be committed in villages and throughout the countryside with the deliberate intention of terrorising the people and so making it unnecessary to leave troops in occupation of small places or to protect the lines of communication. In large places like Brussels, where diplomatic representatives of neutral Powers are eye-witnesses, there appear to have been no excesses.

The reaction to such stories in Biggleswade is not hard to imagine and the outrage would have been amplified in that the possibility of a German invasion of Britain was felt to be quite real. For many years before the outbreak of the war, many fictional accounts of such an event had been best sellers with the public. One of the first great spy novels, *The Riddle of the Sands*, set during the long suspicious years leading up to the Great War would have been read by many. The story was one that built in excitement as two young men on a sailing holiday discovered a German plot to invade England. In an age where reading was more popular than it is today, the stories emanating from the invasion of Belgium would have struck a chord, and the fiction of Erskine Childers would be added to throughout the conflict by publications such as John Hannay's *The Thirty Nine Steps*. Germans made acceptable villains and a Parliamentary Recruiting Committee was soon busy at work setting up the production of a number of posters urging the country to 'Remember Belgium' and to encourage recruitment.

As well as the stories of atrocities, readers in Biggleswade were remarkably well informed about the progress of the war in those first few weeks. Columns of the *Chronicle* were dedicated to coverage of events on what were to become known as the Eastern Front and the Western Front. Articles entitled 'Stories from the Front' described a range of situations involving troops and civilians, and recounted both success and setbacks. The mood of these reports was bullish and the importance of maintaining morale was evident throughout them.

So what exactly was happening on the continent? At the start of the hostilities the German High Command was aware that the fighting of a war on two fronts would be unlikely to lead to victory. Therefore they felt it was imperative to deliver a knockout blow to one of their major enemies before the other could mobilise its forces. The Schlieffen Plan was their solution to this situation. In essence this would allow them to defeat France before Russia could move its armies into the field. The plan had been devised in 1899, revised in 1906 and assumed that it would take Russia six weeks to get herself ready to fight. This, it was felt, would give Germany plenty of time to defeat France. The plan required Belgium to allow the German Armies to pass through her country, for the German armies to sweep southwards and capture Paris, thus bringing the French to defeat.

The French meanwhile had their own plan that they hoped would bring them victory. Following their defeat in the Franco-Prussian war in 1871 they had come to the conclusion that the way to recapture past glory and to defeat their enemies was a return to what they did best, and that was the emphasis upon attack. Thus Plan XVII would see invasion of Germany, drawing upon the heritage of *la gloire* from the time of Napoleon. All-out attack combining infantry and artillery would see the recapture of Alsace and Lorraine, and, in theory, would lead to the defeat of Germany. The plan did not include the British and was a reactive one, in that it waited upon Germany making the first move. The French stuck rigidly to this plan, even though the Schlieffen plan swung into action, and they failed to acknowledge the development of warfare since the time of Napoleon. Thousands of Frenchmen, dressed in their distinctive red and blue, advanced into the killing fury of the Maxim machine gun and the destructive power of modern artillery. Casualties were enormous and the French lost over a tenth of their officer corps during this fighting.

The German advance into Belgium was also not experiencing the smooth ride that had been expected and the resistance of the Belgian armies, fortified cities and towns was proving to be a problem for them. Indeed this slowing down of the German advance would prove to be critical for Germany's long-term chances of victory.

So these were the opening moves of the Great War that the British Expeditionary Force would find itself involved in following its embarkation for France. That this army was small in comparison to both the German and French is undeniable, but it was well trained and in all senses of the word, professional. Men, horses and equipment were shipped across the Channel, although not as quickly as our French allies would have liked, and disembarked at the ports of Boulogne, Rouen and Le Havre. They were escorted by the Royal Navy and to the great credit of the 'Senior Service' no ship was lost. Landings began on 9 August, with the 'Tommies' receiving a very warm welcome from French civilians, and fourteen days later on 23 August this small 'Contemptible' army, as the Kaiser is supposed to have labelled them, would cut its teeth at the Battle of Mons where its accurate and withering fire would surprise the enemy. Men from Biggleswade numbered amongst this regular army in both the infantry and artillery.

The battle that took place at Mons saw the British outnumbered by just over two to one with 70,000 British troops facing 160,000 Germans. The ratio of guns was similar with 300 to 600. The battle was very different from those that we associate with the Great War, for it was fought in the open and was not the kind of trench warfare that the Western Front conjures up. The advancing German First Army had no real idea of the whereabouts of the BEF but, upon encountering them a frontal attack was launched. The British infantry at Mons drew upon their marksmanship with the Short Magazine

Lee Enfield 303 rifle. The men were trained to a very high standard and could fire at least fifteen aimed rounds per minute, and the story goes that this fire was so precise and devastating that the advancing Germans believed that they were facing machine guns. What is true is that the British Army did reward its soldiers with extra pay for proficiency with the rifle and that this speed and accuracy of fire was put to very good use at Mons. The advancing Germans made a good target for such well-trained men as they moved forward in block formation and, by the end of the day the German First Army had suffered over 5,000 casualties. British losses amounted to around 1,600 – much of these coming from artillery bombardment. The German soldier had learned a painful lesson at Mons and as one captured German was to say, 'that the Russians can't shoot at all, that the French are not good shots, but that the English shoot and kill.'

Equally effective at Mons was the performance of the British Artillery but, although the advance had been halted, the sheer numbers of the advancing Germans meant that the BEF would have to retreat. This withdrawal was to be exhausting and prolonged, but it was a retreat and not a rout and the pursuing Germans became very wary of the rifle proficiency of their khaki-clad opponents. It was during this retreat that the growth of one of the most famous myths of the First World War would occur – 'the Angel of Mons.'

The *London Evening News* of 29 September reported an unearthly intervention as the BEF retreated from Mons as ghostly archers, supposedly Henry V and his bowmen from Agincourt, appeared in the skies, firing their arrows and so causing the Germans to fall back. The story took popular hold in Britain and was seen by many as proof that God was backing the Allied cause.

Men from Biggleswade and the surrounding villages certainly took part in the fighting at Mons, with the 1st Bedfordshire Battalion amongst those that were blooded there. Their war diary tells how the men had been digging shallow trenches and firing pits when the Germans began their attack by shelling the area. The 1st Bedfords then engaged the Germans as they advanced through the streets of Mons, and after a fierce fight, they pulled back. The 1st Bedfordshire Battalion had been in Ireland at the start of the war but it was quickly dispatched to France, arriving there on 16 August. Indeed news that the 1st Bedfords had been in the thick of the action and involved in very hard fighting quickly reached Biggleswade when Private Forder wrote and described in this letter home:

> We had been fighting eighteen hours and had lost about 300 killed and wounded. I have been through six engagements and am ready to go through six more. There ain't half some Germans — about ten to one of us — so you can tell we have been very busy, but we give them more than they want. We dropped them by thousands; but they still kept sending more.

The real impact of war was now being felt in the town when Mrs Joseph Bilcock of Benson's Row heard that her brother, Private Edward Lake of the 1st Bedfords had been killed in the retreat from Mons, having been shot through the lungs. Four years later the hand of tragedy was to touch Mrs Bilcock again when she would lose her husband to an aeroplane bomb. Others would survive to fight on, such as Private William Goodwin from Shortmead Street who was wounded in the shoulder at Mons, whilst some would be captured and would spend the rest of the war as POWs. One of these was Private Frank Watson of Stotfold who had been called up as a reservist, but had been captured by the advancing Germans on 3 September. The rest of his war was grim to say the least. He spent time carrying out forced labour in Germany and Russia, suffering from frostbite to both his hands and feet. He, together with many other POWs from the Biggleswade area gratefully received food parcels as a part of 'The *Biggleswade Chronicle* British Prisoners of War Fund.'

During the fighting at Mons a platoon of the 1st Bedfords found themselves involved in a somewhat unusual situation involving the invading German troops. Both sides had dug makeshift trenches and faced each other over a gap of about 70yds, when one of the Bedfords hoisted an improvised bullseye target above the shallow trench. German marksmen then took turns to fire single shots at this target, and the hits were signalled up by the Bedfords, and bullseyes were greeted with a huge cheer. After a while the Germans reciprocated, putting up a target of their own and the 1st Bedfords were able to show their expertise in the use of firearms. Both German and British enjoyed the moment and each celebrated their marksmanship with cheers and songs. This 'target practice' would put to good use by both sides in the weeks, months and years to come by those who survived this initial fighting.

Letters from the front gave a surprising amount of information about the fighting at Mons, as the following missive from Grenadier Guard L. Goodwin of Great Barford shows. Writing to friends he reported that:

> We marched 190 miles in eight days. We were marching day and night, and when we did get a stop we had to entrench ourselves and lie with bayonets fixed and ten rounds of ammunition loaded, so you see that there was no chance of getting any rest. I was in three battles; in the last of which I was wounded. I have seen some awful sights. The first fight at Mons was terrible. We did cut the Germans up there, and our Battalion never lost a man. The next fight was at Landrecies. I was in a big house in the middle of the town, and we knocked the windows out and made holes in the brickwork to fire through; and the Germans again lost heavily there. We were fighting in a wood when I got shot.

Private Goodwin was subsequently captured by the Germans but was later to regain his freedom when counter-attacking French troops secured his release.

Casualties were not only restricted to the fighting in Belgium and Northern France, and those preparing to leave for the front also suffered injury and death. Two territorials encamped near Biggleswade were injured in September, one being kicked by a horse, whilst another hurt his big toe on a bale of corn!

A much more tragic event was to take place eleven miles northwards up the Great North Road at St Neots. Walter Ralph Davidson Taylor was a trumpeter with the Territorial 1st Highland Brigade, the Royal Field Artillery. This territorial force was encamped at St Neots, having previously been quartered at Bedford. On Monday

31 August, together with other soldiers from the Royal Field Artillery, Walter Taylor had gone to the bathing sheds at Eynesbury, on the River Ouse but on arrival had found that this was a ladies bathing day, so they had sat on the banks of the river, some distance away from the sheds. Three local girls, Alice Mead, Flossie Peacock and Maud Andrew had gone along to enjoy a swim in the Ouse and Alice started to swim out across the river. As she swam across she called for her friends to follow. They did so, however, one of the girls got into serious difficulties, and then the two of them, Flossie and Maud, started to struggle. Walter Taylor and Driver William Carr did not hesitate and both ran and dived into the river to help the girls. Trumpeter Taylor was bringing one of the girls back when one of the other girls caught hold of him. Driver William Carr then reached the three of them and swam back to the bank with one of the girls. Meanwhile Walter Taylor, with Maud Andrew clinging round his neck, disappeared beneath the water. The other watching soldiers, who could not swim, had managed to get hold of a punt and they were able to rescue Maud Andrew when she came to the surface, but they were not able to get to Walter Taylor and he went down for a second time and did not reappear. The local police recovered his body a half an hour later and it was discovered that he had become entangled in weeds and had become trapped beneath the water. Walter Taylor was only seventeen but his courage and gallantry on that summer's day saw him lose his life in saving the lives of those three teenage girls. He is buried in St Neots Cemetery.

Memorial for Walter Taylor who gave his life in saving three girls in the River Ouse at St Neots.

Across the Channel as the retreat from Mons continued, British troops found themselves tired, dusty and pressed by the enemy. This point is emphasized in the war diary of the 1st Bedfords that tells of the men being 'tired and footsore'. However, the BEF in retreat continued to prove to the following Germans that they were a force to be reckoned with though, and their pursuers' losses persisted. At Le Cateau on 26 August the British retreat came to a halt and a decisive rearguard action took place with the Germans again suffering sorely in the face of accurate rifle fire from the BEF. This rearguard action by II Corps proved to be very costly, for the British lost over 7,800 men, but it did allow the retreat to continue in good order. Once again the 1st Bedfords were in action here and the war diary reveals how well organised this rearguard stand was, and how they covered the withdrawal of the artillery.

Douglas Haig commanded the other British Corps, I Corps, and he had a narrow escape in the retreat, for his driver took the wrong direction and almost ran into advancing German troops who fired on Haig's car. Quite how the war would have progressed if Haig had been captured or killed here is a beguiling question.

Six days later the first man actually from Biggleswade was to lose his life. The incident took place at Nery and was one of those uplifting, backs against the wall situations where the British people seem to show great resilience. The battle that took place at Nery on 1 September would see the winning of three Victoria Crosses, the entire German 4th Cavalry Division being beaten off and defeated even though the British troops involved were outnumbered by five to one. The day had begun with thick fog and both German and the British soldiers were not aware of how close they were to each other. A scouting patrol of the 1st Cavalry Brigade of the BEF had ridden out at around 5 a.m. to look for signs of the enemy. As they were about to return they encountered the enemy when the fog started to lift, so they galloped back to warn their comrades and raise the alarm. At first Colonel Pitman, the commanding officer, refused to believe the news that the patrol was giving him, but that soon changed as German shells began to fall close to the encamped British troops. The mist had now all cleared and what was apparent was that the L Battery of the Royal Horse Artillery was limbered up, and prepared to move off rather than fight. Amongst the gunners of L Battery was Horace Bryant of Biggleswade, a regular soldier aged twenty-one. Horace was the only son of Mr and Mrs Joseph Bryant of Stratton Park Cottages and he had sailed for France in early August. The Germans were within 60yds of L Battery and Horace Bryant was amongst the first to fall, as shells, shrapnel and machine gun bullets hit the gunners. The artillery reacted to the German attack as quickly as they could, but out of the six guns of L Battery three were destroyed at once, whilst the other two were damaged and only one of the 13-pounders could be used. The remaining gun took on the twelve German guns that overlooked them from the ridge close by and what was to be known as 'Dorrell's Duel' commenced. Sergeant Major Dorrell took command after the officers were either killed or seriously wounded, and gradually put out of action the German guns, firing until the last round had been used. This allowed reinforcements to arrive and they attacked the Germans from the flank, capturing all of their guns apart from four. These were the first German guns to be captured by the BEF, and to add to the success the whole German 4th Cavalry Division was driven off.

The *Biggleswade Chronicle* was to report Gunner Bryant's death later in September and again at the start of October:

> We extend our sympathy to the parents in the loss. They at least have the satisfaction of knowing that he died for a noble cause, that of fighting for the weak and oppressed and for liberty and civilisation. Gunner Bryant's death we trust will spur many of our young men to come forward and offer their services to the King and country in the place of him who has given all, even his life for the cause of freedom.

The fight at Nery once again confirmed that the British in retreat were deadly and dangerous opponents. Indeed the mood of the men was one of resistance, and they truly believed that they were lulling the Germans, drawing them on and that soon they would turn and fight and drive their enemy back. On 6 September their faith would be justified, as the Allies did exactly that and turned to the attack. The battle of the Marne would show that the Schlieffen Plan was not going to succeed, for the German army was halted here, suffering a distinctive defeat and it found itself in full retreat. The battle took place over a period of five days and for a while the outcome was in the balance, but eventually the German army lost its nerve and started to fall back. This was certainly one of the defining battles of the Great War as the concept of a war of movement would shortly come to a close, and, following the so called 'race to the sea', the trench system that was to stretch from the Belgian coast for over 400 miles to the Swiss border would come into creation.

The death of Gunner Bryant was followed shortly by further bad news for the town when two reservists who were both serving with the King's Royal Rifle Corps were added to the town's roll of honour. Both men, Rifleman Arthur Watts, and Rifleman Arthur Butterworth met their deaths in the fighting that followed the Marne as the BEF pursued the retreating Germans.

Arthur Watts was twenty-six, had completed his ordinary term of service in the army and at the outbreak of the war had been a reservist, who had been employed as a policeman in Gainsborough. He was the son of Mr and Mrs Watts of Shortmead Street and had been wounded in action at the Battle of the Aisne, where the BEF tried to dislodge the Germans from the high ground that was the Chemin des Dames. Arthur Watts had gone missing in this fighting and for many weeks nothing was heard of him, his parents fearing that he had been taken prisoner. His death would not be confirmed until November although he had actually died on 19 September. The tragedy of Arthur Watts' death was compounded by the fact that he was to have been married in December. Rifleman Arthur Butterworth was another casualty of the advance to the Aisne, being wounded as the BEF took on the Germans here. He would succumb to his wounds on 1 October 1914, one of many casualties of the King's Royal Rifles who drove the retreating German armies back towards the heights of the Chemin des Dames. The fighting here was particularly difficult, for the BEF had to cross the River Aisne just to get at the enemy who were strongly entrenched in the banks above the water.

Back in Biggleswade Sergeant Yarrell found himself reappointed as a drill instructor for the recruits of Kitchener's volunteers, and Colour Sergeant H. Farr, formerly of the 5th Bedfordshire Regiment, replaced him in the post of recruiter for the area. Sergeant Yarrell's appointment to the 6th Division of the New Armies showed exactly the difficulty of having to train the influx of volunteers. The BEF was fighting for its life on the continent and casualties were growing daily. This meant that there was a dearth of experienced soldiers remaining in the UK who could take on the tuition of the thousands who were heeding Kitchener's call for men. Sergeant Yarrell was no spring chicken, having served for twenty-one years with the colours but it was increasingly falling to men such as him to try to turn the volunteers into soldiers.

Lord Kitchener has obtained 900,000 recruits, and only 100,000 are needed to make up the first million. So take *your* place in the ranks, young man, at once, and enlist at the nearest recruiting office, for the sake of your King and Country.

Advertisement from the *Biggleswade Chronicle*, September 1914.

At nearby Arlesey this was clearly evident where a sprightly eighty-six-year-old travelled to London and presented himself to help with the training of recruits. Sergeant Kyle was another Sebastopol veteran who could remember seeing Florence Nightingale at work during the Crimean War. He was a tall figure who now stooped a little, and although he had snow white hair he did have a keen eye, a firm and military step and a strong voice – the recruits were pleased to see such a man who had started his military career such a long time ago.

As well as a shortage of trainers for the recruits, there was also a corresponding need for uniforms and rifles, together with less obvious commodities such as blankets. The training was not easy and the standard format was drill, drill and more drill. This emphasis was as a result of the deficiency of firearms and was to have an unfortunate consequence in less than two year's time when the New Armies went into action on the Somme. General Rawlinson, Commander of the 4th Army on the first of July was not convinced that the inexperienced men of Kitchener's Armies could deal with advanced tactics such as fire and movement, so instruction given to the men on that fateful day was for them to form up and advance in waves. This they were good at, for they had spent much of the early months of service being drilled and following such instructions. Although over fifty of the attacking battalions did not employ this tactic for 1 July 1916 over thirty did and, for them, the consequences were tragic.

The insistence on drilling and marching in these initial days did not seem to worry the volunteers though as Private Charter explained in a letter to his family back in the town: 'We are all right and enjoying ourselves.'

Another letter published in the *Chronicle* endorsed this view but, in the interest of national security, did not give the name of the author or the exact location of the training base, other than the south coast:

> We are in the best of health and getting on fine. The sea air suits us fine and we are getting quite fit and if we get on all the while like we are now we shall be ready to have a pot at 'Kaiser Bill' before Christmas. I don't know what he would say if he could only see us lot here, he would be a bit surprised, and would want to make his will at once. The weather is hot during the day, but cold at night and we have all been served with an extra blanket. We have plenty to eat and plenty of work. We do eight hours drill a day, but that's the only way to make us fit for active service.

Indeed many of the volunteers' accommodation in these early months of the war turned out to be tents and the autumn nights saw dipping temperatures. The *Chronicle* carried an appeal for blankets at the start of October from no less a figure than Mrs Thornton of Bedford, who was the sister-in-law of Sir John French, the Commander in Chief of the BEF. Readers were advised that those who could not afford to buy a blanket could send along a contribution towards the cost of one. Meanwhile the town continued to show its commitment to the cause in other ways and the Vicar of Biggleswade organised open-air services for troops quartered in the town. The shortage of blankets was but one example of the difficulties of equipping and preparing the large numbers of volunteers who were forming Kitchener's Armies. Uniform, rifles, accommodation and training by regular soldiers were amongst the others.

Corporal W.H. Hartley was one who had answered the call for Kitchener's New Army and he was one who could call upon previous military service, for he had served with the Yorks Light Infantry. Writing home, he encouraged others from the town to follow and he gave this account of life with Kitchener's 'boys.'

> Reveille sounds at 5am. The first thing is to make our beds up, wash ourselves and by the time that this is done, orderly men, who are appointed each day, are then back from the cook-house with tea and biscuits for those who go on early morning parade, which is at 6am. This parade lasts two hours and consists of physical training. They are then dismissed for breakfast. Food is very good: for breakfast: 1 pint tea, 1lb bread (which has to last a man all day), corned beef or brawn, sometimes bacon. Breakfast finished we then fall in on parade at 9am. We then go for a route march or field training. This parade lasts until 12 noon. Diner is served at 1pm and consists of boiled and roast meat, potatoes and soup; sometimes we get haricot beans but no pudding. Next parade at 2pm which is generally musketry lasts until 4pm. Then tea and that consists of tea, 1 pint, cheese, jam and occasionally a little cake. I may mention that the cheese we get is that which was captured from the German ships, and incidentally is not too bad. Our barrack rooms are

large, but somewhat overcrowded, but all the boys are jolly anxious to get away to help our boys across the water.

At the front more obvious requests started to be made, and the officer commanding the 1st Bedfords made an appeal for socks, cardigans, warm underclothing, briar pipes and cigarettes. Morale continued to remain high within the BEF and its killing power continued to be reported upon and communicated to avid readers back in Blighty. Percy Mosley had been brought up in Biggleswade and his parents had previously run the town's post office. He was serving at the front with the Postal Section of the 15th Infantry Brigade as a sapper. He commented upon a letter taken from a captured German officer. In the letter this German had told his parents that 'the English soldier is the best trained soldier in the world' and went on to comment that 'the English soldiers' fire was ten thousand times worse than hell', adding that if 'the Germans could only beat the English all would be well, but he was afraid that they would never beat the English devils.'

Following the battles at the Marne and the Aisne both sides turned their attention towards the Channel and each became involved in what has become known as the 'race to the sea'. This saw both the Axis and the Allied forces moving northwards and trying to outflank each other. This 'race to the sea' saw casualties continue to multiply in the BEF and letters home confirmed the losses being faced as the conflict moved back northwards. By October the two sides were facing each other from Nieuwpoort on the Belgian coast southwards for around 400 miles to the Swiss border. The BEF soon found itself back in the maelstrom as the Germans attempted to break through to go on to capture the channel ports. Their belief was that this would see the BEF defeated and lead to Britain's exit from the war. Only the town of Ypres stood in their way. In October this was the last Belgian town remaining in allied hands – by 1918 the name would be indelibly inscribed in the history of the Great War.

Ypres in 1914 was a town that had seen German troops pass through it in early October as they headed north. They had not left a positive impression, as they had wrecked the town's telegraph system and had demanded a tax of 70,000 francs to ensure the good behaviour of the citizens of the town whilst they billeted themselves there for three days. The town possessed an imposing cathedral and a cloth hall that both revealed how the town's history was based in trade and religion. These buildings were easily visible for miles around, as the town sits in a flatland basin surrounded by higher ground, and they were imposing sights. Over the next four years they would be gradually destroyed, as would the town itself, until it would be said that a man on horseback could look from one side of the town all the way across to the other side, as the town was reduced to rubble by the destructive bombardment of the German Army's artillery. The British troops who arrived there in October received an encouraging welcome from the locals, especially the Scottish troops who were given special attention because of the kilts they wore.

The open nature of the fighting changed now with both sides beginning to dig in and the trench system that for so many epitomises the Great War came into being. Initially the trenches were a single line but as the war progressed then this would change, so that by 1916 there would be three lines – front, reserve and support, all connected by communication trenches. The actual trenches also varied, for in France they were deeper as the water level was lower than it was in Belgium. Indeed on the Somme in 1916, a major reason for the failure of the attack on the first day was that the Germans had dug down between 20-40ft in constructing dugouts that were all but indestructible except for a direct hit by a high-explosive shell. In Belgium the water level was reached at about 4ft and this required the construction of a different kind of trench with a raised parapet and parados to offer troops protection. By 1917 the Germans had strengthened their trench lines here, with the construction of reinforced concrete blockhouses that would prove to be more than a thorn in the side of attacking allied troops. However in the autumn of 1914 these developments were in the future, and the outcome of the war rested to a great extent in the attack by the Germans at Ypres.

The 1st battle of Ypres began in October and would continue through to November and proved to be a very close-run thing. It would see the Germans almost break through and would see the blooding of the first territorial battalion, the London Scottish, to fight in the war so far. It was a battle that stretched the BEF almost to breaking point as more and more of the 'Old Contemptibles' became casualty figures.

Private Basham of the Bedfordshire Regiment wrote home on 18 October 1914, emphasising how hard the fighting was and describing the desperate situation facing the BEF as it fought for its life around Ypres:

> Still in the land of the living, and a little war-wearied for after a week of horrible and heavy fighting we fellows all feel the necessity to get away from the boom of guns and the crack of rifles. In the midst of a shell-shattered village with pigs, cows and a dog or two all wandering disconsolately about streets heaped with the debris of cottage homes, here and there houses afire, we are sitting on the edge of bomb-proof trenches. All the company's officers are either wounded or dead.
>
> If there is a man in England skulking to preserve to himself a few years of life, let him imagine us burying our dead and setting our teeth as we face Maxim fire galore, rifles innumerable, and shells by the hundred. And still we stick on unrelieved!
>
> We want men to fill the gaps
>
> We want men to relieve men — men that need rest and a washing day, men that need shaving and rebooting. And I make this appeal because I am with those fighting the fiercest on the German flanks.

Another letter published in the *Chronicle* revealed just how hard the BEF were being hit at Ypres and Sergeant Andrews wrote:

> Our regiment is proving its fighting qualities, but our losses are heavy. Our Regiment's history should be great, and read by all in Bedfordshire, and then I'm sure that recruits would come up much easier. Nobody knows the daring and pluck of our boys, as all the officers called us at the first instant of the engagement around Ypres. Well, we have lost nearly all of our officers, only three were left in the field on November 5th, when we were relieved from the trenches for a short spell.

The fighting at Ypres did not abate and was to take the lives of more men from Biggleswade. Firstly Private George Goodship of the 2nd Bedfords was killed as the battalion fought close to Gheluveldt at Becelaere. Initially the battalion had attacked but then it had dug in, and men were lost in both attack and defence. George Goodship was one of those who were killed in action on 26 October as the battalion fought desperately at Becelaere, just before they were relieved by the Scots Guards. George Goodship was initially reported as missing in action but in 1915 it would be confirmed that he had died during the 1st battle of Ypres. George Goodship had been a professional soldier, having joined the Bedfords when he was just a boy. At the start of the war he had been with his battalion in South Africa but, on return, he had served in Flanders since October, fighting through the early weeks of that month to try to stem the German advance. Today his body rests in Harlebeke Military Cemetery.

Then in late November Mr and Mrs William Rowlett of Sun Street were to receive the dreaded news that their son Fred had been killed on the last day of October. Fred had sailed to France with his battalion on 5 October, although they had not reached Calais and Dunkerque as scheduled as the troopship was recalled. Eventually all of the battalion reached France by 7 October and they began to advance and marched all of the way to Ypres. Fred was in the Special Reserve of the 3rd Bedfords prior to the war, but he had gone abroad with the 2nd Bedfords. Indeed 60 per cent of the initial BEF that crossed the Channel in 1914 came from those 'on reserve.' At Ypres Fred Rowlett was with his friends Harry Day and Arthur Hallybone as they increasingly began to be involved in the struggle to resist the Germans. They first encountered the enemy on 18 October on the Menin Road, outside the town. This is the road that would later see thousands of Tommies march along it as they went up the line. It would see the construction of huge canvasses to try and restrict the Germans' view of the troops moving up to the front, but in 1914 it was the road that led to the neighbouring town of Menin. That initial baptism of fire saw the 2nd Bedfords shelled and receive a number of casualties from shrapnel. For the next two weeks they were engaged on a day to day basis with their foe, and the number of those killed or wounded rose. German snipers and artillery took their toll of the battalion. On 30 October, Fred Rowlett had been on hand to help his friend Harry Day when he had been struck by a shell splinter in the foot. On the following day the battalion was moved forward to a small fir wood about 250yds in front of the line and were told to hold this position. As soon as day dawned they found themselves under shellfire from the enemy and they received orders for an orderly retreat back towards Ypres. The battalion's losses were severe on this day and Fred Rowlett was amongst those who were killed. His friend, Private Hallybone saw him die and would later write home to his mother who lived in Shortmead Street: 'I expect that you heard about Fred Rowlett. I was with him at the same time he got his brains blowed out on 31st October.'

As this was a letter to his mother, rather than a letter to Fred's next of kin, it seems likely that this was close to the truth, for many letters written by comrades in the trenches to the families of those who were killed often spared them the horrific nature of some of the deaths.

It was a shrapnel shell that accounted for nineteen-year-old Fred Rowlett and further details of this would come to light in early 1915 when Private John Dennis wrote to his cousin in Biggleswade:

> I should like to tell you a bit about the war but I am not allowed to say. I had one big shock when we were at Ypres when young Fred Rowlett got killed. We were having a laugh together when a shell burst over our heads and a piece of shrapnel hit him on the side of the temple and knocked his brains out.

The usual strength of a battalion was around 800 men, with about 200 held in reserve. By the end of 1 November 1914 the 2nd Bedfords were down to four officers and between 350 and 400 men. The fighting that would later become known as 1st Ypres was hitting the BEF hard and the actions at the end of October were defining ones in the outcome of the Great War. The German Army came within a whisker of achieving the breakthrough it was so desperately seeking – to capture the channel ports, and so defeat the BEF. Sitting astride the Menin Road, the Worcestershire Regiment was to play a pivotal role in the outcome of the 1st Ypres. When it seemed that nothing could prevent the German attack from breaking through and taking Ypres, the 2nd Worcesters had charged the enemy and had thrown back the German assault. The importance of this battle can be seen in that 31 October would become known as Ypres Day and those who had survived the fight would take great pride in the wearing of blue cornflowers in memory of those who had died. For the Worcesters, the day would be remembered as Ghevulet Day.

Readers of the *Chronicle* continued to be surprisingly well informed about the grim and critical nature of the fighting at Ypres, for letters were published each week in the 'Local War News' section. Letters about the war were printed with the following proviso:

> The Editor is always pleased to receive letters for publication which have been received by relatives from the gallant lads who are fighting our battles, or are in training for same, or in hospital suffering as a result of their patriotism. Many hundreds of our readers look eagerly for the letters about the war each issue and we are deeply indebted to those who have made this feature of the *Chronicle* a link between friends who are separated by thousands of miles of sea and land. We always make a point of omitting any private matters and also take every care that nothing that can be of use to the enemy is published. Further we undertake to take every care of all letters entrusted to our care and to return same as soon as possible. Once again we thank all that have granted us the use of their letters in the past and we have every confidence that the practice will be continued.

Under a subtitle 'Sergt. Harper Recovering' the *Chronicle* reported in November that Arthur Harper had a sister living in Biggleswade and that he had written to her from hospital where he was recovering from bullet wounds to the thigh. He was a regular soldier with the 11th Hussars and had written to his sister in graphic detail of the struggle at Ypres:

Our worst day was the October 31st. we went into the trenches on the previous night and the Germans shelled us heavily with big guns. The first shell hit the Squadron Sergt. Major. After that it was awful. Two officers, a sergeant and several men were buried alive. I had part of the trench on top of me three times but I got away with a good shaking. One poor chap was partly covered; his arms and body were showing from under the soil. He looked up pleadingly and we got him round the shoulders and started to pull him out but his legs had been blown to a pulp. There was 75 went into our trench and either 41 or 42 were killed or wounded.

Within a week the fighting at Nonnesboschen, near Ypres, again saw the Germans perilously close to breaking through. It is from this battle that the infamous and incredulous comment of a captured German officer was uttered. When asking what reserves the BEF had, he was told that there were none and that if they had succeeded in breaking the BEF line then Ypres would have been theirs for the taking, and the prospect of victory on the Western Front so much closer.

On 7 November another man from Biggleswade was killed in action to the south of Ypres. William Gray was one of two brothers who would die on the Western Front. William was eighteen and his brother Leonard would be nineteen when he was killed four years later. They were the sons of William and Fanny Gray of Sun Street. William was a regular soldier with the 1st Bedfords and he had been in the thick of the fighting at Mons, the Marne and the Aisne. As with many of the soldiers who died in the Great War, William Gray's grave was lost in the continued fighting and he is commemorated on Le Touret Memorial. This loss did not deter his younger brother Leonard from enlisting before he reached the age of seventeen. Perhaps revenge was a deciding factor here but the sad fact would be that Len Gray would follow his brother when he too was killed in action in 1918 during the German advance that was known as the Kaiser's Battle.

News arriving in Back Street revealed another casualty for the town when Mr and Mrs Housden heard that their son Tom had been wounded in the shoulder during the struggle for Ypres, and that he was now being treated in Stationary Hospital, Rouen. Tom Housden had been in the Special Reserve when war broke out and was serving with the 2nd Bedfords in Belgium when he was wounded.

Mr and Mrs Buck of Bensons Row also heard news from their son George concerning the fighting at Ypres. He was with the 1st Royal Dragoons when he had a very close shave on 13 November that saw his parents told at first that he had been killed. Their relief was great when they received the following letter from their shaken son. He wrote:

I will tell you the reason that they reported me killed. It was on the 13th November, our regiment lost 58 horses during one afternoon in a camp we had occupied for nine days. I was left in charge of the horses, when a shell burst one yard from where I was lying under some straw. Rather lucky for me, as two other chaps that were lying next to me were blown to pieces and I helped to gather up the remains next day. I had my own rifle blown away, but I escaped with a twisted neck. When I came down the lines the next morning, one of the officers was asking if they had found my remains. Previous to that I was hit by shrapnel, but not much, only a slight bruise. Since then they have started telling me I am a cat with nine lives. One horse was shot under me. Never mind, do not worry, cheer up and look on the bright side of it and all being well I shall be home for a short spell later on.

Another letter received in Biggleswade showed the importance of parcels that were sent to the troops from home. Private John Dennis with the 2nd Bedfords wrote to his Aunt and Uncle: 'I am getting plenty of food, plenty of tobacco and fags and plenty of clothes, so you can see I am all right in all ways.' The only complaint that he had was that he was always short of writing paper and that he did not get enough letters from Biggleswade.

The part played at 1st Ypres by the 2nd Bedfordshire regiment received the appreciation of the 'top brass' for Lieutenant General Sir Henry Rawlinson commended them as follows:

> You have been called upon to take a conspicuous part in one of the severest struggles in the history of the war, and you have had the honour and distinction of contributing in no small measure to the success of our arms and the defeat of the enemy's plans.
>
> The task which fell to your share inevitably involved heavy losses, but you have, at any rate, the satisfaction of knowing that the losses you have inflicted upon the enemy have been far greater. The Division have gained for themselves a reputation for stubborn valour and endurance in defence, and I am certain that you will only add to your laurels when the opportunity for advancing in the attack is given to you.

How comforting these words would have been to families in Biggleswade is hard to judge, especially when further sad news came to the town of yet more fatalities, both from the 1st Bedfordshire Battalion who were fighting close to Festubert.

First of all, George Tear, a Private with the 1st Bedfords was initially reported missing and then confirmed as being killed in action on 22 October. He was on Special Reserve at the start of the war and this son of Fred Tear of Shortmead Street embarked for the Western Front where he was involved in much of the early fighting. His parents had not heard from him since early October but then their worst fears were confirmed. This thirty-one-year-old's body was another that was never to be found. Soldiers during the Great War did have identification tags but they were made of leather, and as such they would rot if the bodies were buried or would start to fall apart if the corpses were left in the open for months. Rats not only ate the bodies of soldiers in no-man's-land but also gnawed at the leather of the 'dog tags'.

The sad tidings of George Tear's death were quickly followed by similar news, when Elizabeth Smith heard that her husband had also been killed in the fighting to the south of Ypres. George Smith had been a member of the Biggleswade Town Silver Prize Band and had been on Special Reserve before joining the 1st Bedfords. He also had fought through all of the initial engagements in Belgium and France and had had some narrow escapes, notably when one of his chums was shot down right next to him. His good fortune in surviving that came to an end on 27 October when he was reported as missing in action. George's battalion, the 1st Bedfords were on the point of being relieved by the

1st Battalion Manchester Regiment when they came under attack on 26 October by the Germans, and it was during this that George Smith and thirteen of his comrades were killed and wounded. The war diary for the battalion tells how aggressive the Germans were in this sector of the front, constantly sapping forward and making attacks at various hours of night and day. Just three days before he was killed George's wife had received a last ever letter from him. No trace of George Smith was ever found, and today his name sits on Le Touret Memorial.

A third fatality must have caused much suffering within the Thomason household situated at Brooklands Cottages, for Private George Thomason's father was far from well. To compound the matter, news of his son's death did not immediately arrive and the War Department's letter to Joseph Thomason was delivered by mistake to a family in Bromham before it reached its proper destination in Biggleswade. George Thomason had been a regular soldier who was in the seventh and final year of his service, and, but for the war, would have gone on to the Reserve. At the outbreak of fighting he had been in South Africa but had quickly returned with his regiment and was with the 2nd Bedfords when they embarked for the front. He was involved in the hard fighting of 1st Ypres and had even given his last drop of water to a wounded comrade, a Private Woodcock, during the two weeks he spent in the trenches. On 31 October he was to lose his life to a German bullet as the 2nd Bedfords fought at Inverness Copse, outside Ypres, The battalion came under shell fire from dawn and the pressure grew as the Germans advanced to try to take this small wood. The battalion hung on grimly until late afternoon when they were ordered to fall back. George Thomason was not with them, and his body was to be lost as the struggle to break through at Ypres continued.

So the Battle of 1st Ypres ground to a halt during the first weeks of November as the weather worsened, the Germans accepting that their attempt to break through had not succeeded. The cost to the BEF though was high and 10,500 soldiers died in that first desperate struggle for Ypres. Less than 2,000 of these men would end up with a known grave as the shifting nature of the initial fighting saw graves lost. Both sides settled down to wait to see what the next year would offer in terms of opportunity for victory. Those who had believed or expected that it would all be over by Christmas had been wrong. On the Western Front shelling and trench raids continued, but no major offensive would take place until the spring of 1915. Meanwhile 1914 had one more decisive event to see with the cessation of fighting in many places along the front line on the fourth Friday of December, Christmas Day.

German troops, especially those from Saxon regiments, were the initiators of this remarkable truce. Along the front line British Tommies were surprised to see the German soldiers putting up Christmas trees, decorated with candles and then to hear them singing carols on Christmas Eve. This surprise turned to astonishment as German soldiers started to climb out of their front line trenches on Christmas Day and call over to their British equivalents. Cautiously the British Tommies climbed out of their trenches and both moved towards each other, greeting and then exchanging cigarettes, alcohol and food. Officers were at first uncertain about how to deal with this situation, some turned a blind eye, whilst others took the opportunity to see the German lines in daylight. There was also the chance for both sides to bury the dead of no-man's-land. Incredibly a football match even took place involving the Bedfordshires that resulted in a 3-2 victory to the Germans.

The truce continued for some days in some sections of the front until the top brass of both sides ordered that it should cease. Even so New Year's Eve was celebrated, the Germans an hour earlier that the Tommies because of continental time, and although there was no fraternisation in no-man's-land, there was little shelling of each other's trenches.

Reports of these remarkable events were published in both national and local papers, so the people of Biggleswade would have been aware of the truce. Indeed the *Chronicle* of 8 January 1915 included amongst its 'Local War Items' column two reports. The first, entitled 'A Christmas Armistice' came from a letter from Private Albert Bygraves, who confirmed that the 2nd Bedfords had participated when he wrote to his cousin:

> We have had our Christmas in the trenches with the Germans. There was not a shot fired all Christmas. We were shaking hands with the Germans and exchanged cigarettes, and the next day all the Germans and all of us were on the top of the trenches talking to each other.

The second report was entitled 'German and British exchange smokes at Yuletide.' This article referred to the letter of a soldier from Cambridge who wrote home as follows:

> On Christmas Eve we started to sing carols and songs, and so did they. They shouted across 'if you won't shoot, we won't.' so we agreed. Then a German officer came half-way, and one of our officers went to meet him. So there and then they arranged to have an armistice of 24 hours. The Germans had lighted candles on top of their trenches which looked very pretty across the white ground, for the ground was covered in frost. Then a German brought some cigars over, and we took them some cigarettes.
>
> Christmas morning — everything is quiet. Not one gun to be heard, except someone on our right who is not going to keep up Christmas, and keeps on now and again. We walk about just as we like for war has stopped for one day. The Germans have some in front of their trenches and ours, so they come and bury them, and we help. Then we exchange cigarettes for cigars, and laugh and joke with one another and have a very good time. I myself got some German money, five cigars, and six names and addresses, so I can prove that I have been over to the German trenches. Their trenches are only 50 yards away from ours, so we did not have far to go. This lasted all day, and we were singing together, and even had our photos taken together, Germans and all, but I don't expect I will be able to get one. Still they might be in the papers. So that is how I spent my Christmas.

Families and their loved ones at the front were able to keep in touch via a postal service that was quite remarkable. Letters from home would usually reach the front within two or three days, whilst those from soldiers writing home took a little longer, as they were subject to a form of censorship to prevent details of location or forthcoming action from being disclosed. Many soldiers often used postcards to write home and the tone of them was usually upbeat so as not to cause concern for families and loved ones. The British Tommy was not without invention, and codes were quickly devised whereby their kin could see where their men were actually fighting. A simple ruse that many soldiers used was to use capital letters in their letters and postcards in inappropriate places. Fitted together these spelt out the names of the place where they were fighting.

The reliable nature of this postal service could however worry those at home in Britain when news from their sons and husbands dried up. Clearly this would cause alarm and trepidation, with families beginning to fear the worst. This was certainly the case for the family of Herbert Stocker who lived in Gladstone Terrace, off Sun Street. Their son was a Corporal with the 2nd Bedfords and was a regular soldier who had seen service in South Africa. In September of 1914 he had enjoyed a spell of leave at home in Biggleswade before rejoining his regiment at 1st Ypres. It was here, during the fight against the Prussian Guards that Corporal Stocker was badly wounded, and despite the efforts of some of his friends and fellow soldiers from Biggleswade, they were unable to bring him back with them during the fierce fighting. He was officially declared 'missing in action' and for over a year his parents clung to the hope that he might be a prisoner of war. They wrote to the War Office and to the Red Cross and in November received the news that they must have dreaded, when a letter from the former which informed them:

> In reference to your enquiry regarding Corporal Stocker I much regret to say that we have received a report dated the 20th November from Pte Arthur Keave who says that since he came home Lance Corporal Holmes, now in the 4th Bedfords at Harwich, told him that Corporal Stocker was shot through the head and killed.

Corporal Stocker it transpired, had died on 8 November. His body was not lost though, as many were, and he was reinterred at Harlebeke New British Cemetery in the early 1920s.

So the first year of conflict had come to an end, seeing four months in which the fighting had begun as a mobile war and had developed into a static war with both sides entrenched. The popular image of the Great War with soldiers living in the trenches now began to take shape. The trenches of 1914 would be developed as the war progressed but the origins of the formidable defences faced by attacking troops had their origins in these initial months of the conflict. Soldiers quickly established routines in the front line, and as mistakes were made they learned from them. Days started with 'Morning hate', an artillery bombardment from both sides. This was followed by 'Stand to' where troops would man the fire steps of the trench in case of enemy attack, and if this did not materialise they would settle down to breakfast. This would be followed by repairs to the trench walls to try to prevent them collapsing. During the day men who were not on sentry duty tried to grab a few hours of sleep and resisted the temptation of looking over the parapet for snipers practised their deadly work on the careless and the curious. For sustenance men from the BEF relied upon a standard diet of tinned food such as bully beef, plum and

Corporal Herbert Stocker.

apple jam, and Maconochies, a form of soup made from carrots and turnips that when cold was terrible but when hot was edible. Added to that, they had a daily bread allowance and hard tack biscuits. Water was brought to the front line in empty petrol cans that were supposed to have been 'fired' to remove the smell of the fuel. This did not always happen, and some soldiers said that they could tell if the water had been brought to the front line in either an Esso or a Shell can! Most activity took place at night and men would go out into no-man's-land to repair barbed wire or to carry out trench raids. Sometimes there would be confrontations between such working parties in no-man's-land, but equally there were occasions when German and British soldiers thus engaged, ignored each other and simply carried out necessary repairs. Life in the trenches was not easy and the problem of rats and lice was constant, together with shelling and sniping. German trenches were usually better constructed than those of their British adversaries for they were intent upon holding on to the land they had initially taken. The British trenches were not as well constructed and did not have the deep bunkers and the concrete pillboxes that would feature strongly in German trench construction of 1916 onwards. Men did adjust though to this troglodyte existence, and many would later tell of the camaraderie that developed there. Sightings of the enemy were infrequent and men could complete many tours of the front line without seeing a single German. This was after all, to the main, an artillery war.

The original BEF had acquitted itself with distinction but had suffered crippling losses, losing much of its pre-war strength. By the end of the fighting at 1st Ypres the total casualties for the BEF on the Western Front so far amounted to 3,627 officers and 86,237 other ranks. The Territorials had seen action from late October and were now in the thick of the fighting. Back in Britain, Kitchener's volunteers were still undergoing training but their day would soon come. As far as Biggleswade was concerned, 251 men were serving their King and country, whilst ten had paid the ultimate sacrifice, and the roll of honour for 1914 read as follows:

    Gunner Horace Bryant, L Battery Royal Horse Artillery, killed in action
    Private Arthur Butterworth, King's Royal Rifles, died of wounds
    Private Arthur James Watts, King's Royal Rifles, killed in action
    Private William Gray, 1st Bedfords, killed in action
    Private George Thomason, 2nd Bedfords killed while giving water to a wounded comrade
    Private George Goodship, 2nd Bedfords killed in action at 1st Ypres

Private Fred Rowlett, 2nd Bedfords, killed by shrapnel at Ypres
Corporal Herbert Stocker, 2nd Bedfords, killed in action in the Ypres Salient
Private George Tear, 1st Bedfords, killed in action
Private George Smith, 1st Bedfords, killed in action

If 1914 was full of hope for a quick resolution to the war then 1915 would confirm that this would not be the case, and the previously unknown place names of Neuve Chapelle, Festubert, Aubers Ridge, Gallipoli and Loos would become all too familiar for the people of Britain, and Biggleswade.

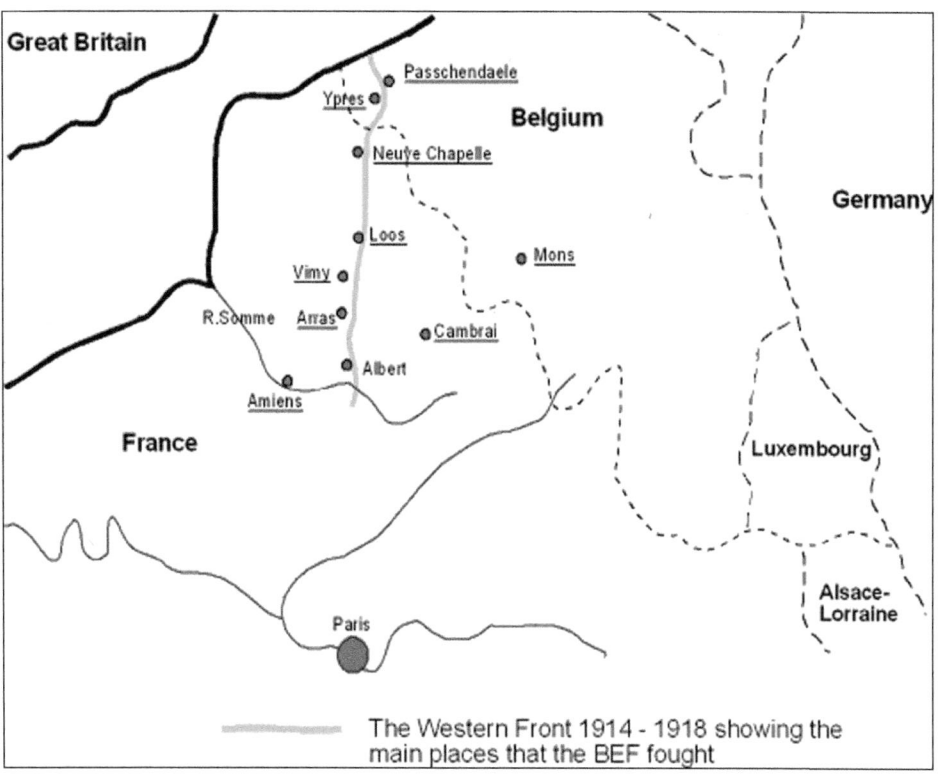

The Western Front 1914 - 1918 showing the main places that the BEF fought

# TWO

1915

A Widening Conflict

The start of a new year brought renewed hope that victory might be achieved, yet the reality was that the BEF had suffered hugely, and the professional nature of that army had altered beyond all recognition. The makeup of the BEF now changed as a matter of necessity, and more and more of the Territorials and Kitchener's New Armies found themselves in the front line. Recruitment in Biggleswade continued and there was a rush after Christmas to enlist, however it was the marital status, or rather lack of it that attracted commentary in the *Chronicle* of Friday 8 January. In the 'Local War Items' column words were not minced and the headline ran 'Single men still hang back.' The article read:

> Last week there was quite a big rush of Biggleswade men to the colours, but the honours went not to where they should have done, for the single men, although there are scores without any ties in the town, hung back, and out of nine men who were enrolled, only one was a single man — all honour to him. Surely the single men of Biggleswade and districts are not going to shirk their responsibilities and leave it to the fathers of large families to leave their homes and take the place of those whose duty is to bear arms to preserve our hearths and homes and thrust back the ruthless invader.

A week later the next edition would hammer home this theme when it published the strong words of Dr Macnamara, Secretary of the Admiralty: 'the man who is prepared to enjoy life under the British Flag without, at a time like this, having the grim determination that he will hand on that Flag as free as he found it, is not worthy of the name of a British citizen.'

This would be a recurring theme for the *Chronicle* throughout the remaining years of the conflict, through the Derby Scheme and then conscription, where it would actually name and shame men in the pages of the paper who had failed to report for service under the heading 'Have you seen these men?'

It was certainly true that recruitment had slowed and Biggleswade, together with many other towns had seen women issuing white feathers to those they felt were hanging back.

Recruitment poster for 5th Battalion Bedfordshire Regiment.

The reasons for men holding back are clearly varied, but accounts in the press certainly would have made many wonder about the wisdom of enlisting for a life in the trenches, as well as the sight of those who had been invalided home from the front. The *Beds Express* of 9 January contained an account from a Private Fred Ashwell of Letchworth that described graphically conditions in the firing line with the Bedfords Regiment:

> Up to the knees in water and mud, their ceaseless vigil was kept; taking shots at any German who showed himself, or taking a turn of rest asleep in the mud and water; hardly a day passing without some comrades being wounded or killed. One day a mate was jumping on his bag of sand to get it into the shape he wanted and in doing so his head must have showed just above the trench — he fell dead, shot through the head. The Germans are (sic) splendid shots. If you put your finger up out of the trenches they could hit it.

Life in the army no longer seemed to be the great adventure that it had in the early autumn of 1914. However the focus on the war in Biggleswade appeared to remain strong, even if the opportunism of some might have caused the raising of an eyebrow today. C.E. Batten owned and ran a drapery shop in the town, and regularly placed advertisements in the local press. The one that promoted his January sale certainly had a 'flavour' of the conflict that was taking place across the Channel. Mr Batten announced that his Great War Sale would be starting on 15 January, and the advertisement in the *Chronicle* of 8 January incorporated such phrases as 'These are stirring times', 'This will be a stirring sale', and 'All prices slaughtered'.

The week of the sale saw another promotion stating the Mr Batten was making war on all usual prices, and announced 'The Greatest War in History compels us to hold the Greatest Sale on Record'.

However recruitment continued and by mid-January there were 265 men who had taken the King's Shilling. Recruits included three brothers, Fred, Albert and Walter Haynes from Hitchin Street who all enlisted in the 7th Battalion, Middlesex Regiment. Sometimes men would take the option of joining a regiment other than their local one. This could be because of a girlfriend in the area, simply the desire to travel, or often the glamour associated with some regiments. The Middlesex Regiment is one such example, and the Haynes brothers were possibly attracted by the nickname of this regiment – 'the die-hards'. Another trio of brothers also had enlisted in early 1915, but these had not done so within Britain, for they had joined up in their new home of Canada where they had recently emigrated. Albert Figg, Ernest Figg, and Harry Figg all enlisted in the Canadian Army and they were joined in so doing by another former resident of Biggleswade, Harold Morgan who was made a sergeant, whilst Albert Figg had been given the rank of Corporal. Both of them had worked as telegraph boys in Biggleswade before they had left for a new life in Canada.

Three other recruits, this time from Biggleswade, all enlisted at Ampthill and all were married men. They were Frank Jones, Arthur Boness and Dick Bryant, and all joined the Duke of Bedford's Regiment.

One of those serving already with the Bedfords was Private Charles Carr, a popular man in the town who was affectionately known in Biggleswade as 'Little Tich'. He was a regular in the BEF, having joined at the age of sixteen, and prior to that he had worked as a butcher's boy in the town. Little Tich would be a regular correspondent for the next three years as he saw service on the Western Front, and his letters were published periodically in the *Chronicle*. At the outbreak of the conflict he had been with the 2nd Bedfords in South Africa, but an attack of pneumonia prevented him from sailing with his comrades for the Western Front. When he did eventually make it to the front he quickly found himself in action, and in his first five minutes in the trenches he had a narrow escape when the soldier standing next to him was wounded. During shelling from the Germans the very next day he saw the three men closest to him in the trench buried alive. The desperate efforts of Little Tich and others to dig these men out were successful though. He was then present at the Christmas Truce and shouted greetings back over to the German troops, remarking in a letter home that opinion of the Kaiser was pretty much the same for both English and German soldier alike! Over the New Year period Little Tich was amongst many to suffer from the chilling cold, and he succumbed to frostbite and was evacuated to Rosemount hospital in Aberdeen. Writing home he told how he had been afflicted for over three weeks, and that his feet were so badly affected that he had been unable to walk, only getting out of the front line by being carried by one of his comrades. His letter from Rosemount was clearly a reflective one:

> I was weak and ill when I went out, but I love my regiment as I love my life. My regiment has suffered; many of the brave lads I used to know I shall see no more until we answer the roll call on the great judgment morning. 'God bless them.' I wish this awful war was over.

Private Carr was not the only Biggleswade soldier suffering, for Lance Corporal George Knott, who was serving with the Coldstream Guards in the Salient was also hospitalised with frozen feet. He found himself in hospital in Stoke-on-Trent.

Others from the town who felt the full fury of the harsh winter were Privates Housden, Bailey and Loveridge who were also hospitalised with frozen feet.

As soldiers convalesced they were able to recount first hand what they had experienced, and also proudly show off some of the souvenirs they had got their hands on. One such soldier was Private Albert Bygraves of the Machine Gun Section of the 2nd Bedfords. He had been involved in all of the fighting around Ypres but had been taken ill. He was invalided back to Blighty to allow him time to recover. Initially he was sent to hospital in Birmingham and then he was given a period of leave back in Biggleswade. Here he was able to tell of the souvenirs he had acquired, and they included shrapnel from Ypres, the strap from a German soldier's helmet and a bullet from a German rifle that had struck the machine gun he had been firing. Other curiosities that found their way to Biggleswade included a dead German's topcoat that was on display in one of the windows of Mr H.T. Church's furniture store in the Market Place. The coat revealed shrapnel holes in both the left arm sleeve and in the back, and it had been sent to Mr Church by a friend in London who had bought it. This trade in relics and souvenirs would feature strongly throughout the war, and many of the soldiers fighting at the front saw this as an opportunity to get themselves extra funds to spend at the local estaminets on egg and chips, beer or *vin blanc*. These were greatly appreciated in comparison to the rations that they received in the trenches. The extract that follows from a letter home from Private Ryall to his mother in Hertfordshire certainly shows this: 'When I come home, mother, whatever you do don't put any bully beef or jam on the table.'

The bad weather that so affected men such as Little Tich and Lance Corporal Knott continued to mean that no new offensives could be mounted and the early months of 1915 did bring something of a respite for those in the trenches. However it did not always follow that the front line was a peaceful place for although major attacks and assaults were on hold the artillery of both sides continued to shell the enemy's trenches on a regular, if not daily, basis. In a war where artillery was the chief cause of death, the early months of 1915 saw the maintenance of casualties and fatalities. Many of the BEF who were injured or killed received head wounds, for their soft caps offered them little protection from artillery or mortar shell. Indeed the number of such wounds caused those in command to come to a decision to introduce steel helmets, although it would not be until early 1916 that this would be implemented.

If the danger from enemy shelling remained ever present then the risk of being killed, wounded or captured increased with the growth of trench raids. In simple terms these were forays across no-man's-land where the aim was to capture enemy soldiers, bring them back to your own trench lines and get information from them. This information was deemed to be invaluable in assessing the strength and morale of the enemy opposite, and was often used in the planning of larger attacks. Sometimes the raiding troops would strike very lucky and capture an enemy officer, who might just have copies of orders that would be very useful in the plotting of future offensives, or even give prewarning of an enemy assault.

The raids were dangerous to say the least with officers selecting volunteers carefully. Those chosen would often arm themselves with studded clubs, cudgels, large sheath knives, grenades and pistols. To add to their camouflage they would blacken their faces with burnt cork and wear balaclavas rather than caps, or later, helmets. Crossing no-man's-land carefully was the aim and they would freeze if Very lights were fired. They would gradually approach the enemy's trenches, listening intently for the sound of sentries' conversation until they got close. Then the raid would kick off and quickly the raiders would infiltrate the trench line, fighting, killing and capturing before they made a hasty exit to return to their own lines. High Command continually stressed the importance of these raids, for as well as gleaning information they felt that they were required to keep troops reminded that they were on the offensive. These raids would also prevent the adoption of either stalemate or live and let live conditions. For the Allies there should be no let up in the drive to oust the invader from French and Belgian soil.

The first casualty of the New Year for Biggleswade saw Private Ernest Emery of St John's Street dying after he was hit in the head by a stray German bullet whilst in the trenches around Ypres on 8 February. His death was a prime example of the danger posed because of the wearing of soft caps, as a letter written to his grieving mother showed. Ernest Emery was serving with the 1st Battalion of the Wiltshire Regiment and it was his Sergeant in 'A' company who wrote to Mrs Emily Emery:

Dear Madam,

I am writing these few lines with sorrow in my heart. On the evening of the 8th inst. the Company then being in the trenches about midnight a spare bullet entered that portion of the trench in which your son was stationed, striking him on the skull. At first we thought that it was not too serious, but I am sorry to say that he died during the following day. So, I, on behalf of the men of the Company write to you to express our deepest sympathy for your loss. One and all sincerely hope and trust that you will bear up under such circumstances. I am pleased to say during the short time that he had been with us that he was well liked by his comrades, who now mourn the loss of another comrade. So we wish for you to be of good heart as is possible under such circumstances.

I beg to remain, yours sincerely,

A. Goulding,
Colour Sergeant,
'A' Company, 1st Battalion, Wiltshire Regiment

Private Emery had joined up in September 1914 and after training found himself at the front in the Ypres Salient. Prior to the war he had lived in London and worked in the cloth trade and, it was here, at Waterloo Station that his mother had seen him for the last time. As he bade her farewell he had said to his mother that 'It will be a noble death', leaving her with a feeling of dread that he would never return. He was aged twenty-one when he was killed at Ypres.

The death of her son left Emily Emery wanting to know more about the way that he had died, and, like many others within Britain, desperate for more information. Death on a foreign field was particularly hard for those who remained in Britain as there was no body to see, nor was there a grave to visit. Mrs Emery wrote back to Sergeant Goulding asking for further details as to exactly how her son had met his end. Being the professional that he was Arthur Goulding wrote back shortly before he, himself was killed. His return letter to Mrs Emery was dated 22 February and ran as follows:

Dear Madam,

In answer to your letter in hand I will endeavour to give you the full particulars of your son's death. Of course, though I am hundreds of miles from you, it hurts me just the same to write this as if I was saying the words to you. I have had several of his companions around and have gone thoroughly into the case for you. He was in the trench at or about 1 a.m. on the 9th, a bullet came through the top sandbags, striking him in the cheek or near the jaw bone and came out through the skull. He was taken down to the dressing station at or about 2 a.m., of course being previously bandaged up and made as comfortable as possible. The stretcher bearers carried him down to the dressing station, where he died at or about 4 a.m. During the two hours from the time he was wounded, until he went to his Maker, I am sorry to say that he never made a murmur of any description, as he was in a state of coma. We had him buried in the grounds of a Chateau, alongside other fallen comrades. There is a cross with his full name and number on the same.

Now Madam, you may think this is a brutish letter, but really I am no hand at writing letters on the subject, though I always like to let people know how their loved ones have departed, for there is no knowing when I may require someone to do the same sad service for myself, but we never study that question, nor did your son.

There may be a slight discrepancy in this to my last letter, please excuse the same. I now close with deep sympathy, begging to remain, yours truly,

A Goulding
C.S.M.

P.S. — I was in another trench to that which your son was in. This letter is written roughly 100 yards from where the sad event took place.

In just over a month Sergeant Major Arthur Goulding's words did indeed prove to be prophetic and he was killed in the continuing fighting at Ypres. However his body was lost in that fighting unlike Ernest Emery, who was buried and whose grave can now be found in Kemmel Chateau Military Cemetery.

Also during February more shocking news was to arrive in the town when the mother of Private George Dean received confirmation that her son, who had previously been reported as missing, had in fact died as a prisoner of war and that he had been buried at Douai. George Dean had served as a regular for eight years before the outbreak of the war, and being on special reserve he had soon found himself in the thick of the action with the 2nd Bedfords. His death must have been particularly hard for his mother as she was totally blind and had depended on her son, who had lived at home after his demobbing from the regular army following service in India. George Dean's grave was lost and today he is commemorated on the Ploegsteert memorial in Flanders.

News of another captured prisoner also reached Biggleswade in February, but on this occasion with less painful consequences. This time the reports that reached the town confirmed that Private Sam Bilcock was alive after initially being posted as missing. His parents were aware that he had been wounded. Towards the end of February his capture was confirmed when a postcard from their son was received at 8 Benson's Row by his worried parents, endorsing the fact that he was a POW.

From further afield came the news that a well-known figure who had lived in the town for years, working for the brewers Wells & Co. had died from heart failure in Egypt. He was Major Archbutt who had moved from the town to manage Bells Brewery in Lancashire and at the start of hostilities he had been commissioned in the 9th Manchester Territorials and had volunteered for service overseas. Many who remembered him from his time in Biggleswade mourned this popular figure.

The Bedfordshire Regiment had certainly had a hard time in the six months that it had been at the front and the casualty figures that were released in mid-February confirmed this – sixty-two officers and 1,262 men were killed, wounded or missing. If this was the case for one regiment then the figures for the whole of the BEF were indeed alarming and the War Office's notification in February drove this point home when it offered the following advice: 'Disabled soldiers who are certified as requiring artificial limbs, etc and surgical appliances should make application in writing to the secretary to the Commissioners to the Royal Hospital, Chelsea, who are authorised to supply them at the expense of public funds.'

However, those who had been wounded seemed to be a hardy breed, for they quickly returned to the front. Lance Corporal George Dickens was one such soldier. He had been wounded early on whilst fighting with the 1st Bedfords. After recovery he returned to the trenches, only to be struck down by enteric fever and was placed in hospital for two months. Meanwhile Lance Corporal George Knott of the Coldstream Guards was recuperating back in Biggleswade after his treatment in Stoke for frostbite to both of his feet.

As the weather improved the pressure on the BEF to take the offensive increased, and this would result in the offensive that took place at Neuve Chapelle in March. This was to be the first large-scale attack that the BEF would undertake under prompting from the French. Neuve Chapelle is located on a flat plain, south of Lille and the aim of the attack was to show both commitment to the Allied cause and to take the high ground known as Aubers Ridge. The offensive was to be combined with a French one to the south at Vimy Ridge, and the first target was the area of enemy line that jutted out towards the allies at Neuve Chapelle. Such a feature was known as a salient and it was this that the British would attack in March. The assault was carefully planned, for there was a need to ensure that shells were used accordingly and not wasted. Both sides had expected that the war would be one of movement and therefore shell production had concentrated upon shrapnel, and for the British heavy naval rounds also, as this was where the need was seen to be. As such there was a real shortage of shells that were especially suited for trench warfare, and so shells were rationed and stored for major offensives. This can clearly be seen during the First Battle of Ypres where the British Artillery was restricted to just nine rounds per day towards the end of October 1914.

On 10 March 1915 at 7.30 a.m. at Neuve Chapelle 342 guns of the British artillery began to bombard the German trench line, using a majority of shrapnel shells that it was hoped would cut the barbed wire in front of the enemy trenches. The advance followed this bombardment as the artillery shifted beyond the German line in an attempt to stop German reinforcements from getting through. On the whole the attack went well and objectives were taken, but the problem was one that would go on to haunt commanders throughout the war – that was communication between attacking troops and their commanders behind. Messages usually had to be relayed by runners for telephone lines were quickly blown up and, of course there were not the portable wireless/radio communications that we take for granted today. At Neuve Chapelle this was crucial for although the initial objectives had been taken, no orders were given to the reserves to follow on to consolidate the gains. This pause allowed the Germans to stiffen their defences and the battle continued for the next two days. Neuve Chapelle could well have seen a real breakthrough after the advances made by the British in the first few hours, but the problem of communication and exploiting success became very evident. Neuve Chapelle did provide lessons for both sides and the effective use of artillery was one of these, together with the need for adequate supplies of shells. For the Germans the battle convinced them of the need to increase the number of trench lines, so that there would be a second and even a third line of defence should the first line be broken. However the crucial lesson of Neuve Chapelle was that of command and control of attacking troops, and the difficulty of communication once the fighting had commenced. It was a problem that would plague commanders for virtually all of the war.

Amongst the British regiments that fought at Neuve Chapelle were the Bedfordshires, with the 1st and 2nd Battalions figuring prominently and there were, of course, casualties. These include the first man who had enlisted from Biggleswade in 1914. He was Private Walter Storton whose death was officially confirmed when Private J. Albone wrote to his parents in Clifton: 'if you see anybody from Biggleswade tell them Storton is dead. He was killed close to me.'

Walter Storton had been a Wesleyan local preacher, a class leader and a teacher, and his parents had lived in town for some years before they moved to Kempston. After enlisting he had trained at Landguard in Suffolk before being drafted to the front. He had been moved from the 3rd Bedfords to the 2nd at the start of 1915 and was twenty-seven when he was killed at Neuve Chapelle 10 March.

By 1915 recruitment had started to slow throughout Britain and newspapers began to try to drum up support. Advertisements featured frequently, right through the Derby Scheme and up until the introduction of conscription at the end of 1915.

In April of 1915 the same paper proudly printed its Roll of Honour (see Appendix 3) for Biggleswade with the names of 342 men who were serving on 22 April and included the following comment:

> Biggleswade has thus a splendid record, and those that once spread white feathers in the town, must now feel somewhat sorry. Because 342 have offered themselves, however, it does not mean that that all the young men left behind can consider Biggleswade has done all it should do. There are still many eligible young men in the town and their

country needs their help in this great struggle, the greatest in the world's history. 'Men and still more men are wanted' is the cry, and we believe that Biggleswade will continue to respond.

The town was responding in other ways though and its proximity to the major north/south route, the Great North Road, saw troops billeted in the town regularly. Towards the end of April a large contingent of Royal Engineers became the latest to arrive in the town. The soldiers forged strong links with the townsfolk and, if or when, they went on to suffer wounding or worse on the Western Front or other fronts, the families they had stayed with shared the grief of that news. One such example was Sapper Horace Green who actually had relatives in Biggleswade and who was drowned when his ship was torpedoed en route to Egypt in 1917.

On the Western Front April 1915 saw the use of gas by the German army at the 2nd Battle of Ypres. A previous attempt to use it on the Eastern Front had failed because the gas had frozen in its canisters, but between 22-24 April, French, French Colonial, British and Canadian soldiers were to encounter this frightening development in the ways of waging war. Chlorine was the gas that the Germans released on that fateful Thursday and, as the yellow cloud drifted slowly towards the Allied trenches, soldiers initially reacted with a mixture of curiosity and confusion. When the gas cloud reached the Allies' front-line trenches those initial reactions turned to panic as the choking gas took its toll on the troops. The French colonial troops were affected badly and they broke in the face of this terrifying introduction to the battlefield. This brought about the possibility of a significant breakthrough for the Germans. However German troops were as uncertain as the Allies and the impact of this gas attack was not followed up. Two days later chlorine gas was again used, but this time it was against Canadian troops and again breakthrough was perilously close. However the Canadians did not break and held their ground in the face of this shocking new weapon. 'The Brooding Soldier', a striking monument to the Canadians resolve can be seen today at St Julien, the very site that the Canadians stood and fought rather than flee this terrifying introduction. The Canadian Corps would continue to fight at Ypres during much of 1915 and it was here that Herbert Stirling Morgan of the Princess Patricia's Light Infantry was killed on 8 May. Bert Morgan had joined up with his brother Harold in Canada, both having emigrated there from Biggleswade. Bert had enlisted on 24 August 1914 just three weeks after the outbreak of the war. In Canada he had worked as an electrician, but after enlisting he soon found himself back on familiar territory, for the Patricias arrived in England in October 1914. They spent two months in the UK before crossing to France. The Patricias were an experienced battalion, for when the call went out for volunteers experienced men were first sought. Bert Morgan was certainly a candidate for he had served for seven years before emigrating, three years with the Rifle Fusiliers and four years with the Berkshire Volunteers. The Patricias first major action was at Bellewaerde Ridge during 2nd Ypres, when the battalion took part in the battle of Frezenberg with devastating costs. From battalion strength of 650 officers and men when they went into the line on 6 May, they were reduced to 154 when they came out, just over two days later. Bert Morgan was one of those who did not come out, being killed in action as the Germans tried to take the ridge. He was thirty-two when he died and, like so many who fell at Ypres, he has no known grave, and is commemorated on the Menin Gate.

The use of gas sparked off outrage from the Allies and its reporting in the British press simply served to confirm the brutish nature of the German Army. Letters from soldiers serving at the front that arrived home in Biggleswade corroborated this view. Sapper Bertram Wheatley of the North Midland Signal Service wrote to his father regarding the use of gas and the fact that there were still men in the town who had not come forward to enlist:

> I am sorry to hear there are still a number of young men in Biggleswade who turn a deaf ear to their country's call. I sincerely hope that after they have read the account of the last German murderous invention they will answer the call to arms ... only this week I had a conversation with some of our lads who had encountered the awful gas fumes and their experiences were simply awful. To overcome any that may appear, we now all carry respirators.

The issue of respirators to the troops was certainly an improvement on how soldiers had tried initially to counter the effects of gas, for they had urinated on handkerchiefs and had then held them to their mouths and noses, the ammonia of the urine offsetting the chlorine within the gas. The Bedfordshire Regiment would get first-hand experience of gas also during 2nd Ypres at the infamous Hill 60. Any high ground around Ypres gave its occupants a significant advantage and Hill 60 was a prime example of this even though it was only 60ft above sea level. It was here that Private George Bland of Arlesey saw the silver ring on his finger change colour to green because of the effects of gas. Writing home to his mother he told of the fierce struggle to capture the hill and then the desperate defence to try to hold on to it. In the letter he was able to tell how the Germans had now started to use gas shells but that it was the gas pumped out from the enemy trenches that was most feared. However there were problems with this way of using gas as his letter went on to say – 'Not a man could stand, owing to the terrible stuff which streamed from their trench to ours, but the breeze changed and drove it back into their trench.'

George Bland was eighteen in 1915 and, although he would survive 2nd Ypres and go on to win the Military Medal, he would be killed two years later at Passchedaele, 3rd Ypres on 4 October.

Within the pages of the *Chronicle* a graphic description of the use of gas was given with the publication of a letter from Captain Harold Green where he told of the gas coming rolling along the ground, being greenish in colour and then fortunately the wind changing to blow it away from his trench. Private Charles Butcher was another who experienced gas first-hand. He was another reservist who had been called up right at the start of hostilities and had fought at Mons. In a letter home to his wife in Biggleswade he apologised for not writing sooner:

> I have been busy and we have had a rough time of it lately. They put that poison gas over us what you have read about in the papers and I can tell you it was horrible stuff. It did make me feel bad, but I am glad to say I got through alright.

In the fighting at Hill 60 Private Fred Senior was wounded as one of his frequent letters that were published in the *Chronicle* tells:

> I have caught one at last. I got it in the shoulder. You need not worry about me as it is not serious. I caught it on May 5th near the hill.

Fred Senior suffered badly from gas poisoning as well as the shoulder wound, and had been carrying dispatches when he was hit. His platoon had originally numbered 57 men, but by the time he was wounded he was one of only 12 who were left. Fred Senior was brought home to Margate Hospital to recover and would then be able to convalesce in Biggleswade before returning to the front.

On the same day that Fred Senior was wounded Private Arthur Endersby was not to be so lucky, for this Biggleswade man was killed in the fighting at Hill 60. The 1st Bedfordshire Battalion certainly came under a severe onslaught here for as well as gas the Germans had attacked with grenades and machine guns. Indeed the war diary of the battalion tells of the desperate nature of the fighting with both sides occupying the same trenches and of a fierce grenade battle to try and control the trench line. Private Endersby was killed during this struggle and although his body was buried the grave would be lost in the continuing fighting. His name is now to be found on the Menin Gate Memorial in Ypres.

Private Edward Warner of the 1st Battalion of the Bedfordshire Regiment had won the Victoria Cross four days earlier during the fighting at Hill 60. This brave man from St Albans had been on the Western Front right from the beginning and had fought at Mons, Le Cateau, the Marne and 1st Ypres. When the Germans attacked Hill 60 with gas on 1 May the Bedfordshires had been forced to withdraw from Trench 46 where they had held the line. Private Warner though realised that this undefended trench's loss would be calamitous and single-handedly defended the trench against the advancing Germans, even though he was breathing in the gas. He then returned to his battalion and persuaded others to return with him to Trench 46 and the German attack was stopped. Edward Warner paid the ultimate sacrifice the very next day when he died as a result of the effects of the gas. Once again his grave was lost as the fighting continued and his name rests on the Menin Gate.

Further casualties at Hill 60 included the following men from Biggleswade. Private Robert Brown from Back Street was wounded in the hand and Private Edmund Garner, the grandson of Charles Wade of Sun Street was wounded in the leg, arm and head by shrapnel.

In Langford Road, Biggleswade Mr and Mrs James Carr also received news that was not welcome. Their son Sydney who lived in Doncaster had been on the special reserve and had been sent to the front in December 1914. This Lance Corporal had suffered serious wounds whilst fighting with the King's Own Yorkshire Light Infantry near Ypres and had died of these wounds after being taken back to hospital in Boulogne on 30 April. Later, in May, further news reached Biggleswade of yet more casualties with Private Charles Jefferies receiving a bullet wound to his foot whilst going into the trenches for the first time at Ypres, and then Private Alfred Mahoney of the 2nd Bedfords who had fought right through 1st Ypres being wounded by a shell splinter. Both men would return to the front line after treatment, and the two of them would see the war through.

1915 – A WIDENING CONFLICT

The news of casualties and death must have had a sobering effect upon those who had not yet volunteered but further pressure for them to enlist came in the form of printed letters in local papers such as the *Chronicle*, and Recruiting Marches. During the middle parts of May evidence of both of these occurred. The 3rd and 5th Bedfordshires continued their recruitment drive with such a march, starting in Baldock and wending its way across both Hertfordshire and Bedfordshire, seeking to recruit 100 men. It arrived in Biggleswade on Tuesday 8 June and would complete its 225-mile march at Bedford three days later. Such marches usually contained a brass band, recruitment officers, medical officers as well as NCOs and ordinary soldiers.

It was hoped that such a stirring sight would motivate men to enlist and an appeal in the pages of the *Chronicle* from the Lord Lieutenant of Bedfordshire, Mr S.H. Whitbread supported this:

> MEN JOIN THE NEW BATTALION,
> MOTHERS LET YOUR SONS GO,
> SWEETHEARTS PERSUADE YOUR BOYS,
> ALL JOIN IN AND HELP.

As well as recruitment marches through the town the *Chronicle* had no hesitation in publishing letters from serving soldiers that called on those men who were hanging back to enlist. Corporal William Franklin was a regular soldier with the 1st Bedfords, and he had seen action at Mons, the Marne and 1st Ypres, where he had been badly wounded.

Recruitment march of the Bedfordshire Regiment in Biggleswade, April 1915.

After treatment back in Britain he was sent to the training area at Languard prior to returning to the Western Front. From there he wrote the following missive that increased pressure on those who had not yet taken the King's Shilling. He wrote to the editor of the *Chronicle*:

Dear Sir,

Could you kindly find space in your valuable columns to insert this appeal to my fellow townsmen. Surely there will be no hesitation on the part of any man, who is fit to come forward and offer his services for his King and country. Perhaps the atrocities in Belgium committed by the German Army have failed to rouse them from their slumbers and we Englishmen boast of our patriotism, but perhaps now the sinking of the Lusitania, which has resulted in the loss of 1,500 innocent women, children and men may have the effect of awakening them.

I hope this appeal to every able-bodied man will be the means of his enlisting in the Army at once, and so enable us to end the war as speedily as possible and cleanse the world of this tigerish nation, known as Germans. Hoping this will cause no untoward offence.

I am sir, yours truly,

W. Franklin

William Franklin was spared from having to return to the fighting on the Western Front though, for his wounds proved to be too severe. Instead he found himself in very different circumstances when he was assigned as Quarter Master Sergeant with the Garrison Battalion in the Port of Sudan on the Red Sea. He was much taken with the fact that he was able to keep a lot cleaner and warmer than he had been able to on the Western Front, and he wrote home in 1916:

We are half a degree south of the equator, so you will have a good idea of how warm it is. We are able to indulge here in that natural blessing, a bathe. In the Red Sea the water is always warm. Warmer than the Ivel you know. The only danger is sharks.

William Franklin went on to say that he missed his comrades in France and Belgium but that he was confident that it would not be long before Germany was defeated.

In Biggleswade there was the familiar sight of soldiers returning on either leave or recuperating from wounds who also encouraged men to come forward. Amongst these were two good friends, Fred Senior and George Dickens who were able to spend some weeks in the town during June. Fred was recovering from the injuries he received at Hill 60 and George was getting over a bout of inflammation of the intestines. George was a Lance Corporal with the 1st Bedfords and he had been in the thick of the fighting since the outbreak of the war. During the skirmishes that took place in the build up to the 1st Ypres he had been wounded in the thigh at the fighting at La Bassee, and had escaped unscathed from the battles at Mons, the Marne and the Aisne. His recovery from this wound had seen a return to the front line but he had then gone down with enteritis. Fred meanwhile was able to give a sobering account of the fighting at Hill 60 and told how his platoon had only 20 per cent of its fighting strength left. A photograph of these two friends appeared in the *Chronicle* of Friday 25 June, under the title of 'Two Biggleswade Boys who have been doing their bit.'

Others returning to the town were not so likely to recover and Private Eli Loveridge had been invalided out of the army following a wound to his right foot at Neuve Chapelle that had left him lame. Eli Loveridge's war did not end here though and he would later re-enlist and take part in the Battle of the Somme in 1916. The Day family of Shortmead Street also received disturbing news during June for Mrs Day heard that the third of her sons, Gunner Fred Day, had been wounded in both the arm and the leg, thus joining his other brother Harry who had been wounded at Ypres. The third brother, Chas had been captured whilst serving with the 1st Bedfords and was a prisoner of war in Germany. All three brothers though would survive the war.

In July Mr and Mrs Gauge of Cemetery Lodge, Biggleswade had a shock when they answered a knock at their door for there stood their son William, who had left the trenches on Saturday morning and had arrived in Biggleswade by 10.30 a.m. on Sunday. He had been at the front since October 1914 and certainly had interesting tales to tell his parents. In November of that year this Private of the 2nd Bedfords had been reported as missing, but he had been able to make it back to his own lines. During the fighting at 1st Ypres he had had a very lucky escape when a German bullet had ripped through his rations pack before lodging in a tin of bully beef. During his leave in Biggleswade he delighted in showing the very tin of bully beef that had saved him from a serious wound, and from a more sombre point of view he told friends and family that he thought that there were only about 200 men remaining out of the original 1,000 of the 2nd Bedfords. In 1915 he had fought at Neuve Chapelle and again came through that without a scratch. His good fortune would desert him though later in the year during the fighting at Loos.

Evidence of the pressing need for more recruits came during 1915 with the forming of Bantam Battalions. Here there was a definite turn around, for men who had earlier been rejected because of their height were now encouraged to try again. Clearly the casualties being experienced by the BEF were a real cause for concern. Posters and advertisements called for 'little men with stout hearts' to answer the call, and even identified the height that they could be – 5ft to 5ft 2in. Such an advertisement appeared in the pages of the *Chronicle* at the start of August 1915 and targeted seventy-five of these men to volunteer for the Luton Platoon of the East Anglian Bantam Battalion. They were encouraged to make their way along the Great North Road to Sandy where they could enlist.

It was not only on the Western Front that the BEF was in action and men were needed, for the widening nature of the conflict saw an attempt to break this deadlock by the opening up of an Eastern Front via Allied action in the Dardanelles at Gallipoli. The aim was a simple one in that the allies planned to progress through the Dardanelles Straits, and then go on to capture Constantinople. It was hoped that this would draw German troops away from the Western Front and perhaps even knock Turkey out of the war. In February and March of 1915 there had been naval bombardments of the Gallipoli peninsula that

Recruitment poster for Bantams from Bedfordshire.

guarded the straits. This had been to try to knock out the Turkish artillery there, but had not been successful, mainly due to the number of mines that the Turkish navy had laid and three battleships had sunk. It had become clear that the only way to pass through the straits was for allied troops to land on the peninsula and destroy the Turkish defences there. This would allow for safe passage through the straits. In April the first of these landings took place involving British, Australian and New Zealand troops. Further landings in May and August would prove to be as unsuccessful as the earlier ones and British, Australian and New Zealand Divisions would incur over 100,000 casualties before the campaign drew to a close in December.

Amongst those battalions who found themselves fighting at Gallipoli were the 5th Bedfords and they served here between August and December. The 5th Bedfords were originally a territorial battalion and one of its companies, D company had its base at Biggleswade, just off Hitchin Street. Men from Biggleswade certainly numbered amongst this battalion and company, as well as within others fighting here. The 5th Battalion had its baptism of fire in the middle of August with the ill-fated attack at Sulva. Casualties were heavy at Gallipoli and soon word was reaching Biggleswade of those who had been wounded or killed, and they included thirty-year-old Lieutenant Laurence Foster who was the cousin of the vicar of Potton. He was killed whilst serving with the Durham Light Infantry on 8 August. Other casualties included Private Albert Milton from Hitchin Street, who was wounded and then shipped to Alexandria for treatment. His parents found out about their son's wounding from another son Victor who was also serving in the army. He was with the 4th Bedfordshire Regiment and was undergoing training before he would be sent overseas. His brother had written to him from Alexandria. Many of those who were wounded at Gallipoli were shipped to Egypt for treatment and then possibly back to England, if they did not respond to the initial care. Others, once recovered usually found themselves shipped back to Gallipoli.

Corporal Austin Skuse had a very lucky escape during September at Gallipoli and he wrote to a friend in Biggleswade to tell how he had been blown 30ft by an exploding shell, and that his mess tin had saved him from further injury for it took the impact of a piece of the shell. He too was hospitalised in Alexandria, suffering from shock and the effects of gas. Less lucky was Private Dick Bosworth of Hitchin Street who was wounded for a second time during the war. He still carried a piece of shrapnel in his arm from the fighting at 1st Ypres, when he had been driving a transport wagon and had been hit by a piece of metal from an exploding shell. Dick Bosworth was serving with the 1st Battalion of the Border Regiment, having been called up as a reservist in August 1914, and his wife received news of this second wounding with trepidation. That concern increased when she then received news that her husband was indeed missing. Mrs Bosworth received no further news and she wrote to the War Office in desperation. She would eventually be told that she should prepare herself for the worst, as no trace of her husband could be found. This later changed and his body was discovered. He is buried in Green Hill Cemetery in Gallipoli.

British, French and Australian soldiers found Gallipoli quite inhospitable and the heat was a factor for many, even though sun helmets offered some protection. The heat was so fierce that flies thrived in the conditions, and soldiers told of the need to have to wipe away swarms of them off their food just to be able to eat. As a result sickness and illness were common with soldiers suffering from diarrhoea, dysentery, malaria and stomach disorders. Letters published in the *Chronicle* brought home the conditions that soldiers found themselves fighting in. One from a Sergeant Major Milton was very graphic and explained that:

> This is not ordinary warfare. It is simply horrible. We have some chaps here who have been to France and they say that it is not a patch on this. First, there is the heat to contend with, and that nearly cooks you. Nearly everyone's face is raw already. There is no water on the place, and the dust-clouds nearly choke you. Then the high hills and boulders are larger than our houses. You have to get over them the best way you can. Another nuisance is the large number of different sorts of insects. Then there are the snipers. There are heaps of those, including women. We caught three yesterday, and one of them was a woman. They are all very good shots and they have tons of ammunition and foodstuffs, and clothes with the German Eagle on.

First-hand evidence of the conditions in Gallipoli also came from Sergeant W.H. Matthews who had taken over recruitment in Biggleswade after being invalided home from the peninsula. Sergeant Matthews told of the dreadful conditions faced by the Mediterranean Force, as the allied troops fighting there were referred to, and corroboration of those conditions reached the town in late September with news of another death. Leslie Whitbread was a private with the 6th Battalion of the Manchester Regiment; a territorial force that had been at Gallipoli since May of 1915, and the regiment had been involved in heavy fighting at Krithia. Leslie Whitbread had succumbed to the terrible conditions that the regiment had found themselves having to live under, and he had contracted dysentery. This resident of Biggleswade was then placed aboard His Majesty's Troopship *Cawdor Castle* to be brought home, but on 11 September he suffered a sudden relapse and died at sea.

The Gallipoli campaign did not succeed and was called off in December, but not before another soldier from the Biggleswade area had died. George Ashwell had been a bricklayer who had lived in the town for some years before the war and had worked for the builder William Battson. He had enlisted as a sapper in the Royal Engineers, and during the fighting in Gallipoli he had been wounded. The wounds proved to be deadly for he died from them on 5 December.

By this time the attempt to open up another front that might lead to victory had failed and the allies withdrew their troops from the peninsula, having suffered the huge casualties shown below:

Australia:	19,441 wounded and missing	8,709 killed
New Zealand:	4,852 wounded and missing	2,721 killed
United Kingdom:	52,230 wounded and missing	21,255 killed

Bearing in mind the determination that the small Belgian army had shown in resisting the German invasion of their country it is not surprising that the Turkish Army should show similar resolve in the defence of theirs.

Whilst the Gallipoli campaign was being fought there was no let up on the Western Front, and September saw the opening moves of what would become known as the Battle of Loos. The pressure for the battle came from the French who wanted a more visible commitment from their British Allies and the choice of Loos was pressed upon the British. It was an area that Sir John French, the British Commander-in-Chief, would not have chosen for it was badly suited for an Allied attack. This mining area offered much more for defenders than for attackers, with cover being provided by miners' cottages as well as the slag heaps that the Germans had occupied and fortified. This attack would also see the BEF use gas for the first time against their German foes but not all too successfully, as some of the attacking troops found the gas blowing back on them.

The 2nd Bedfordshire Battalion was amongst those who went into action again at Loos and they found themselves initially untouched as they reached the first German trench line, with practically no casualties. As they continued their advance they came under very heavy rifle fire. This caused the battalion to have to change their tactics and they rushed forward in smaller groups, eventually taking the second German trench, Gun Trench. Amongst the casualties was Private William Gauge who had escaped serious injury at Neuve Chapelle, and who had only been on leave in Biggleswade during July. Bill Gauge perhaps had a premonition, for as he left the town in July, he told friends he did not think that he would return to England again. These words proved to be prophetic for Bill Gauge was shot in the head during the advance on 25 September. News of his death came to Biggleswade informally at first, for his good friend Private Alfred Lovett wrote to his mother in October saying: 'My old chum Bill Gauge got killed right beside me. He had a bullet right through the head so it was instantaneous. You break the news to his mother. Remember me to all.'

Later in October Mr and Mrs Gauge would receive official notification that their son had indeed been killed at Loos by a bullet through the head whilst he was throwing bombs at the Germans. Bill Gauge's body was lost on the battlefield and today he is commemorated on the Loos Memorial. His close friend Alf Lovett would not escape from the Battle of Loos unharmed, for he was wounded and was hospitalised in France. Alf Lovett would wear his wound stripe with pride on his uniform for this was the fourth time that he had been wounded since he had entered the fray in October 1914. Another injured soldier from the town was Private Sidney Daisley who suffered a wound to the top of his head on 26 September as the 8th Bedfordshire Battalion attacked Germans who were located in a quarry at Loos. Both Bill Gauge and Sidney Daisley would perhaps have had better luck if the British Army had been able to introduce steel helmets earlier than they did in 1916. The soft caps that the BEF wore up until then offered little protection and head wounds continued to be a major cause of death or serious injury.

Sidney Daisley returned to the town to convalesce, and he was joined there by Private Arthur Webb and Private Charles Butcher, who had both been with the 1st Bedfordshire Battalion right from the start. Both had seen action at Mons, the Marne, the Aisne, Ypres and now Loos. When they arrived home in November both still had mud on them, and Charles Butcher would tell how he had been a victim of gas. Arthur Webb would see out the war and win the DCM but Charles Butcher would fall at Passchedaele during October of 1917.

The year 1915 had seen the British Army take part in offensives that it was not especially trained for, not properly equipped for and that had been fought to show its French allies that it was on the Western Front as a committed partner. The regular army, professional though it was and highly skilled, had been used to fighting in colonial wars that were very different to the trench warfare it now faced. The territorials had been formed for the defence of Britain and the static war of the Western Front was again a type of fighting that they had not been prepared for. Both had fought with resilience and determination but, by the end of 1915, the original BEF was almost decimated and the territorials had paid a very high price.

The scene was now set for a major contribution from the citizen, volunteer armies that the Kitchener recruitment drive had called for. Recruitment was drying up though, and the talk of conscription was in the air. Before this came in at the start of January of 1916 the government tried one more recruitment drive – the Derby scheme. This was devised by Lord Derby and eligible men were written to and invited to join up, with the proviso that they could choose which regiment they wanted to enlist in. Conscription would not allow this choice.

The end of the second year of the war also saw the end of Sir John French as Commander-in-Chief of the BEF. He came under increasing criticism with the outcome of the battle of Loos, where the failure to back up the initial attack was seen by many as a lost opportunity. He paid for this with his job and he was replaced by Douglas Haig.

So the second year of the war drew to an end and this time there would be no ceasefire for either the Christmas period or for the New Year. The fraternization of 1914 was not to be repeated and the High Command of both sides stressed this. Close to 1,000 men from Biggleswade and the outlying villages were now serving in the armed forces, and many of those who had heeded Kitchener's call would be nearing the end of their training and take their place in the offensives of 1916.

THREE

1916

Enter the Citizens' Armies

1916 was in many ways a pivotal year in the Great War. It would see the only major naval battle between Britain and Germany at Jutland, the drowning of Lord Kitchener en route to Russia and the Battle of the Somme, for many the defining battle of the war.

The start of the new year brought further bad news to Biggleswade when the Gauge family of Cemetery Road heard from the War Office that their second son had been reported missing. He had been trained with the 3rd Bedfordshire Battalion and had then been sent to the Balkans to support Serbia after Bulgaria had entered the conflict on the side of Germany and her allies. He had, in fact, gone missing on 7 December, but it was only in the New Year that word of this reached his family. This must have been a very difficult time for the Gauge family following the death of Bill Gauge at Loos. The last sighting of Stanley Gauge had been in the fighting in Serbia, but he had then gone missing. His comrades had believed that he had been captured. This would be confirmed later in the year and Stanley Gauge would spend the remainder of the war as a prisoner of war.

Better news came in the form of the award of the Distinguished Conduct Medal to Private Arthur Webb, who had been on leave in the town towards the end of 1915. The *London Gazette* of 14 January reported that in recognition of his services on the Western Front he had been awarded the DCM. Arthur Webb had been on reserve at the start of the war and was working in the Wells and Winch brewery. As a reservist he was called up immediately war broke out and he quickly found himself across the Channel and in the thick of the fighting, seeing action at Mons and all of the major engagements of 1914 and 1915. The action where Arthur Webb won the DCM concerned the carrying of rations to the front line at Ypres during a fierce German artillery bombardment. For two days this artillery attack had prevented the troops in the front line from receiving rations. Arthur Webb was having none of this and persuaded his commanding officer that he could get through to those men. He was allowed to try and he set off with his wagon through the area being shelled. The danger was immense and the horses that pulled the wagon were wounded with shrapnel, one of them being hit by eighteen shrapnel balls. Private Webb succeeded in his quest, the food getting through to the grateful 1st Bedfordshires in the front line. The citation for the award of Arthur Webb's DCM read:

'For conspicuous gallantry; he succeeded in driving up by daylight, a wagon of supplies to B Company of his regiment, which had been without rations for days along a road which was under heavy shellfire, and although warned that it would be impossible to get through.' Private Webb would go on to survive the war but he would not be the only man from Biggleswade to win a DCM in the early days of 1916.

During January Lance Corporal Arthur Blanshard was serving with the 7th Battalion of the Bedfordshire Regiment on the Somme. In this period both the German and British were at work, tunnelling beneath each others' lines and mines were laid and exploded regularly. On 18 January the Germans blew such a mine under the Bedfords' trench line and supported this with machine-gun fire and gas shelling. This was followed up on 19 January by trench mortars and rifle grenades, and some of the Bedfords were sheltering underground in one of the mine shafts that was being worked at when it partially collapsed. Arthur Blanshard and James Ivory, who were both Corporals in the 7th Bedfords, went into this mine shaft to rescue the men who were trapped and suffering from the effects of gas. Their swift and brave action in bringing out these men saved many lives and significantly reduced the number of casualties. Both men were awarded the DCM for conspicuous gallantry in saving their comrades under very difficult circumstances.

The early months of 1916 saw the continuing training of the volunteer armies and a letter from Bert Tasker that was published in the *Chronicle* in March showed that the volunteers were in good spirits. Bert Tasker had worked in the post office in Biggleswade and, as many workers chose he had enlisted in the battalion associated with his work. For him it was the Post Office Rifles in 1914. His letter told that he expected to go over to France sometime during April after he had completed his last musketry course, and described the camaraderie amongst the recruits. He was less enthusiastic about those who had not volunteered yet, and especially scathing about those who were conscientious objectors:

> For a man to go before a tribunal and say he would not defend his own mother and loved ones from the Hun if England had been in the position of Belgium is absolute cowardice and rot. In my opinion there are no conscientious objectors; those that appear before the various tribunals as such are nothing but traitors. That is the idea of a rifleman — Bert.

Training of men for the front was also taking place in Canada and here a very different tragedy was to take place. Laurie Brown was a Private with the 11th Canadian Mounted Rifles and was another of those who had left Biggleswade for a better life abroad. His mother and father still lived in the town and they heard the shocking and surprising news that their twenty-seven-year-old son had died, not on the Western Front but in a training accident in Canada on 28 February.

Towards the end of April news of another soldier making the ultimate sacrifice reached the town when it became known that Lance Corporal Joseph Loveridge had been killed in action with the 2nd Battalion of the Yorks and Lancaster Regiment. The War had certainly been eventful for Joseph Loveridge who had seen action right from the onset. In the early fighting of 1914 he had been badly injured when shellfire caused a tree to fall onto his leg. After recovering he went back to the front and was gassed, which meant that he had to return home for a period of treatment in the UK. After recovering he was then sent to Gallipoli where, once again, he saw further action. From Gallipoli he had been posted back to the Western Front and at Ypres in the spring of 1916 his war came to an end. Even though this sector did not see the intensity of fighting there was at the Somme in 1916, the daily routine of trench raids and artillery duels maintained the high casualty rates for this part of Belgium. Over the course of the four and a half years of conflict a quarter of a million British soldiers died in the Ypres Salient. Joseph Loveridge was one of these casualties as his battalion was in action on 20 April, and sadly, this soldier's body would be added to the increasing number of those whose grave was lost as the fighting continued. Today Joseph Loveridge's name is to be found on the Menin Gate in Ypres

By the spring of 1916 plans were already in place for a major Allied attack later in the year and this would eventually lead to the Battle of the Somme – but more of that later. Both at home and in France the war had other aspects. In Biggleswade Elphicks of Shortmead Street continued to supply the town's need for literature on all things military with a special book offer of the following titles, all at 1s each:

> OUR NAVY – OUR ARMY. IN PEACE AND IN WAR, BEAUTIFULLY ILLUSTRATED IN COLOUR
> OFFICIAL CRESTS OF THE BRITISH ARMY. 108 DESIGNS BEAUTIFULLY LITHOGRAPHED IN GOLD AND COLOURS. SUITABLE FOR PRESENTATION.
> OFFICIAL CRESTS OF THE ROYAL NAVY SHOWING 108 CRESTS OF H. M. SHIPS BEAUTIFULLY DESIGNED AND LITHOGRAPHED IN GOLD AND COLOURS. SUITABLE FOR PRESENTATION.
> FLAGS OF THE BRITISH EMPIRE AND NATIONAL FLAGS INCLUDING CODE SIGNAL FLAGS; ADMIRAL'S FLAGS OF DIFFERENT NATIONS; BRITISH SEMAPHORE; SIGNS AND SIGNIFICATIONS. SPECIAL COAST FLAGS. MORSE CODE AND SIGNALS FOR PILOTS; ETC
> REGIMENTAL RIBBONS AND BUTTONS OF THE BRITISH ARMY REPRODUCING THE DISTINGUISHING COLOURS OF EVERY REGIMENT. INFORMATION IN SUCH A COMPACT FORM IS MOST USEFUL TO EVERYONE.

The last comment would have sounded very attractive for any passing German spies in the Biggleswade area! On the home front there were increased demands being made upon the public, and, following Zeppelin raids in parts of the country blackouts were in force during the hours of darkness. This required houses and shops to ensure that no light escaped from their windows, and all blinds and curtains were to be drawn at night. In nearby Sandy Henry Kemp, a hairdresser, was fined for his carelessness when local magistrates ruled that failure to draw his blinds after nightfall was worthy of a £2 fine. Henry Kemp was not alone and three other defendants found themselves also £2 poorer.

Over in France football continued to give troops a welcome relief from serving in the front line. Private Alfred Endersby, whose brother Arthur had been killed in 1915, wrote home telling how much soldiers got from a game of football. His letter home in May proudly informed of a football competition where the 6th Bedfords beat the Leicesters

3-2 in the final, and he explained that this victory was well deserved – 'as far as football was concerned we were all over them.'

His letter also told of a fine day with a band playing and this put him in mind of Broom Fete on August Bank Holiday. Less welcome was a raging toothache that he had and sore feet, but he was pleased to be able to tell that he had heard that his cousin Herbert was recovering from wounds he had received during the fighting in the Balkans.

Another letter received during May came to the family of Private Archie Boness. Having recovered from an earlier wound he told of being inspected by Sir Douglas Haig, the Commander in Chief of the BEF, who had congratulated the 8th Bedfordshire Battalion on its steadiness and for not giving way when recently resisting a German attack. Archie Boness would go on to see further action in France, notably on the Somme where he would see tanks in action at Flers during September but would not survive to tell the story.

May of 1916 also saw the first Derby Scheme recruits from Biggleswade join up, and the return to the army of Eli Loveridge. This young man had been serving with the army in 1914 in Africa. He had then fought with the 2nd Bedfords during 2nd Ypres where he had had been gassed, and he was then badly wounded in the ankle at Neuve Chapelle. This had led to him being discharged from the army as being medically unfit. Indeed he was in receipt of an army pension of 6s 3d a week, but he gave this up and re-enlisted at the end of April, joining the 3rd Bedfords. Perhaps the news of the death of his brother Joseph at Ypres on 20 April was the reason he chose to return to the ranks. Whatever his motif was he would quickly return to action and the Somme beckoned him.

Less welcome news though reached Biggleswade during May and this concerned two brothers Frederick and Herbert Cartwright-Wells. Both of these had been in action with the 8th Bedfords in the Ypres Salient near the Yser Canal Bank, and both had gone missing in the fighting. During June their parents, who lived in West's Yard, would receive a postcard from Germany from their son Frederick stating that they were prisoners of war.

In the same action that had seen the Cartwright-Wells brothers captured, another man from Biggleswade was less fortunate. Walter Gatward was twenty-six and he had been employed at Hill Farm, Old Warden before becoming a horse keeper in Potton. He had been a regular churchgoer and worshipped at the Wesleyan Church in Biggleswade with his wife and their two young children. His wife Daisy received her last letter from him on the very day that he was killed. On the night of 19 April, Private Gatward and the 8th Bedfords had faced a determined attack by the Germans on the Yser Canal, outside of Ypres. They had suffered a two-hour artillery bombardment and then German troops attacked, seizing a part of the British trench line. The Bedfords resisted strongly though, and eventually were able to recapture the section of the trenches that had been lost. That the fighting was fierce can be gauged by the casualty figures for the Bedfords with thirty-five killed, ninety eight missing, believed killed, and sixty-five wounded. Walter Gatward was among those who were killed in this action and is buried close to where he fell in Essex Farm Cemetery, Ypres. His grave sits very close to one of

Private H Cartwright-Wells, POW.

the most visited plots in the Salient, for a few feet away rests Private Valentine Joe Strudwick of the Rifle Brigade who was one of the youngest to be killed when he fell in January 1916, aged just fifteen.

At the start of June more bad news reached Biggleswade with the reported death of Sergeant Harold Morgan of the Alberta 49th Regiment of the Canadian Infantry. Harold Morgan was another of those who had been brought up in Biggleswade but who had left for Canada. He had enlisted in 1915, had later been promoted to sergeant and had seen his brother Herbert killed in 1915. Now in the same area, the Ypres Salient, he too was to die. Harold Morgan died defending an advanced trench against a German attack on 2 June, and like his brother his body was lost on the battlefield and his name sits on the Menin Gate. Some years after the end of the war a signaller with the 49th Alberta Regiment published his diary that covered this period, and his entry for the day that Harold Morgan was killed was graphic:

> After we pass Zillibecke with the ammunition we witness some gastly (sic) scenes in the communication trench leading up to Maple Copse and Lover's Walk. The great sandbag wall has been smashed up by German shells and the trench is one string of dead and wounded — you can tell which are the dead for they are quiet when we unavoidably tread on them in the darkness, but the wounded moan. Our stretcher bearers are already at work, but the situation is far beyond them. There are cries everywhere for water and our water bottles are soon emptied. The front line is one mass of fireworks, and there is considerable shelling and bombing going on. All other bombardments we have been through seem almost insignificant compared to what is going on now. Nearby explosions follow one another so closely that at times there is nothing but one great ear-splitting roar around us. The earth is shaking and dirt is being rained down on us. It seems impossible for anyone to live through anything like this.

Harold Morgan did not.

Three days later the man who had been responsible for the recruitment drive of 1914, Lord Kitchener was drowned when, en route to Russia, his ship HMS *Hampshire* struck a mine off the Orkneys. Newspapers that covered the story gave glowing tributes to the man who had done so much to raise the Volunteer Citizen Armies, but some of them also ran questionable advertisements such as this example.

> LORD KITCHENER
> EVERYBODY SHOULD HAVE
> A PLACE FOR THE LATE
> LORD KITCHENER'S PHOTO
> IN THEIR HOME
> PRICE, COMPLETE 4/6. CASH WITH ORDER
> THE BROMIDE ENLARGING COMPANY
> 44, WANDSWORTH ROAD., LONDON S.W. 3

On the Western Front the loss of the man who had been the prime mover in the expansion of the BEF was felt by those very men who had responded to his call as they were about to enter the fray *en masse* for the first time. The Battle of the Somme was about to commence.

The advance at the Somme had been agreed by the French and the British in late 1915 and the location had been chosen, not for its strategic importance but rather for the fact that it was here that the British and the French armies met. Indeed, Douglas Haig, the Commander in Chief of the British Expeditionary Force would have preferred to have seen the main Allied offensive take place in Belgium at Ypres, where a breakthrough could have had a huge impact upon Germany's ability to continue the war. However, Haig did not get his way and the joint attack over an eighteen-mile front was planned, initially with both of the Allies providing equal numbers of men. The plan had to be changed when the Germans attacked at Verdun in February and the French commitment had to decrease. By June the French at Verdun were becoming desperate, with casualty figures of 257,000 and the pressure on the British to attack at the Somme increased.

The Somme had been a relatively quiet sector of the Western Front until the arrival of the BEF in July 1915. The British soldiers who arrived there from Flanders took over a section of the front from the French, and they were certainly pleased to be there after the conditions they had faced at Ypres. The rolling countryside reminded many of the countryside of home. However between their arrival and the end of the year the hitherto peaceful nature of the area changed, and trench raids, increased artillery bombardments and tunnelling made it a much more violent place. In the six months of 1915 over 1,600 men of the BEF were killed in action. The start of 1916 saw no let up in this aggression and by the end of June over 6,000 soldiers of the BEF had already died here.

The scene was now set for what would become the most infamous battle of the Great War for Britain. After a seven-day artillery bombardment all was ready for 100,000 British troops on the morning of Saturday 1 July to make their mark, and advance through and beyond the German lines. These men were all volunteers, whether original BEF, Territorial or Kitchener's New Army. By the end of that day almost 60,000 of them had become casualties, with nearly 20,000 dead. It was, and still is, the worst day experienced by the British army in terms of those killed, wounded and missing. The battle would continue for another 148 days by which time the advance would be roughly six miles, but even so, the first day objective of the capture of Bapaume had not been achieved.

Throughout the battle men from Biggleswade and the surrounding areas would be involved and would play their part, with twenty-seven being killed and many others wounded.

Saturday 1 July dawned bright and sunny and, for three hours after sunrise, the guns of the British artillery continued their assault on the German lines. This was augmented by

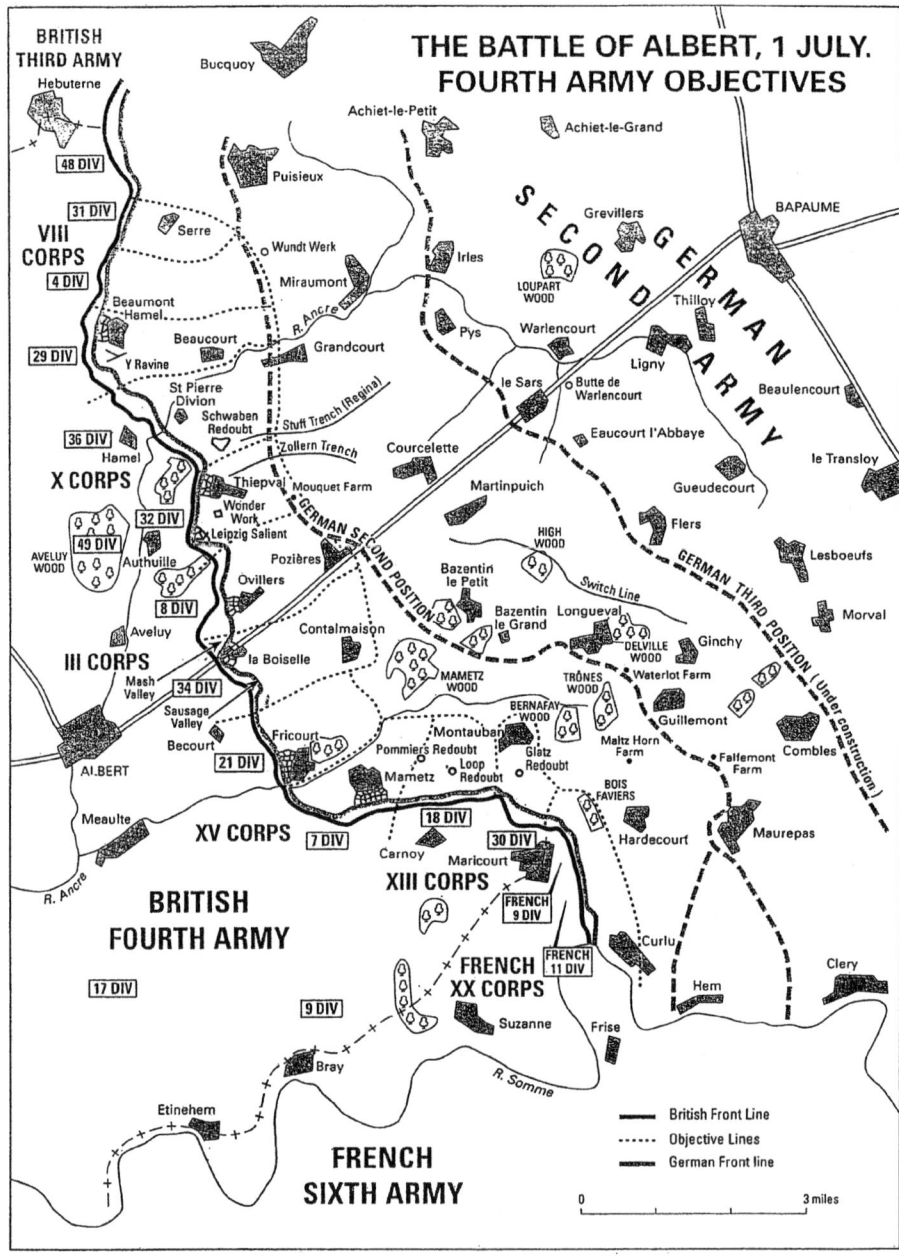

Map of the Battle of the Somme.

thousands of mortar shells fired from British front-line trenches. The noise was so great that many men were later to tell that their ears bled from the constant artillery barrage that increased in the minutes just before zero hour, with mortars also increasing their bombardment of the German lines. At 7.20 a.m. the first of the mines exploded on that date was detonated at Hawthorn Ridge and Private Sidney Leonard Chambers of the 16th Middlesex Battalion, known as the Public School's Battalion prepared to go over the top. Len Chambers, whose father Jacob lived at No. 27, Drove Road, Biggleswade, was amongst those who were charged with capturing the crater that the mine created. As well as destroying German troops such mines also saw the formation of highly advantageous positions if they could be occupied. The lip of the crater gave the chance for an elevated position from which troops could fire down on the remaining enemy. Attacking in support of the Lancashire Fusiliers Len Chambers and his fellow soldiers went forward into a hail of machine gun bullets, and faced a swathe of uncut German barbed wire. They stood little chance and Len Chambers was amongst the heavy casualty figures for the battalion. Further to the south Private Edmund Stratton of the 7th Bedfordshire Battalion must have heard the sound and felt the shock of the Hawthorn Ridge mine, to be followed by sixteen other mines between 7.28 a.m. and 7.30 a.m., as he prepared for his part in the 'Great Advance.' Edmund was twenty-nine, the son of Mr and Mrs Fred Stratton of Sun Place and had been amongst the first to enlist from Biggleswade when he joined up in September 1914. Following training he had been on the Western Front for eleven months prior to the attack on the Somme. On this fateful day he was in 'C' Company of the 7th Bedfordshires under Captain Clegg and they were charged with capturing Pommiers Redoubt. As Edmund was clambering over the parapet he was hit by an enemy bullet and became the second man from Biggleswade to die on that fateful date. The 7th Bedfordshires were successful and they did capture the redoubt, but with very heavy casualties, for around a third of their battalion strength was killed or wounded. The news of the death of Edmund Stratton reached Biggleswade before official confirmation arrived telling that he had been killed. Private Arthur Stocker, who was with Edmund Stratton in the 7th Bedfordshires wrote home explaining how his friend and comrade had died.

Len Chambers lies today in Hawthorn Ridge Cemetery No. 1, only yards away from the crater that remains from the explosion on 1 July. Edmund Stratton's body was yet another that was lost in the continuing fighting and he is commemorated on the Thiepval Memorial.

The first day on the Somme was soon to claim another man from the town when Private Charles (Chas) Pepper succumbed to the wounds he received on that day and died at Heilly Casualty Clearing Station, Mericourt L'Abbe. Chas Pepper died on 6 July aged twenty-one. He had enlisted six months earlier and prior to this had worked for a builder in Biggleswade. His training had been with the Bedfordshire Regiment but he had been attached to the Essex Regiment, and it was with them that he was to advance on 1 July. News of Chas Pepper came when Private Fred Pressland wrote to tell that his friend was missing. Chas Pepper had been in France for just a month before he was killed on the Somme. The sheer number of casualties from these first few days can be seen in that Chas Pepper shares a grave with two others who died on 6 July. Casualty Clearing Stations such as Heilly were inundated with wounded men who were sorted into categories and then treated. Some had no hope of recovery but were given pain reducing shots of morphia, whilst others received basic surgery under terrible conditions as surgeons often ran out of anaesthetics. Men died in large numbers as is evident in the need to bury more than one man per grave. Between 1-3 July, 7,000 casualties arrived at Heilly, mainly by train, for No. 36 and 38 Casualty Clearing Stations were right next to the railway line. As well as this high number of British wounded, the hospital treated around 150 wounded German prisoners. Later in the month the hospitals here would treat the author Robert Graves, after he had been given up for dead at a dressing station near Mametz Wood. Graves had been wounded during the attack at Bazentin Ridge on 20 July and, although the dressing station did not think he would survive, the doctors at Heilly were able to treat him and put him on the road to recovery. From Heilly he was taken to a base hospital at Rouen and then back to Britain. Graves' war experience was faithfully recorded in his classic work 'Goodbye to all that'.

Both Edmund Stratton and Chas Pepper were a part of the 18th Division that attacked east of Mametz, and both were within touching distance of the famous incident where Captain Nevill of the East Surreys encouraged his men across no-man's-land by kicking footballs towards the German lines. Four footballs were kicked into no-man's-land, and the men of the East Surreys were told that the man who kicked the first one into the German front line trench would be given a prize from Captain Nevill. One of the footballs was even inscribed 'The Great European Cup, The Final, East Surreys v Bavarians, Kick Off at Zero'.

Chas Pepper, Edmund Stratton and Wilfred Percy Nevill were to number amongst the 3,115 casualties suffered by the 18th Division on Saturday 1 July 1916.

If three men from Biggleswade were to die as a result of the advance on day one then ten others would be wounded in the first few days of the battle, with one other being injured the day before the battle commenced. By the second week of July news was reaching Biggleswade of these men from the town who had been hurt in the first few days of the battle. Firstly it was learned that George Fairbanks, a Private with the Highland Light Infantry had been hit by shrapnel in the hand and shoulder and had been taken back to a hospital in Boulogne. George had been in France since February and had had an eventful time. Just prior to the Somme he had been struck and wounded on the head by a pick axe whilst putting up tents. When he was taken to Boulogne it was discovered that he was only seventeen and this was two years below the age limit for soldiers serving abroad. After his wounds were treated he was returned to Britain. The war was not done with him though and two years later he would return to the front line, and his date with destiny. As George and Caroline Fairbanks were hearing about their son, so was Harry Milton's father receiving news that his son had been wounded in the ankle on 3 July. Two other wounded men lay out in no-man's-land whilst the battle continued with different fates. Private Charles Kemp had been wounded badly in the back and he had to stay in a shell hole until 2 July when an officer heard his cries and went out to bring him in.

Private Cooke of the London Scottish was wounded during the advance and also lay in a shell hole amongst those who had died. He though was captured by the Germans and would spend the rest of the war as a prisoner.

Private Albert Clark had been wounded by shrapnel on the day before the battle started and wrote home telling how he was wounded when one of his own side's shells burst close by. His letter, written from his hospital bed in Birmingham told:

> I was wounded on June 30th by a shell bursting on my dug out. I am covered with shrapnel in my left knee, both hands and face, but since I was brought over from France on Tuesday the nurses and sisters have worked day and night on me, and I am pleased to say that I am getting on fine. Some of the shrapnel has been taken out. I must have been lucky to escape as I did. I had a near go of losing both eyes. I have two black eyes, but they are looking better. It happened just before the big attack which, as you know the Allies made, and made good progress. We sent over some smoke bombs and one happened to land in our dugout and I got plenty of shrapnel. I didn't see anything more of my mates so I think they must have been buried. There were a lot of casualties in that front line trench in the last 48 hours. I am going on well.

Reports of other casualties arrived in the town thick and fast. At the same time that Edmund Stratton's death was learned, came the news that Lance Corporal George Gurney, one of the original BEF of 1914, who had served since the outbreak of war and had already been wounded three times, had been wounded in the wrist and the thigh on the Somme. In the action where he had been injured he had also been awarded the Military Medal. Private Fred Senior was with George Gurney and the 2nd Bedfordshires on 1 July and indeed helped him to the dressing station even though he too was wounded. Fred Senior was a prolific writer and his letters featured regularly in the pages of the *Chronicle* throughout the Great War. He also had considerable combat experience and had fought right through from November 1914. Now he wrote home telling of how he had been wounded on the Somme: 'I have stopped two this time in my left arm, but not bad. I may have to go under an operation to have the bullets taken out as they did not go right through this time.' The Somme had already been eventful for Fred Senior as he had taken part in a successful raid on German trenches on 25 June and he was then awarded the Distinguished Conduct Medal for his part in a bombing attack on German trenches on that first day of the battle. The citation for his DCM read 'For conspicuous gallantry during an attack, when he led a party into the enemy dugouts and took many prisoners. Later he displayed great coolness and courage in carrying messages under shellfire.'

Private Alfred Lovett was another with the 2nd Bedfordshires on 1 July. He was one of four brothers who were the serving sons of Mr and Mrs H. Lovett of Sun Street. Alfred Lovett had been a reservist before the outbreak of the fighting and he would be the only one of the brothers to survive the war, despite being wounded five times. Previously he had been wounded in the head, neck, arms and hand. Now on the Somme he was wounded in his cheek. This plucky young man wrote home later in the month – 'Fritz

Private Fred Senior, DCM.

tried again to do me in, but failed. I have got a bullet in my cheek but am still smiling.'

Other casualties included Private Jerry Yerrill, a widower of Sun Street who was hit in the back but who would go on to survive the war, as would his brother James who was wounded on the Somme also. Private Eli Loveridge, who had been pensioned out of the army after being badly gassed at Ypres, was wounded in the foot at the start of the Battle of the Somme. After his gassing at Ypres he had spent some time back in Biggleswade but had then had re-enlisted. He would survive the war but grief had come to the family when his brother Joseph had been killed in action at Ypres two months before the Somme. Private Horace Bridge of the Machine Gun Corps was another who was a casualty on the Somme when he was brought back to Wales for treatment to a wound to the head, but he did not see out the war. He was killed in action during the 3rd Ypres, better known as Passchendaele, in October of 1917. His brother Thomas was killed twenty-six days earlier during the same battle.

News of the fighting on the Somme came to Biggleswade via both the national and local press. The *Chronicle* published letters from men who were fighting in the so-called Big Push and equally ran questionable advertisements such as the one that appeared in the edition of 14 July. Here a quarter page was taken by W. Albon & Co. of Shortmead Street who advertised their shoe, boot and bags sale. The header for the advertisement contained the words 'The British Great Offensive' flanked by a Union Jack!

Over the next few weeks the newspaper, in line with hundreds of local newspapers across the UK would include growing details of the number of casualties from the Somme, together with photographs of those men who had been killed. On 21 July the *Chronicle* told of another associated with the town that had been killed as the trickle of casualties and deaths increased. This time the paper told of Sapper Frank Sharp of the Royal Engineers who had been killed in action on 12 July. Frank Sharp was originally from Royston in Hertfordshire, but he had settled in Biggleswade where he had worked as the manager of M.J. Allen, the builder. Frank Sharp was twenty-nine when he was killed on the Somme.

The fighting on the Somme was to continue until 18 November by which time much of the terrain had become the muddy, lunar-style landscape that is so associated with the Great War and was a far cry from the verdant fields strewn with wild flowers, notably poppies, across which the attack of 1 July had taken place. The breakthrough that had

W. Albon's questionable advertisement for the sale in his shop, using the Battle of the Somme phrase, 'the British Great Offensive'.

been the original aim had developed into a struggle of attrition that saw some of the fiercest fighting on the Western Front. A further twenty-four brown envelopes would be delivered in Biggleswade by the postal services and they would bring the dreaded telegrams informing residents that their sons, fathers or husbands had been killed on the Somme.

On 11 July the 2nd Battalion of the Bedfordshire Regiment attacked at Trones Wood at 3.10 a.m. and despite very difficult conditions they took their objective and held on to it. Dense undergrowth and a hostile response of shell and machine-gun fire did not deter them, but Private Arthur Dellar from Biggleswade was amongst the 244 from the battalion who were either killed or missing in the taking of Trones Wood. His death would not be confirmed until the start of the next year though. The *Chronicle* of 11 August actually published a lengthy article on the fighting that it had secured from the adjutant of the battalion.

Towards the end of July cousins Arthur and George Boness of the 1st Bedfordshire Battalion were killed in action in the desperate fighting close to High and Delville Woods. The 1st Bedfordshires attacked at Longueval in support of the 1st Norfolks, and although their objectives were taken the casualty rate was very high with ten officers and 342 other ranks being either killed or wounded. Both Arthur and George Boness were killed on 27 July, both were reservists and both now left widows and families back home in Biggleswade. Arthur was thirty-one and George was thirty-nine when they were killed in the attack at Longueval. George Boness was one of five brothers who were serving in the BEF, and he had volunteered in December 1914. His war was intensive to say

Private George Boness, killed on the Somme in 1916.

the least, and before the Somme he had been in action at Ypres, Festubert, Loos and Dickebusch. During the advance on 27 July he had been amongst a group of men who had been buried when a German shell landed next to them. George Boness was dug out by comrades but they discovered that an artery in his shoulder had been severed. Those comrades tried to bind up his shoulder but it was to no avail and he died half an hour later. Neither Arthur nor George Boness has a marked grave and their names sit near to one another on the Thiepval Memorial to the Missing.

A former resident of Biggleswade, who had worked as an apprentice printer at the *Chronicle* had also been killed in July. He was Sergeant Gilbert Way Albone and was twenty-eight. He was killed on 15 July when the 6th Bedfordshires, another of the Kitchener battalions that were literally blooded on the Somme, attacked Pozieres Ridge, which after Thiepval was perhaps the most strategically important section of the Somme. This attack was typical in terms of casualties that were experienced during July and out of a battalion of around 800 who attacked, thirty-five were killed, 183 were wounded and a further twenty-five were reported as missing in action. Machine-gun fire wreaked havoc amongst the attacking Bedfordshires and Sergeant Albone was one of those killed in action that day, being buried on the battlefield by three of his platoon. His body would number amongst the 'Missing of the Somme' when the grave was lost in further fighting and today he is yet another commemorated on the Thiepval Memorial. Pozieres Ridge would not fall until it was captured by the Australians during their bloody baptism on the Somme.

During August further fatalities for Biggleswade included twenty-year-old Cliff Huckle of the Royal Army Medical Corps and twenty-year-old Steve Runham of the 6th Bedfords. Cliff Huckle had only been in the RAMC for ten months, and on the Western Front for three weeks before he was killed on 1 August.

His family were informed of his death and told that he had died as a result of wounds received whilst treating wounded soldiers and that he had been buried by a chaplain who had preached in Biggleswade. Steve Runham was killed by shell fire on Monday 7 August whilst with a trench mortar battery

Private Arthur Boness.

Private Cliff Huckle, killed on the Somme whilst treating wounded men on the battlefield.

in a front-line trench at Bazentin-le-petit Wood. Trench mortars always attracted immediate response from the Germans, and Steve Runham was one of eight other men from the 6th Bedfordshires to die that day. His commanding officer wrote to tell how death had been instantaneous and that he had been buried just behind the allied front line. That grave again would be lost in the continuing fighting and Steve Runham is yet another commemorated on the Thiepval Memorial. In just under a year Steve Runham's brother Chris would also be killed on the Western Front at Arras but on the Somme he also was in action and was wounded in the fighting at Delville Wood. Here he was hit by shrapnel in the face and down the right hand side of his body but he carried on helping other injured soldiers until he lost consciousness from loss of blood. Chris Runham had served for a year and a half on the Western Front, and was a Corporal in charge of bombers, as the section of a platoon who threw Mills bombs was called. The fighting at Delville Wood was grim and it was no surprise that the Tommies referred to it as Devil's Wood.

September would see the highest number of casualties for the town, with eleven men from Biggleswade being killed. At the end of August, thirty-two-year-old William Warner, a private with the Sherwood Foresters was wounded in the head and neck. He was taken to a Casualty Clearing Station on 26 August and even though he was operated on he gradually got worse, and died on 3 September. His widow and their six children would later receive a letter from the Duke of Bedford expressing sympathy for the loss of her husband. Other men from Biggleswade were perhaps more fortunate during August and both Company Sergeant Major Cecil Walker of the Bedfords and Private Sidney Brown of the King's Royal Rifles were wounded but would survive. Sidney Brown wrote home with details of his brush with death. His battalion was advancing by Delville Wood when he was hit in the thigh – the piece of shrapnel entering from one side and exiting from the other side of his leg. As he was hobbling back another shell landed close by and he was hit again. This time he was rendered unconscious and lay out in the open for hours. His trouser leg had been blown away and much of his tunic was also torn open. Eventually he was brought back, given hot tea and rum followed by morphia and an operation successfully removed the shrapnel from his right side.

Fighting in this month saw the first ever use of the secret weapon that the British hoped would end the stalemate of the trenches and bring about victory. Tanks were used for the first time ever in the attack at Flers and forty-two-year-old George Jackson from

Biggleswade was killed here on 15 September. There was much debate regarding the most opportune time to introduce the tank, some being of the opinion that its impact would be lost if it was to be sent into battle in a dribble rather than *en masse*. Those of this view felt that the Germans would be able to devise defences against the tank and, that if just a few were initially used, then there would be no breakthrough that could lead to victory. By September 1916 Haig could not afford to wait, and thirty-two of the monsters prepared to go into action on that Friday morning, but nine of them would break down before reaching the jump off point, and in fact only fifteen reached enemy lines. Those that did go forward had mixed results, generally enjoying more success in the middle of the area attacked than at the flanks, and the village of Flers was captured. The British press later reported this in glowing terms – 'a tank is walking up the high street of Flers with the British Army cheering behind.'

The impact of the tank was considerable, for although the vast majority broke down on that first day of use they did have a severe psychological effect upon the Germans, who were shocked at the appearance of these metal monsters. For over two years the British had explored ways in which the impregnable barrier of the enemy's trenches with their swathes of barbed wire could be breached. Vehicles with huge caterpillar tracks, armoured roving vehicles and gun-mounted trains all came under consideration before the 'landship' was decided upon. Their development and production was a closely guarded secret, and the name tank derived from the attempt to disguise this development, and later shipment to the front as water tanks. Two types of tanks that were produced were used on the Somme, the male and the female. The male tank was bigger and armed with a 6-pounder gun, whilst the female's main armament was a heavy machine gun. The conditions inside the machines were terrible, not only being cramped, with a crew of up to eleven, but also exceedingly hot. These early machines had a top speed of 4mph, and were steered by the slowing or stopping of one of the tracks, whilst the other one continued to move. The noise inside was dreadful and crew communication was only possible by shouting, written note, or signs. The petrol engine's heat and fumes made life within the tank uncomfortable to say the least, for ventilation was minimal. There was no suspension also and the ride for the crew over uneven ground jarred their bones, and the 6-pounder gun had to be moved manually to be aimed and fired. However the tank did bring something extraordinary to the battlefield and it was able to traverse the extended coils of German barbed wire, thus offering a fascinating glimpse of possible victory.

The action at Flers would claim the lives of other men from Biggleswade, notably Edward Cecil Batten, Charles William Swepstone, and Archie Boness. Edward Cecil Batten was initially reported as missing, having taken part in the attack at Flers with the King's Royal Rifles. He was a private with the 9th Battalion, the Prince Consort's Own, as they advanced during late morning when they came under heavy machine-gun fire. Edward Batten was one of the battalion's many casualties, his body being another that would not be found and again his name is to be found on the Thiepval Memorial. Archie Boness and William Swepstone had been serving with the 8th Bedfordshires along with George Jackson. William Swepstone had suffered shrapnel wounds to both hands late in 1915, and had only recovered after being treated in Boulogne Hospital. This time he would not survive.

Private George Jackson, killed at Flers 1916. He was the oldest soldier from Biggleswade to die during the Great War.

Two other men from the town were the final casualties for the Flers battle with twenty-year-old Robert Lovett also of the 8th Bedfordshires, the first of three brothers who would die during the war, and Maurice Woodward of the King's Royal Rifles, who was killed on his way to a dressing station whilst helping a wounded comrade. Maurice Woodward was only eighteen and as such should not even have been abroad, for soldiers were supposed to be nineteen at least before they served overseas. Maurice had slipped through the net though and had been in France since May.

George Jackson, William Swepstone, Archie Boness and Robert Lovett had found themselves under heavy fire as the German positions that the 8th Bedfordshires were ordered to attack had escaped the lengthy artillery bombardment that had been planned, and their situation became more perilous when tanks that were supposed to support the advance did not arrive. Archie Boness died one day before his twenty-fourth birthday, and he was the third cousin within the Boness family to die on the Somme. The bodies of Archie Boness, William Swepstone, George Jackson and Robert Lovett were lost during the fighting and they are now amongst the 72,000 commemorated on the Thiepval Memorial to the Missing.

The overall casualties for the action at Flers were considerable, with around 30,000 killed or wounded. Amongst those who were killed was thirty-seven-year-old Lieutenant Raymond Asquith of the Grenadier Guards, the son of the Prime minister,

September was particularly cruel to the Lovett family of Sun Street for Alex Lovett, brother of Robert was killed three days after his brother when the Canadians went into action for the first time here. Alex Lovett had emigrated to Canada six years before the war started and he had joined the Canadian Expeditionary Force when the call came for the Dominion to join the fray. On 18 September as he went into action with the Manitoba Regiment he had died instantly of concussion when a shell exploded close by.

Robert Plumbridge of the Machine Gun Corps was another casualty in early September. Bob was only sixteen when he enlisted and had been in France since January. He was reported missing on 6 September and his body would never be found. For some months his anxious parents clung to the hope that he might somehow be alive. However, early in 1917 exactly what happened to him became known and it was reported by the Red Cross that he had been out as a member of a four-man machine-gun team just after the capture of Guillemont when a shell fell among them. No trace was found of Bob Plumbridge and today he is commemorated on the Thiepval Memorial.

Private Bob Plumbridge, Machine Gun Corps – the 'Suicide Club'.

Other fatalities this month included Lance Corporal Albert Haynes of the Middlesex Regiment, William Smith of the Hampshire Regiment, and Fred Wells of the Suffolk Regiment. Albert Haynes had been a teacher in Biggleswade before the war and after enlisting he had served in Gibraltar and Egypt and his letters home featured regularly in the pages of the *Biggleswade Chronicle*. Albert was one of five brothers who had enlisted and of his other brothers one, Herbert would contract trench foot whilst another Walter would number amongst the casualties when he was killed almost a year later in 1917.

William Smith had fallen in an attack at Thiepval on 3 September. He had been one of those who had been rejected several times when he had earlier tried to enlist because of problems with his feet, but had eventually been accepted into the 3rd Bedfordshires which was a battalion that acted as a home defence militia and trained men for service abroad. William had moved on and had seen service in Salonika, but here he had been taken sick and upon recovery he had been sent to the Hampshire Regiment. He was with them as they advanced on that September morning. Today he is commemorated on the Thiepval Memorial only yards from where he was killed in action.

Fred Wells died of the wounds he received at Thiepval and today his body lies in Puchevillers Military Cemetery on the Somme. Private Wells had died in the capture of the Schwaben Redoubt, perhaps the strongest German trench system on the Somme. This fortification had been captured by the 36th Ulster Division on 1 July, but their courage and bravery had not been enough for them to hold onto the Redoubt. They were the only division north of the Albert/Bapaume road to take all of their objectives on that first day but their success was their undoing, for the supporting divisions were unable to make the same headway, and the Ulsters found themselves isolated and under attack from three sides. They had to retreat, leaving the Schwaben Redoubt back in German hands until the end of September when it was captured by the 18th Division. Amongst the battalions that attacked and captured the Schwaben Redoubt were the 7th Bedfords, the Shiny Seventh, and during the fighting Second Lieutenant Thomas Adlam won the Victoria Cross when he stormed a German machine-gun emplacement even though he had been wounded in the leg. Tom Adlam was a Salisbury man by birth but, after the war, he settled in Sandy, Bedfordshire for some time and became the chairman of the British Legion there between 1922 and 1926.

The last casualty for the month was Private Harry Wagstaff of the 4th Bedfords who was wounded in the attack on Schwaben and Thiepval. He had been advancing at about 1.00 p.m. when a piece of shrapnel hit him, going through his trouser pocket, tobacco tin and then deflecting into his stomach. He would be less lucky in just over a year's time when he was killed at Passchendaele.

Other men from Biggleswade were also wounded in the fierce fighting of late September. Private Jack Cartwright of Sun Street was hit in the chest in the fighting for

High Wood whilst serving with the London Regiment. Unusually his parents were able to cross the Channel and visit him in an army hospital in Boulogne. Jack Cartwright would go on to recover from this wound and survive the war. Other casualties in September included Lance Corporal Reg Boness and Private Bert Pressland, both of the Bedfordshires.

October would see continued losses for the families of soldiers from Biggleswade and Harry Huckle, one of those who had joined up under the Derby Scheme and who was forty, was killed in action as the 2nd Bedfords attacked on the morning of 12 October close to High Wood. They were the only battalion that day that managed to capture and keep hold of the German frontline at Gird and Bite Trench, but Harry Huckle lost his life in this fighting.

Fred Land was another to succumb to wounds in October. He had been with the 7th Bedfords, as they had stormed Thiepval in September, and had been shot in the back. As soldiers advanced they sometimes missed Germans who were either wounded or hiding. Often these wounded or hidden men would fire on the advancing Tommies after they had gone by them, literally shooting them in the back. Fred Land was one of those who received such a wound, and although he lingered on for days he died on 9 October. Fred was only nineteen and had been so enthusiastic about serving, having joined up when he was below age, and he had to train at Ampthill up until he reached nineteen. He had not been in France long when he was wounded at Thiepval, and although he was taken to a general hospital he could not be saved. The shock to his mother was great for Fred was her only son and she was a widow.

Francis Taylor, a former school teacher at Alma Boys School, of the Middlesex Regiment was also killed in action at Morval on 7 October. Francis Taylor was thirty-two and the son of Alfred Percival and Mary Taylor, of 66 Shortmead Street. In the same regiment was Private Alwynne Turnery whose parents lived in Havelock Road. He had an incredible escape when he was hit in the chest but cigarette cards he was carrying in his pocket stopped the German bullet. Not so lucky was Private Ernest Pope of the Royal Sussex Regiment. This unfortunate young man was only twenty and the only son of Walter Francis and Sarah Pope, of Dunton. He was about a mile behind the front line when a German shell exploded close by and killed him outright. Shelling of the support and reserve lines was quite usual, for logically this prevented or reduced the number of troops, who could reach the front line as reinforcements.

In Biggleswade itself tragedy was about to strike when Corporal Edgar Waite of the Royal Engineers was accidentally killed on 4 October. This twenty-two-year-old was serving with the Signals section and his death came as a terrible shock to his parents in Monmouthshire. The threat of death on the Western Front was always there in parents minds for their sons, but to be killed in an accident at home in Britain would have been totally unexpected.

November saw the reality of the Battle of the Somme brought home to everyone in Biggleswade when the film of the battle was shown twice daily at the Empire Cinema in Hitchin Street, and the film included footage of the Bedfordshire Regiment. Indeed some of those who watched the film may have recognised soldiers as many of those serving from

Biggleswade were in the Bedfordshire Regiment. This film had a profound effect throughout the country and brought home to many the reality of the Western Front, even though some scenes were staged. At one screening the words 'My God they're dead' were heard.

At around the same time as this film was being shown in Biggleswade news reached the town that Corporal George Gurney had been awarded the Military Medal for gallantry. The Somme had certainly been eventful for George Gurney for apart from winning the Military Medal on the first day he had also been wounded in both the thigh and the wrist. During November he was on sick leave in Biggleswade, but this modest man was very reserved about the award of the Military Medal, which he officially received in May 1917, and simply told those who enquired that he had received it 'for hanging on.' His modesty was mirrored though by his bravery and he had seen action right from the start at the 1st Ypres, having fought in the repulse of the Prussian Guards. He had later been badly wounded in the leg but had returned to duty in France upon recovery in time for the Somme. The Western Front was not yet done with George Gurney and he would see further action during 1917 and then, during the Kaiser's battle of 1918, he would lose his life. His body was never recovered and today he is commemorated on the Pozieres Memorial.

Casualties for November were indeed high for Biggleswade and a further seven men were killed before the battle ground to a halt. The first of those to die was Private Sidney Circuit who died on 6 November whilst serving with the Middlesex Regiment. He was followed by Sergeant Reg Peddar of the Machine Gun Corps and Harry Rowlett of the 4th Bedfordshires. Reg Peddar died as the battle was entering its closing stages when he and two of his comrades were killed by shellfire on 3 November. Harry Rowlett died in the offensive on the Somme on 13 November as he attacked with the 4th Bedfordshires just south of Beaumont Hamel. Attacking at 6.45 a.m. the battalion suffered heavy casualties in achieving their objectives. Harry Rowlett fell next to his officer. He was only twenty-four.

The last actions of the Battle of the Somme took place on 18 November and by now winter's grip was fierce. As the troops prepared for the assault snow was falling and the battlefield was made even worse by having to move forward across half-frozen mud. As the men went in at 6.10 a.m. the snow changed to whirling sleet, and it became increasingly difficult to locate objectives and keep one's bearings. Amongst those attacking was Private Arthur Rainbow, who was with the 7th East Surreys, better known by the name 'The Buffs'. Their objective was Desire Trench and they took it, but communication was lost with them and all of the runners who were sent forward to ascertain their position were shot dead by German snipers. Eventually the Buffs had to withdraw, but Arthur Rainbow was not amongst those who came back. Reports suggested that he had been wounded and captured, and confirmation of that came early in 1917 when it was confirmed that he had died from his wounds on 17 January whilst a prisoner.

Other fatalities in the attack on 18 November included Edmund Sells of the Royal West Surreys and Fred Skilliter of the Essex Regiment. Edmund Sells was initially reported as missing during the final attack on the Somme, but it was confirmed early in 1917 that this former carman had indeed been killed in action. In his last letter home Edmund had told his wife how awful it was in the trenches with shells bursting all around. He also told how grateful he was to have survived so far and said that it was a mystery how any

Private Edmund Sells.

man gets out of it. On Saturday 18 November Edmund Sells did not get out of it and he was killed in action with the Royal West Surreys as they attacked at Grandcourt.

Fred Skilliter's young face stared out from the front page of the *Chronicle* of Friday 22 December under the heading 'The Great Dead'. He had been conscripted at Easter, and after training had been on the Western Front for just five weeks when he was killed. Fred Skilliter's platoon sergeant wrote home to the Skilliter family who lived in Rose Lane, telling them that Fred had been killed in action less than six months after joining up. Sergeant Betts wrote:

> You have probably heard by now from the War Office of the loss of your son, Pte. F.C. Skilliter, No. 28484, and I am writing to offer you my deepest sympathy in your bereavement. He was in my Platoon and he met his death on 23.11.16. He suffered no pain, death being instantaneous. He had not been with us long and we are sorry to have lost him so soon. All the men join me sending their sympathy in your sorrow.

Sergeant Betts also wrote to another in Biggleswade. This time it was to Miss Evie Matthews, Fred Skilliter's fiancée. He told her:

> It is a hard matter for me to put together this letter to you. Pte. F.C. Skilliter was I believe a great friend of yours, and I therefore feel it my duty to inform you of his fate. On 23.11.16 he was killed. I regret to have to inform you this, although I am glad to say he suffered nothing. I should like to offer you my deepest sympathy in your time of sorrow.

Fred was only twenty-five and again his body would have no permanent resting place and, together with over 72,000 others, his is just a name inscribed on the immense Thiepval Memorial to the Missing. The sight of his young face gazing out from the front page of the *Chronicle* must have haunted and saddened both his parents and his fiancée for a long time.

The final person associated with Biggleswade to be killed in the latter stages of the battle was Henry Wall who had emigrated to Australia four years earlier when he was sixteen. He died fighting with the 6th Battalion of the Australian Infantry as they took part in a bombing raid on the German frontline. Earlier he had fought at Gallipoli and had been wounded in the arm. After recovering he had arrived on the Western Front and the Somme. At first he was registered as being missing and his parents, Henry and Flora who still lived in Drove Road clung to the hope that he was alive. They wrote to his battalion asking for information and soon they received a reply. The Reverendd Carter wrote:

Dear Sir,

You have my deepest sympathy, but I fear I cannot help you in your anxiety. Your son has been missing since a bombing raid by our men on the Somme front, 11.11.16. Some say he was seen killed, but it has not yet been officially confirmed, though it is probably true. May God soon send us victory and peace.

Yours sincerely,
George W. Carter

Henry Wall's body was never found and he had in fact died on the day that two years later, would see the war come to an end. Today he is commemorated on the Australian Memorial on the Somme at Villers Bretonneaux.

The battle of the Somme was a tragedy in terms of the number of British and Empire troops who were killed and wounded, but the British Army that emerged from it had learned painful but significant lessons that they would put to very good use in the remaining years of the war. The British Army that went into the Somme was, to the main, an amateur one. The Army that emerged from it was a professional one. Both infantry and artillery tactics developed hugely as a result of the Somme and this changed the way in which the BEF fought. This was especially the case during the final 100 Days of the war when the British Army proved to be the best that there was in the field (see appendix 4). The horrors of the Somme had been a difficult and harrowing experience but the British Army that emerged from it was the one that would go on to win the war. How much of a consolation this would be though to the bereaved families of those whose fathers, husbands and sons had died on the Somme is another matter.

Not all casualties for the latter part of 1916 were on the Somme and the war continued in the Ypres Salient. The nature of the fighting here for the BEF during 1916 was like a nagging toothache that simply would not go away. The area that the BEF held here continued to see them dominated by the German army who occupied most of the high ground and, as such, overlooked the British trenches. Casualties continued on a daily basis either as a result of enemy shelling or from trench raids. One such casualty was Herbert Goss of the 8th Bedfordshire Regiment on 27 July. Herbert Goss was the only man from his regiment to die on that day. He was out with a party of men from his platoon in the early hours of the morning when he was hit

Private Fred Skilliter, killed on the Somme in December 1916.

by bullets from a German machine gun. Working at night always brought the danger of being detected and sound from no-man's-land usually resulted in artillery, mortar or machine-gun response from the enemy. Herbert Goss was well thought of in his platoon and his grieving parents received letters from both his commanding officer, 2nd Lieutenant Buck and from Herbert's best friend John Newman, also from Biggleswade that told of the high esteem he was held in. When the 8th Bedfordshires were moved to the Somme during the late summer John Newman received serious wounds from shrapnel and was hit in both hips and on one hand during the Flers attack on 15 September.

At Loos fighting also continued and twenty-eight-year-old Private Frank Kefford was one of those who died during October. Frank had joined up in February 1915 and had sailed to France nine months later in November. On Halloween in 1916 he had been out with a bombing party carrying out a trench raid on German lines when he was wounded. At first he was reported as missing, and indeed in 1918 rumours started to circulate that he was a POW but later it was confirmed he had been killed and buried by the Germans. Wherever that grave was, it was never found by the British after the war and today Frank Kefford's name can be found on the Loos Memorial.

The final casualties of 1916 were Private John Lincoln and Rifleman George Wagstaff. John Lincoln was a private with the 2nd Battalion Norfolk Regiment and he had been serving far away from his native Biggleswade, fighting throughout the siege of Kut, to the south of Baghdad. This town, in what is now Southern Iraq, had been initially captured by the British under General Townsend, but the Turks had recovered and their counter-attack had seen the town besieged from December 1915. For four months the garrison held out, but relief columns could not get through. John Lincoln was amongst those who were captured by the Turks when Kut surrendered at the end of April, and for months his mother and father worried greatly about the fate of their son. His parents were relieved to receive a postcard from him in November that said: 'I am alright at present … This is the first chance we've had to write.' That relief quickly changed to grief when the next communication they received told that he had died whilst a POW on 15 December. The treatment of the POWs from Kut was very harsh, and over 3,000 men died as a result of forced marches of over 1,200 miles, and beatings. The fall of Kut was a disaster for the British and a huge boost to the morale of the Turks, representing yet another victory following on from that at Gallipoli just months earlier.

George Wagstaff's death was rather different, for he had died two days before John Lincoln, on 13 December at the age of twenty-eight. He had enlisted early during the war and was with the Post Office Rifles. However he had not seen action and had died as a result of appendicitis in a London hospital.

So 1916 came to a conclusion and there was still no end in sight to the fighting. By now the ranks at the front were starting to receive the first conscripted men, as well as those from the Derby Scheme, and, as the war progressed, and casualties mounted, these men would increasingly be called upon.

FOUR

1917

Soldiering On – Arras, Passchendaele, Gaza and Cambrai

The winter of 1916/17 was a dreadful one and the cold experienced by soldiers in the trenches was numbing. However, in spite of the horrors of the Somme, the morale of soldiers appeared to be holding out. Gunner Harry Watts of Sandy wrote home that he had witnessed the surrender of many Germans and these prisoners were very demoralised, and that he expected the war would be over in four or five months.

Harsh as the winter was, fighting continued and shelling and trench raids featured on some part of the Somme every day. During one of these actions Private Horace Smith of Hitchin Street and serving with the Duke of Cambridge's Own, Middlesex Regiment, was killed on 17 February, one week before the German army withdrew from the Somme to take up a stronger position on the newly constructed Hindenburg Line. Horace's father heard of his son's death when a Sergeant Kempley wrote to him telling how Horace had at first been reported as being wounded, but that his body had been found and had been buried. Horace Smith was only nineteen and had only been in France for a few months. Today his body rests in Regina Trench Cemetery on the Somme.

Alex Drysdale, in the 4th Battalion of the Bedfordshire Battalion, was wounded badly on 5 February. He had been with the battalion close to Beaumont Hamel when he had been wounded. He was then taken back to England and treated in hospital in London, but on 1 March he succumbed to those wounds and died. His parents though would be able to see him buried, for his body was brought back to Biggleswade and he was interred in the town's cemetery. Herbert Boness, whose brother George had been killed on the Somme in July 1916, was another wounded early in the New Year. He had been hit in the knee whilst with the Bedfords and the wound was bad enough for him to be brought back to 'Blighty' where he was treated in Manchester Hospital. Fred Pressland was a further wounded in these early weeks of 1917 and he suffered a wound to the head as the Essex Regiment cautiously advanced.

After the German withdrawal, the BEF advanced cautiously and came across some nasty and deadly surprises that the Germans had left behind. Dugouts were booby trapped, animals were slaughtered and water supplies were poisoned. The Germans were determined not to leave anything behind that the Allies could use and this scorched earth policy shocked the advancing troops. The booby traps that were left were ingenious and claimed many lives. Wine bottles were attached to explosives by wire and stoves had gun cotton hidden in them. The results caused the Allied soldiers to have a more cautious approach as they moved forward and occupied German trenches and dugouts. George Senior, whose brother Fred had won the DCM on the Somme, was a Corporal with the Royal Berkshire Regiment and he wrote home to Biggleswade telling what the Germans had left behind: 'He hasn't left a house standing and has cut down the trees and mined all the roads.'

During this German withdrawal Private Arthur Garner was killed instantly by shellfire. Arthur Garner was aged twenty-nine and had left Biggleswade to make a new life for himself in Australia some years earlier. Arthur had some military experience, having served with the Bedfordshire Yeomanry for five years before emigrating. Joining up at the start of the war he had seen service at Gallipoli, where it had been mistakenly reported that he had been wounded at Suvla Bay, and then in Egypt. When the Australian Infantry had been sent to the Somme in July 1916 he had gone with them and had seen much action during the four months that the battle had raged. He was killed near Wallencourt on Wednesday 28 February and his body rests in the CWG cemetery there.

Another veteran of the Somme battles of 1916 was also killed in the pursuit of the Germans as they withdrew, and he was Private George Street of the Machine Gun Section of the 6th Battalion Northamptonshire Regiment. George Street was from Edworth near Baldock but he had been living with his uncle in Saffron Road in Biggleswade when war broke out. In the town he was well known and his death was mourned by his relatives and members of the Methodist Choir where his singing had been much appreciated. News that he had been killed in action on 17 February did not reach Biggleswade until the end of March.

If the German defences on the Somme were strong then what confronted the BEF as they faced the Hindenburg line appeared to be virtually impregnable. During the winter of 1916/1917 this defence line had been built and it included concrete bunkers, machine gun nests, heavy belts of barbed wire and deep tunnels for moving troops around. To break this line would indeed be a difficult task.

Private Arthur Garner (right). Sergeant Major A.E. Field (left), another man from Biggleswade who emigrated to Australia, survived the war.

Private George Street (standing).

In March of 1917 another of those who had been conscripted from Biggleswade was killed when Walter Walker of St John's Street died. He had been called up in August of 1916, had trained with the Bedfordshire Regiment but found himself serving with the 2nd Battalion of the Northamptonshire Regiment. On 6 March Walter Walker was severely wounded in the stomach and high up on the leg. He was taken to a casualty clearing station but, as the nursing matron described when she wrote to Walter Walker's widow explaining that it 'was practically hopeless from the first'. Walter Walker was buried in Wimeraux Military Cemetery.

Further bad news reached Biggleswade later in March but this time from much further afield, From Palestine came news that Lance Corporal George Dickens had been killed in action on Monday 26 March. George Dickens was another who had seen action right from the off, having fought at Mons, the Marne, the Aisne and at Ypres. In 1915 he had been wounded, having been shot through the thigh at the fighting at La Bassee and had spent time back in Britain recuperating before he was sent to serve with the Essex Regiment. Initially he had been with the Bedfords but early in 1917 he found himself in the Middle East as the Allies tried to take Gaza. As with many soldiers returning from wounding he was allocated to a regiment that needed 'topping up'. At Gaza he was with the 4th Battalion of the Essex Regiment. The 1st Battle for Gaza was one of those instances of 'if only.' At the very point that the Turks had given up their defence the attack was called off. The attacking troops of the EEF (Egyptian Expeditionary Force) could not understand why they were being pulled back and it would take two further assaults in April and October for Gaza to be captured. It was here, in March, that George Dickens was killed.

George Dickens' photograph had appeared on a number of occasions in the *Chronicle* together with that of his good friend Fred Senior as they posed for the camera in one of those typical shots that soldiers had taken to give to their relatives. George Dickens stood almost to attention in this photograph whilst his friend Fred Senior sat. The photograph would be used from time to time as news of the exploits of these two friends reached Biggleswade. Now George Dickens's exploits had come to an end.

East Africa, an oft forgotten area of conflict for the Great War, had seen a fierce struggle between the Germans and the Allies, where the German Commander Paul von Lettow-Vorbeck, a master of guerrilla warfare, had led the Allied army of General Smuts a merry dance. Vorbeck refused to commit to a major engagement, preferring to use guerrilla

Privates Fred Senior (left) and George Dickens (right).

tactics to tie down as much of the Allied resources as he could. General Smuts was an experienced and able commander himself and he enjoyed a significant numerical superiority over his German opponent, yet the task he faced in trying to defeat Vorbeck was considerable, for both the terrain and the tactics used by the Germans made victory hard to achieve. The resourcefulness of Vorbeck enabled him to fight on until two weeks after the war in Europe ended and it was on 25 November 1918 that he surrendered with only 175 men left.

Hubert Purser was a forty-year-old veteran of the Boer Wars and the youngest son of Revderend and Mrs Purser of Station Road in Biggleswade. He had been in South Africa when the Boer War had started and had served as a sergeant throughout the fighting, being amongst those who were besieged at Ladysmith. After the Boer War he had returned to Biggleswade, but the lure of the Dark Continent was strong and he had gone back to South Africa where he had taken up farming. When war broke out in 1914 he had volunteered his services at once and returned once more to England. His experience had quickly seen him granted a commission in the Royal Marine Artillery and he had served on the Western Front in the defence of Antwerp. After this he was sent back to Africa where his familiarity with that continent could be put to good use. At first he was employed in training new batteries of heavy artillery but, when Vorbeck began to make himself such a nuisance to the British forces in East Africa, he was attached to the force that was sent to find Vorbeck and defeat him. As Vorbeck's troops withdrew further into East Africa, Bert Purser was amongst those who followed, and it was here in March of 1917 that he contracted malarial fever. For days he hovered between life and death but died on Sunday 18 March. He is buried in Morogoro Cemetery in Tanzania.

On the Western Front winter continued to hold its chilling grip and in Biggleswade the wintry conditions that troops in France and Belgium were experiencing were also in evidence. During March snow fell on eighteen days and there were only sixty hours of sunshine for the whole month. The snow that lay up to three inches over the town would have mattered little though to Private Ernest Leonard who was discharged from the army this month. He was declared as being medically unfit to continue to fight because of both rheumatism and an injury to his leg. Altogether he had served for three periods on the Western Front. Other soldiers returning home included Private J. Spring who had served with the Suffolk Regiment as far back as Mons and who now had been declared medically unfit, and Private Victor Wakes who was home on sick leave recovering from frozen feet. The strain on manpower was evident also in this month for the national

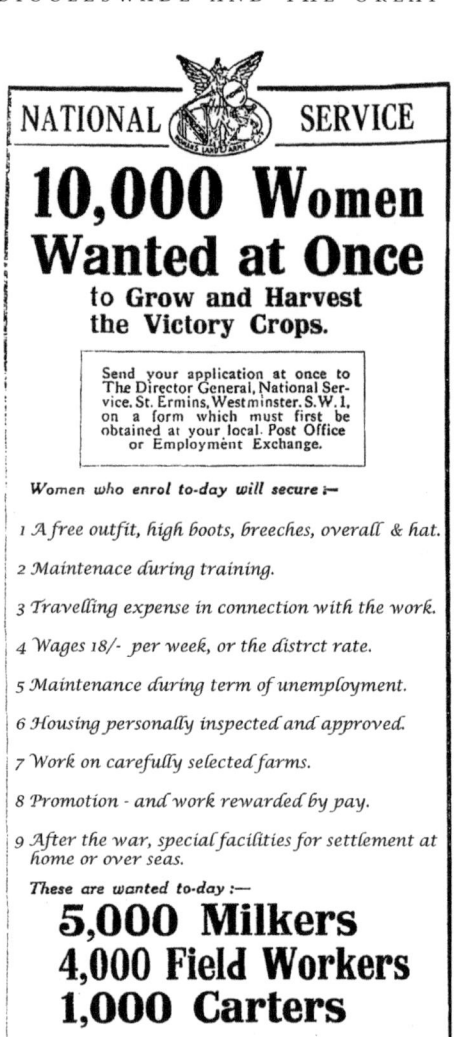

Advertisement for Women's Land Army workers.

newspapers ran advertisements for the Women's Land Army. The *Chronicle* carried an advertisement in its edition of 13 April, and nationally 10,000 women were asked to come forward to grow and harvest the 'Victory Crops.'

The bad weather would continue right through into April when the British would make their next assault on the German front line at Arras. This battle was a commitment from the British to support the offensive of Robert Nivelle, the dashing new Commander in Chief of the French armies. Nivelle had become a national hero during the Battle of Verdun when his troops had recaptured Fort Douaumont, and he had now persuaded both the French and the new British Prime Minister David Lloyd George that he could win the war on the Western Front. So convincing was Nivelle's argument that David Lloyd George ordered Field Marshall Douglas Haig to place the British Army under French control for this campaign. The plan was for a massive French attack on the Aisne, whilst the British were to carry out a supporting/diversionary attack at Arras. For the plan to succeed a creeping barrage would be used by the French as they attacked the German trench line. However it did not help that a French officer had been captured prior to the attack and he had on his person details of the offensive, and therefore the Germans were ready and waiting. Haig was against the plan but was overruled by David Lloyd George, and the British were to carry out the attack in the Arras sector. The British attacked first on Easter Monday, with the Canadian Corps securing a memorable victory at Vimy Ridge. This was the first time that the Canadians had fought together as an army and their planning and execution were exceptional. Attacking in driving snow they took the whole of the German front line that overlooked the Douai Plain. The Canadians, under their excellent commander General Arthur Currie were to forge a formidable reputation for themselves via this success, and by the end of the war they were much feared by the Germans as opponents.

Today critics of the British High Command are keen to point out that the most effective troops within the British and Empire forces were either Australian or Canadian. What those critics fail to allude to is that a huge percentage of the men of those two Imperial and Dominion forces were actually born in UK and that they had emigrated to Australia and Canada prior to the war. They had quickly volunteered to come to the aid of the mother country as is evident from the number of ex-Biggleswade residents from both Canada and Australia who fought during the Great War.

Initially Arras was successful for the British, but by the middle of May the attack had come to a halt. For the French the offensive was hardly successful at all. By the end of the campaign their armies were close to mutiny and Nivelle had been sacked as their commander. For the British Arras was not without gain, for tactics that had been developed on the Somme, were put to good use there, and they would be honed later during the 100 Days that would bring the war to a successful conclusion in November 1918.

Men from Biggleswade certainly featured in the Battle of Arras and there were, of course, heavy casualties. At the beginning of April Corporal Fred Roberts of the 8th Battalion of the Bedfordshires had died of wounds in the trenches at Loos-en-Gohelle, to the north of Arras. He was the only man that was killed that day in his battalion during an enemy bombardment. Fred Roberts had been born, had lived and had enlisted in Biggleswade. In just over one week the actual Battle of Arras began and the 6th Battalion of the Bedfordshire Regiment was involved in the attack on Monchy. The fighting was hard but the British were able to make significant progress as the Germans failed to carry out their new tactic of defence in depth. The idea was that the front line trenches would only be lightly held and that the advancing British troops would almost be encouraged to break through. Strong reserves would then counter-attack and catch the British tired and battle worn. What happened at Monchy was that the German Commander Von Falkenhausen had his reserves too far behind for this to work, and the British were able to consolidate their gains.

Private Alec Ambrose of the 6th Bedfords was killed in the assault on Monchy on 10 April when he was hit by shrapnel. He was quickly attended by stretcher bearers but they were unable to save him and this twenty-five-year-old died without regaining consciousness. Wounded also was another private with the 6th Bedfords, Harry Milton, and this time his wounds were far more serious than those he had received on the Somme. He succumbed to them on 10 April despite the efforts of the field ambulance crew who tried to save him.

Another killed in action in these early moves at Arras was Corporal Dick Alvey. Having lied about his age he had joined the Bedfordshire Regiment in 1915 and had two-years' service under his belt when he was transferred to the City of London Regiment as a Lewis gunner. He died on 11 April just aged eighteen, having fought on the Western Front for just about a year. Dick Alvey was another who should have not been serving abroad, being a year too young to do so.

As the fighting continued further casualties occurred and 23 April saw both the 1st and 4th Battalions of the Bedfordshire Regiment heavily involved. With the 1st Battalion was

Above left: Private Robert Brown, killed at Arras 1917. *Centre:* Punch Brunt. *Right:* Private Jack Gauge, killed at Arras 1917.

Private Robert Brown who had been at the front for over two years as the personal servant of a Lieutenant Fletcher. On the Somme Robert Brown and his brother Andrew had been wounded but both had recovered. Now in the attack on 23 April at La Coulotte to the north of Arras Robert Brown was killed as he advanced next to Lieutenant Fletcher, who was himself killed a few paces further on in the attack. Robert Brown was twenty-nine and one of three brothers who served.

Corporal George Dilley of the Machine Gun Corps was also to lose his life in supporting the Bedfordshires here. Initially George Dilley was posted as missing and indeed his body was never recovered. Today he is commemorated on the Arras Memorial.

Directly to the east of Arras the 4th Battalion of the Bedfordshire Regiment had attacked also on 23 April. They were a part of the 63rd Naval Division that was given the task of capturing the village of Gavrelle and numbered amongst the 'landlubbers' who were attached to the Division. Attacking at 4.45 a.m. proved to be successful and all objectives were taken, although a windmill that stood to the north east of the village of Gavrelle remained in enemy hands and remained a thorn in the British side. Thirty-seven-year-old Alfred Brunt was one of those who were killed in action with the 4th Bedfords as they attacked that day.

'Punch' Brunt was an only son of elderly parents and his death was devastating to them. He was not the only Biggleswade man in the 4th Bedfords to die on that fateful Monday though, for Private Jack Gauge also died in action.

Jack came from a family that was familiar with soldiering for his father, Joseph, had served in the militia. Jack had arrived in France shortly before his nineteenth birthday and had gone to the Somme where he had been involved in hard fighting during the autumn and winter of 1916. As spring 1917 approached he had been hoping for a period of leave, but it was not to be, and he was killed in that early morning assault by the Bedfords on 23 April. He too would number amongst those whose body would be lost in the continuing fighting as the battlefield was churned up by almost ceaseless shell fire,. Today he is commemorated on the Arras Memorial, together with Robert Brown and Alfred 'Punch' Brunt. Another Biggleswade-born man, Percy Cole, was with the 'landlubbers' section of the 63rd Division. He had left the town to go and work Deptford although his parents remained in Biggleswade. He had joined the Honourable Artillery Company Infantry just a year earlier and when this battalion attacked on 23 April he was killed in action. In May his parents received a letter from Captain O'Brien who was Percy Cole's company commander. In this missive the captain gave more details of Private Cole's death and conveyed his sympathy. Percy Cole had been killed outright by a piece of shell and Captain O'Brien pointed out that he had been buried in a marked grave and that the Graves Registration Committee had been informed of the spot. Sadly though Percy Cole's grave was to join the huge list of graves that were lost in the ensuing fighting and the Arras Memorial is the only place that his name is to be found in Northern France. Percy Cole was a fine soldier and Captain O'Brien mourned his loss greatly as he told Alfred Cole, Percy's father: 'I have lost a good soldier and a friend, and one whose presence among us will for ever be missed.'

The fighting on 23 April was indeed fierce and, in addition to the fatalities above, a high number of men from Biggleswade were wounded. Their stories reached the town via the *Chronicle* that published extracts from letters home from these men. The editor of the newspaper would certainly have taken an interest in Private George Harper's letter, for it gave news of a former employee of the *Chronicle*, Bob Wilson, a Lance Corporal in the Bedfords who had been wounded on 23 April. George Harper told how he himself had been hit by shrapnel just as he was about to advance at 5 a.m. The *Chronicle* also reported that Harry Wagstaff had been wounded again, this time in the side. On the Somme he had received a stomach wound, and in just six months after this second wounding he would receive a third wound from which he would not recover at Passchendaele.

Other casualties included Private William White who had been shot in the hand and Private Herbert Boness who had caught one in the hand and knee. Both of these men would go on to survive the war but their scars would always be a visible reminder of their experiences on the Western Front. Herbert Boness wrote home to Biggleswade to tell graphically of the part he played in the attack of 23 April. He wrote to his sister:

> I consider myself to be a lucky man to tell the tale. You'd like to hear about it. We started from our reserve trenches at 8 at night and tramped until about one. Then we rested until about 4.45 when our Barrage started and we knew what it meant and soon we were going over the top. I hadn't gone ten yards before the chap next to me was killed by a shell. It knocked me in a hole, but we had to go on. I got a long way in a trench, then shell hole, talk about Dante's Inferno that's not a patch to it. We got about 50 Germans. I got on a sunken road and was lying up the side of a bank waiting for another move for we were close to the village we had to take, when a shell hit me. I had got my hand on my knee and gloves on. My fingers were open and the splinter of a shell split my glove finger. I got in a shell hole and bandaged my knee up, and eat [sic] a tin of sardines, and bread; my rations for the day. Then I threw my stuff away and made it for the dressing station, 2 miles away. It took me all my time to get along and there was a sniper fetching some of us down. So we got the captured Germans and made them help us down and the sniper left us alone.

The 23 April was not yet done with Biggleswade though and two letters arrived at the home of William and Mary Runham of St John's Street within days of each other. The first came from their son Chris who was a corporal with the 1st Bedfords. Chris Runham had been serving in the army when war broke out in 1914 and he had been sent over to France in December of that year. By 1917 he was quite a veteran, having seen action at Neuve Chapelle, Hill 60 at Ypres, Festubert and on the Somme. This first letter told how he had bumped into a fellow member of the Biggleswade Town band and his spirits seemed high. He spoke of seeing normal activity beyond the German lines and wondered what life was like for those under German rule. In conclusion he thanked God that England was free from the ravages of war and that the youngest son Bob Runham was too young to fight.

The second letter, from Chris Runham's commanding officer, was far less welcome for it told that their son was missing in action and that it was possible he had been captured by the Germans, for a counter-attack had seen him and his platoon surrounded. Chris Runham was a corporal in 'A' Company of the 1st Bedfords and they were given the task of capturing La Coulotte in a diversionary attack that was closer to Lens than Arras. The attack went in just before 5 a.m. and met with fierce resistance, and some of the Bedfords found themselves trapped between the German counter-attack and belts of barbed wire. The Germans bombed the Bedfords with stick grenades and Chris Runham was lost during this assault. Mr and Mrs Runham already knew tragedy for their second youngest son, Steve, had been killed by shellfire on the Somme. They now clung desperately to the hope that their eldest son was still alive. Those hopes would linger on for over a year until Chris Runham was officially confirmed as having died on 23 April, being killed in that action at La Coulotte with the 1st Bedfords. Both of Mr and Mrs Runham's serving sons were now dead and neither had a grave; indeed both are commemorated on memorials in France – Steve at Thiepval and Chris at Arras.

The fighting at Arras showed no signs of abating though, and grim news continued to reach Biggleswade of growing casualty figures for the town. At the start of May Percy Brown, who was a private in the Northants Regiment, was killed in action, whilst Privates John Newman and Jonathan Wade were wounded. Percy Brown had been a keen sportsman before the war and had played for St Ives football team. After enlisting he had trained with the Bedfordshire Regiment but he had gone over to France with the 6th Battalion of the Northants Regiment, and it was whilst serving with them that he was killed in action. Percy's parents had moved from Biggleswade to nearby Sandy and it was there that they heard of their son's death. Percy's younger brother had been badly wounded at 1st Ypres but had recovered. Percy was not so fortunate and his commanding officer wrote to let his parents know of their son's death. Writing to Tom Brown he said 'We can ill afford to lose such men as these.'

Apart from being wounded, John Newman was also diagnosed with shell shock and the fact that he had spent almost three years on the Western Front indicates that the constant shelling did have a traumatic effect for not just new recruits but for veterans equally. Jonathan Wade had left Biggleswade at the age of eighteen in 1908 to go to Canada where he had worked as a farmer. He had enlisted in 1916 and was one of four brothers serving with the Canadian forces. Early in 1917 he arrived back in the UK with the

Private Percy Brown.

Canadian Expeditionary Force and had gone over to France in April in time for the attack at Vimy, where he had been wounded in the hand. In just over six months he would not be so lucky as the Canadians saw action at Passchendaele.

Tidings of a more welcome nature arrived in Biggleswade during May when it was learned that Sergeant Major French of the Bedfordshires had been awarded the Military Medal when, according to his company officer 'seeing a party of Germans evidently on mischief bent, Sergeant Major French went for them single handed, and with the bayonet removed all chances of the Huns accomplishing their desires.'

During the German Spring Offensive of 1918 Sergeant Major French would add to this when he was awarded the DCM. The citation read 'For conspicuous gallantry and devotion to duty. During many enemy attacks in the course of a battle lasting some days, he was constantly visiting all the post, keeping up a good supply of bombs and small arm ammunition, encouraging the men by his cheerful courage and energy, and doing good service everywhere under very heavy artillery and machine-gun fire. When nearly all the warrant and non-commissioned officers had become casualties he helped to reorganise the units, taking his place when necessary in the front firing line. When the order to retire was eventually received he rallied the men and led them into a position to help the troops already occupying the defences.'

Far away from the fighting at Arras was Private James Smith who was with the 5th Bedfords, a part of thethe Egyptian Expeditionary Force, fighting in Palestine, and he was listed as wounded and missing in May. It would later come to light that he had been captured by the Turks, and early in 1918 his wife would receive a reply to her letters for news of her husband, that seemed to suggest this. The chaplain of the 5th Bedfords wrote:

Dear Mrs Smith,

The Captain of C Company, who was wounded, has asked me to answer your letter. Your husband was wounded in the wrist, and was got to the dressing station. The fighting was very hard that day and the next, and he was last seen at the dressing station. Unfortunately the Turks captured some of our wounded, and though we have no news of him, I hope he is alive and a prisoner in their hands, though wounded…I am sorry you have had so much anxiety. Your husband advanced bravely on that day. I hope you will have good news of him.

Alan D. Johnson.

Another man with the same surname, Absalom Smith, was a van dweller who had lived around the Biggleswade area for most of his life. During the earlier part of the war he had been a munitions worker, but he had enlisted in the first few months of 1917 with the Essex Regiment. He had then found himself in Egypt where he was badly wounded towards the beginning of April. Those wounds proved to be very serious for he died on 24 April. Further bad news from afar came with the death of Corporal Harry Garner of the 5th Bedfords during the 2nd Battle for Gaza on 19 April when another attempt to take the fortress was made. This second venture also failed. Initially Harry Garner was reported as missing but this would later change, and his death would be confirmed. Harry Garner had been a 'Saturday night soldier' as the Territorials were known and he had been mobilised during August of 1914. After training he had been sent to the Dardanelles and had survived Gallipoli. From there he had gone on to Egypt where he had fallen foul of the flies that swarmed and he had contracted a fever. Having recovered Harry found himself fighting the Turks at Gaza and he lost his life during a Turkish counter-attack as they pressed for possession of the town.

More fortunate was Private Ernest Brown of the 5th Bedfords, another who was wounded during the fighting at Gaza, but he recovered. His wife who lived in Palace Street eventually received news from her husband that he had been wounded and hospitalised. He apologised for not writing sooner but the wound was to his arm, and it had taken him a week to be able to get the feeling back in his fingers. His missive told of the hard fighting at Gaza and he reflected on the fortunes of his comrades as they continued the attack:

> I am thinking of the boys all the time they were having it a bit hot when I came away, and I expect there will be a good lot gone to their last home before I get back. It was like being in hell.

His own journey from the battlefield to hospital in Egypt took three days, and wounded men had a very uncomfortable ride by camel to get back for treatment. They would be transported in chairs attached to each side of the saddle and the motion of the animal made this a very painful experience for the men.

Ernest Brown was indeed yet another one of those prolific writers home and his wife gave his letters to the *Chronicle* for publication so that the people of Biggleswade would know, firsthand, what the fighting was like, for the interest in both the Western Front and the Middle East was great. One of those letters was published in May shortly after Ernest returned to the 5th Bedfords following recovery from his wounds. The letter shows how much men valued receiving tobacco from home, and more touchingly, what a family man Ernest Brown was. It read:

> Thanks for the tobacco; it was just what we wanted, and it got here just at the right time. It's about the only thing the boys really look for, a smoke. When they get wounded it is the very first thing they ask for … if anything should happen to me look after Elsie, and bring her up to be good. Send her to Sunday school. But I hope that I am spared to come back, but I mean to do my bit as far as I can, so cheer up, and don't worry. I shall be glad when it's over, but we must win. They have been a bad enemy and we must pay them for it.

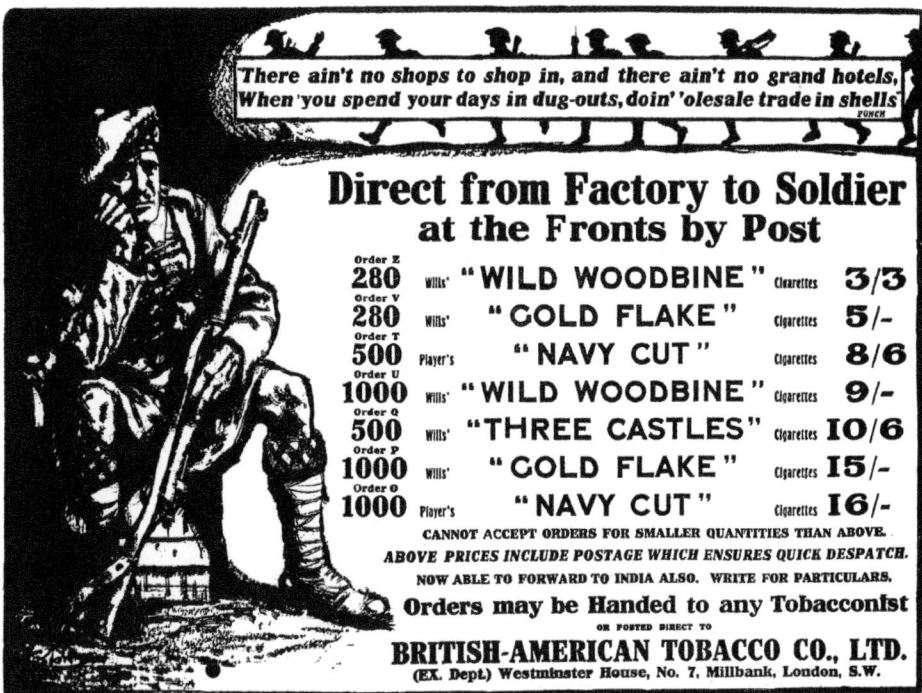

Advertisement used in local and national papers for tobacco for the troops. For many men the receipt of 'smokes' from home was something to look forward to.

For those serving with the 5th Bedfords in this theatre of fighting, leave in the UK was almost unobtainable, simply because of the huge travelling distance involved. Letters were very important to these men, as can be seen by the output of Ernest Brown. The receipt of missives from home, usually about once a fortnight, gave them some contact with their families, and parcels, containing food, clothing and cigarettes were very welcome. Indeed, for many soldiers, the arrival of mail from home was something they looked forward to greatly. Alternatively failure to receive mail was depressing for them, for this was the only link they had with their former lives. Mail was shipped home and vice versa, and there were problems, for German U boats patrolled the Mediterranean, with many a mail sack going to the bottom when ships were sunk.

Quite how hard the global nature of the conflict was could now be seen in the need to recruit more men, and those who had previously been rejected in Biggleswade were summoned to Kempston, near Bedford for re-examination. The *Chronicle* reported the desperate urgency to fill the gaps in the ranks for one person called was deaf and dumb, whilst another was on crutches. What is certain though is that some men were certainly having serious thoughts about the increasing number of casualties and deaths, for they did not respond to call up papers. In early May the *Chronicle* published the names of thirteen men in the following notice:

> The Recruiting Officer,
> No. 2 Sub-Area, Biggleswade,
> Asks for information regarding the
> Following men, as to whether they
> have joined the Army
> are excepted from the provisions
> of the Military Service Act 1916
> are in possession of a definite
> certificate exempting them from
> liability for Military Service
> have removed to another District
> The above information is required to
> complete Records in the Recruiting Office, and
> any communication will be treated in strict
> confidence
>
> | Name | Age | Last Known Address |
> |---|---|---|
> | BAKER, Albert James | 23 | Washingley Lodge, Sutton |
> | CARPENTER, Harry Hubert | 25 | 1, Council Cott., St Neots Rd, Sandy |
> | MITCHELL, Ernest Edward | 30 | 4, Foundry Terr., Biggleswade |
> | GRAVESTOCK, Alfred | 30 | Meeting Lane, Potton |
> | DAULBY, Albert | 32 | Honeysuckle Cottage, Wrestlingworth |
> | WOODWARD, Chas. W. | 33 | Upper Caldecote |
> | WOOLLARD, James | 37 | Dolphin Meadow, Biggleswade |
> | LENTON, Joseph | 38 | Carter's Lane, Potton |
> | WRIGHT, William | 39 | 22, Rose Terrace, Biggleswade |
> | DAVIS, Claude Hugh Clement | 18 | RE Signal Section, Sandy |
> | SMITH, Walter | 17 | Dolphin Meadow, Biggleswade |
> | WORTH, Alfred William | 16 | Wrestlingworth, Sandy |
> | FITT, Arthur | 38 | St Neots Rd, Sandy |
>
> (Signed) M. BOWERS, Lt. Colonel, R.O. No. 2 Sub Area, Biggleswade

By April of 1917 there were fifty-nine divisions serving on the Western Front, which amounts to over 1 million men. The odds therefore of bumping into someone you knew, apart from those within your battalion would have been slim. The odds of meeting a relative would have been even slimmer, especially so for brothers. In the spring of 1917 such a meeting occurred when two sets of brothers actually did so. Chas Northwood was with the Royal Engineers whilst his brother Arthur was serving with the Royal Garrison Artillery when they found themselves serving within 150yds of each other. Such an opportunity was too good to be lost and the two of them managed to meet up behind the lines to enjoy a 'so-called' English beer in a local French hotel. Arthur Northwood was a veteran of the Boer War and he had initially re-enlisted with the trench mortar section of the Royal

Garrison Artillery. On the Somme he had had a lucky escape in July 1916 as the following letter home told:

> We have had two or three days wet weather and the trenches are in a nice state, over our knees in places so you can guess what we are like in our wet clothes night and day, but never mind, we shall get over that if God spares our lives. We have been giving them 'Gip' and they have us too. I had a near shave the other day; a piece of shrapnel missed me by inches and struck a piece of wood in my dug-out in the trench. I have got it for a curio. The officer said to me 'Are you alright?' I said 'Yes my, my name wasn't on it. If there is one made for me, I'll stop it, but thank God, not yet'.

Unfortunately for Arthur Northwood there was one made for him, and it would find the target in 1918.

Private Joe Bilcock also met up with his brother Herbert around the same time in April 1917, Joe serving with the Royal Engineers whilst Herbert was with the Bedfords. Joe Bilcock told of this meeting in a letter home to his wife where he complained that the price of French beer that they had enjoyed had risen from half a franc for a quart to one and a half francs for a quart. With some regret he told his wife that he was going to be a teetotaller now!

Back at Arras the fighting showed no sign of abating and more of the dreaded brown envelopes were received in Biggleswade. During late April and May a further five men were killed. The first of those envelopes was delivered to Mr and Mrs Simms of Back Street and brought them the awful news that their son Harry was dead. Harry Simms had been amongst the earliest to enlist and had joined up with Edmund Stratton who had been killed on the first day of the Battle of the Somme. On 28 April the 6th Bedfords attacked at dawn and had suffered appalling losses at Berlencourt where they had been hit by tremendous enfilade fire from the German held chemical works. Even so, the Bedfords almost took their objective but were forced to dig in where they could. Twenty-seven-year-old Harry Simms had spoken often to say that he felt he would not return home and that dread feeling he had came true when he was killed in action in the attempt to take Berlencourt.

Listed as missing initially was another from Biggleswade on 28 April and he was twenty-five-year-old Private John Lincoln of the Royal Marine Light Infantry. It would not be until later in the year that his wife Ada and young child were to be informed that he had died. No body was ever found and again he is remembered on the Arras Memorial.

Killed on 29 April was Frederick Reynolds of the 4th Bedfords as they attacked the Oppy trench line at dawn. The battalion was at first successful and took their objective, but they were then counter-attacked, and driven out from the captured trench. They then recaptured it but, in this see-saw fighting, Fred Reynolds was posted as missing, and indeed his body was also never found. Today he is commemorated on the Arras Memorial.

The fourth of those brown envelopes came to Frederick Bonfield who lived in the Baulk, and told him that his only son, Percy, had also been killed in action. Percy had been aged thirty and had joined the army during 1916, serving with the Royal Garrison Artillery. He had quickly found himself on the Western Front when he was sent abroad in September, and had survived the later stages of the Somme. He had only written home

Gunner Percy Bonfield.

on 20 May, just three days before he was killed, and had told of recently seeing Sir Douglas Haig pass by in a motor car.

The fifth man to die during May was twenty-two-year-old Harry Grummitt who had survived a bullet wound on the Somme but who now killed as a result of gas poisoning. Private Grummitt was serving with the 6th Battalion of the Bedfordshire Regiment when they came under very heavy shelling on the evening of 22 May. This was followed by gas-shell bombardment during the night, and Harry Grummitt was one of seven men who died. As gas shells fell on the trench line Harry was caught by the gas of a bursting shell before he could put on his respirator. He was taken to an advanced field dressing station where they tried to treat him but without success. His company officer Lieutenant Geoffrey Peel wrote to Harry's parents to tell them that their son had been fatally gassed and had suffered heart failure. Although he was buried, his grave would be added to the growing number of those graves that were lost as the intense artillery fire continued to churn up the ground. The war had not been kind to Mr and Mrs Grummitt for they had already had one of their six serving sons wounded and invalided out of the army, and now they had another one killed. How comforting the words from Lieutenant Peel were to the grieving parents cannot be guessed but they did tell that 'His death was due to heart failure following on gas poisoning and was quite painless.' The *Chronicle* did not mince its words regarding Harry Grummitt's death and in the column entitled war news ran the headline: 'A Victim of Hun's Barbarous Device.' What it failed to recognise was that by this time the BEF itself had become prolific in the use of gas shells and was firing huge quantities of them into the German trench systems.

Officially the Battle of Arras had ended on 17 May but as can be seen above each side continued to shell the other and casualties increased. Over the official forty days of the battle 150,000 casualties had been incurred by the BEF and the Canadian Corps. The first stages had proved to be very successful but the later stages were not, for the BEF was still dogged by the problem of communications and how to bring up supporting artillery once the initial breakthrough had been achieved. 1917 was not yet done with the BEF and Haig's thoughts turned northwards towards the Ypres Salient and in the summer he would launch the attack there he had wanted for so long. The 3rd Battle of Ypres, and the name of the village of Passchendaele, would become as indelibly etched in British military history as the Somme.

Between the end of the battle of Arras and the start of the offensive at Ypres there was a major development within the armies of our French allies following the failure of the Nivelle offensive. By the end of May the French army was on the point

Private Harry Grummitt.

of breaking, having lost over one million men dead since the outbreak of fighting in 1914. Desertions from the front line were increasing and there was serious concern that a whole army mutiny could occur. In the end the French troops took a stance whereby they would continue to defend their country, but attacks were a different matter. Promises of better treatment and increased leave, together with the executions of ringleaders quelled the threat, but the outcome was that Haig and the BEF were now the main protagonists as far as the Allies were concerned. The German Army were not aware of these developments within the French army and did not act upon this.

There was however no let up in the day to day attrition between the opposing sides and, in a war where artillery was the main killer accounting for fifty-six per cent of all casualties coming from this, deaths continued on a daily basis. The months of early summer would confirm this statistic, for news of further fatalities would arrive in Biggleswade with alarming regularity. On June 14 twenty-two-year-old Sergeant Harry Figg of the 49th Alberta Regiment died of wounds. Harry Figg was one of three brothers who had left Biggleswade for Canada before the war but, as was the case with many, he did not hesitate to join up, together with his two brothers Albert and Ernest in January 1915. They had returned to Canada due to ill health but Harry remained, and had even managed to get married during a period of leave in 1916. His wife was now a widow following Harry's death from shrapnel wounds to his back. Harry's father still resided in Biggleswade at No. 125 Hitchin Street and he would hear in July that his son had died in Northern France.

Not all was doom and gloom though that reached anxious relatives back in Biggleswade and the news of Lance Corporal Frank Garner of the Seaforths must have been especially heartening. Frank was a regular correspondent and his letters often found their way to the pages of the *Chronicle*. In July part of a letter to a friend told how Frank was very pleased and surprised to receive a visit from his sister who was serving as a Red Cross nurse in France. He wrote: 'Yesterday was a bright day for me, for my sister paid me a surprise visit ... and she stayed with me for an hour and a half ... She has been on active service 28 months, and me 25. I am still A1, and wish all the best of health. Cheerio. Frank.'

Over in Flanders the early stages of that would become known as the 3rd Battle of Ypres began in June. On 7 June the BEF achieved a stunning victory at Messines Ridge. Here the Second Army under the leadership of General Herbert Plumer carried out one of the most successful operations for the BEF in the whole war. Plummer, or 'Daddy' as he was known to his men, was certainly no 'donkey' as some of the generals of the Great War have been labelled. He was meticulous in his planning and would not risk his men in futile attacks. Before the operation at Messines he had the men rehearse the attack over and over again, using both models of the terrain and specially created practice areas. Also tunnelers had been at work for well over two years and a total of nineteen mines had been dug out under the German front lines. On the eve of the battle, General Plumer had spoken these memorable words 'Gentlemen, we may not make history tomorrow, but we shall certainly change the geography.' On the morning of 7 June those words proved to be very apt for the nineteen mines that had been dug over the last two years were exploded with devastating effect. This was the culmination of an artillery barrage that had started on 21 May and stopped just before 3 a.m. on 7 June. Plumer's Second Army advanced at 3.10 a.m., supported by tanks, gas shells and a creeping barrage that gave them excellent protection. What they found surprised them, for up to 10,000 German soldiers had been killed as a result of the mine explosions and the advancing British troops faced very little opposition. The cessation of the artillery barrage had seen the Germans quickly man their forward trench lines and set up their machine guns. Therefore when the mines exploded many were exposed. Hundreds were atomised where they stood, whilst others who were found by the advancing BEF were without a mark. The shock of the explosion had killed them and it seemed as if they were sleeping when the BEF entered their trench lines. Within three hours all of the initial objectives had been taken and this was indeed a resounding success for the BEF. The noise of the exploding mines was so great that they were audible in southern England, and the story has been told that the Prime Minister, David Lloyd George heard the rumble as he was working in his study in 10 Downing Street. The battle continued for another seven days but, by the end of the fighting the whole Messines Ridge was in Allied hands and, for the first time, in the war the casualties of the attackers were less than those of the defenders.

Private Charlie Albone was amongst those engaged in the attack at Messines. He had previously been with the 5th Bedfordshires in Gallipoli but had been reassigned to a trench mortar battery in Flanders. He wrote home to his brother in Biggleswade telling of the battle in some detail. His letter which was published in the *Chronicle* recounted:

> Talk about a barrage, nothing could live in it. They were throwing shells like a hail storm. I never heard such a noise. No wonder they heard it in London. You should have seen the ground; there was scarcely a square foot without a shell hole. The boys were eager to get at Fritz, and he was not long before he threw up his arms and seemed glad to be taken prisoner.

The fighting at Messines was though to claim the life of Sydney Bygraves who was a private in the Royal West Surrey Regiment. During the battle he had the extremely dangerous job of being a runner. Sydney was not a very strong lad and had tried to join up earlier during the war but had been rejected. By 1916 the need for men saw previous rejections reconsidered and Sydney found himself serving on the Western Front. As a runner it was his job to take messages from the fighting areas back to battalion HQ and then return with responses. As such he had to endure exploding shells, machine gun bullets and trench mortars both from, and back to, the front line. Casualty figures for this work were always high, and at Messines Sydney Bygraves was badly wounded as he carried messages. He would not survive these and died after being taken back through the lines to a base hospital. This twenty-year-old was buried in Lijssenthoek Military Cemetery.

On 8 June the Germans counter-attacked and the 2nd Battalion of the Bedfords, in the front line just outside of Ypres had to face this. In a detailed letter home Private Albert Clark gave a remarkable account of this attack, and the days before it. He wrote:

> I know you like to hear from the boys who have left all to fight for their country. That is why we are here, and why we are keeping bright, because we want to get it finished so as to return to our homes again. I have been helping to hold the trenches for 12 days. And I

Private Sydney Bygraves.

must say we had some warm shops, but I hope it was for the better for us towards getting it finished. The weather has been grand for the boys, or we should not have been able to stick it so long under such a terrible bombardment as we did. Thank God I came out safe, but I was lucky, for I was only buried four times. I escaped without being hit, but it was marvellous, for those of my chums on either side were wounded, and I am sorry to say some were killed. I kept as cool as I could and said to myself, 'What is to be will be.' The more you worry at such times it stands to reason that you are not likely to stick it. One morning the shells and whizz-bangs were flying about and we were in the trenches dodging them the best we could. It's no use running from your position, for you would most likely only run into a shell and lose your life. We lay down in the trenches and were looking through our periscopes, when all at once the Huns were coming over no-man's-land towards our lines, which were only so many yards away. To the Huns' surprise, instead of finding little Belgians there they found the Bedfords, and I can tell you they had a warm reception from us with our machine guns, rifles and bombs. It was a sight that morning, very hot, and what with our guns letting out, a shell dropping here, and a whizz-bang there, and then, we had them well in hand, and I don't think many returned to the Boches' line. After things settled down a bit we started on our rations and soon forgot about it, but old Fritz thought he would get his own back on us, so he greeted us with some Minny Worthers and Tear Shells but we didn't worry, for we gave him as many back as he sent, and a few extra ones thrown in for luck. So we stuck on for 12 days, and then, thank God, we were relieved, and now we are resting, and we have earned it too. The weather is nice for us, and I don't expect it will take many days to get us fit again, and it will be our duty to go back again. I must close now as it's time to get a sleep in some billet. Roll on to the time when we shall all get back to our beds again.

Tres bien,
Pte A. Clark.

The war diary for the 2nd Bedfords confirmed Albert Clark's letter, for on the morning of 8 June they were attacked at 10.30 a.m. by about 300 German troops, but these were driven off by Vickers and Lewis machine guns and Mills bombs.

On 8 and 9 June the Australians were also in action at Messines and another runner was to receive fatal wounds. He was Bob See, a nineteen-year-old who had left Biggleswade three years earlier for a new life 'Down Under.' In April 1916 he had volunteered and been placed in the 37th Battalion of the AIF (Australian Imperial Force) and had sailed for Europe just a year before he died at Messines. On 10 June Bob See succumbed to the wounds he had received a few days earlier and died. His mother who ran a confectioners and greengrocers in Hitchin Street heard of the death of her son when a letter arrived from Chaplain Kennedy Tucker from a casualty clearing station that told: 'I have to tell

Private Bob See.

you of the death of your son Private B See. He was brought in last week suffering from very severe wounds in the legs and arms. Although everything possible was done for him, he passed away on Sunday June 10th.'

Chaplain Tucker went on to say that he could not give any actual details of Bob See's last moments for although he tried to catch sight of every seriously wounded man he could not remember noticing Bob See but thought he must have done. He was able to tell Mrs See that her son had been buried in Trois Arbres British Cemetery and that is where he rests today. Further confirmation of her son's death came from a second letter, this time from the chaplain of his battalion. Chaplain Davidson spoke well of Bob See and how dangerous it was to be a runner, telling how Bob 'never flinched his duty, and on more than one occasion did splendid work'. Ten days later on 20 June yet another Biggleswadian was killed when Private Ernest Woodward of the Middlesex Regiment fell in action at Ypres and joined the ever-expanding number of those whose grave would be lost.

Away from Flanders fields, another tragedy was about to befall the Haynes family of Biggleswade. William and Susan Haynes had already lost one son when Albert had been killed on the Somme in 1916. The grief that was felt within the family was further compounded when news reached Biggleswade that Walter Haynes, a signaller with the London Rifle Brigade, had been killed in France. The fighting at Arras had ceased but still the two sides engaged in daily artillery duels. During one of these Walter Haynes became a fatality when a shell killed him outright as he lay sleeping in the British trenches. Soldiers in the front line were well aware of the dangers from the guns and trench mortars, and some said that they could even recognise the incoming shells by the sound they made in the air. Walter Haynes did not even hear the shell that killed him on 17 June. Whether he died from the shock of the explosion or from shell splinters is unknown but there was a body and that was taken for burial and today Walter Haynes rests in Tank Cemetery close to Arras.

The fighting in this part of France claimed another victim eleven days later. Bombardier William King was serving with the Royal Field Artillery and died instantly on 28 June when a German shell fell directly into a gun emplacement where he was in action. The gun was totally destroyed and Bombardier King was killed, like Walter Haynes, in one of those daily artillery duels that so typified the fighting on the Western Front. Reverend Holden, the chaplain to the RFA wrote to William King's widow and the letter that was delivered to their home in Drove Road told how he had buried him in Roclincourt Military Cemetery, near Arras.

Further north in the Ypres Salient, the 3rd Ypres was about to start up again. After the stunning victory at Messines there had been a lull in the fighting and critics of Haig comment upon the delay to follow up the success of early June. Those who defend Haig stress that this was simply a part of the plan, but what is a fact is that this delay did give the Germans the chance to reinforce their armies surrounding Ypres. When the fighting recommenced there was also a change in command for Hubert Gough, the youngest General in the BEF, was now given the task of driving the Germans from Passchendaele Ridge. Gough had a reputation as a 'thruster'. By this it is meant that he was not afraid to push his men forward, even if this meant that casualties would be high. On the Somme he had been in charge of the cavalry reserves that it had been expected would break through after the hoped-for success of the initial attack. He had been responsible for some of the later attacks on the Somme where he had not endeared himself to the Australians. He had then been in charge of the final action on the Somme in November 1916 when Beaumont Hamel had been captured. Hubert Gough was a personal friend of Haig and certainly knew how hard the war could hit families. His brother, Johnny Gough had won the Victoria Cross during the British campaign in Somaliland in 1903 and was serving as a Brigadier General in 1915 when he was killed at Neuve Chapelle by a sniper's bullet.

On 31 July Hubert Gough was ordered to renew the attack which Haig had wanted for some time. A British attack made much greater sense to Haig here, for if the German line could be broken, then there were real strategic possibilities for the Allies. Behind the German lines was the railhead of Roulers. To capture this would help the Allies greatly and would restrict German troop movement considerably. Equally important was the chance to drive on to the ports of Ostende and Zeebrugge where German U boats were based. Their capture would bring immediate relief for the home population of Britain, and would cease the threat to British industry as it supported the war effort. Following the Somme Germany had resumed unrestricted submarine warfare in the hope that this would defeat the British. The impact of this was considerable and Britain's ability to maintain the struggle was in serious doubt. Haig argued that the capture of the two ports on the Belgian coast was crucial. Only the capture of Passchendaele Ridge would allow this. There was also the real problem of the French armies, who were in some disarray following the mutinies earlier in the year. If the Germans became aware of this then the war could well have been lost. A major attack by the British in Flanders therefore made sense to Haig for a number of reasons, not least that it would likely distract the Germans and disguise the problems facing the French. The attack on 31 July initially was going to be supported by an amphibious landing on the Belgian coast by General Rawlinson's Fourth Army but plans for this were shelved.

The British Army that would attack on 31 July had certainly evolved from that that had gone over the top at the Somme. Its composition had changed also, in that it now was a mixture of volunteers and conscripts. For some of the men Passchendaele would be their first taste of battle, whilst for others it would mean drawing upon the experiences gained in Picardy, on the Somme. When the troops of Gough's 5th Army went in on 31 July they were buoyed by the success of Messines but, as with every attack, the soldiers were both fearful and nervous. A ten-day bombardment preceded the attack before, at 3.50 a.m., the troops went in following a creeping barrage. This was one of the developments from the Somme (see Appendix 4) and gave the advancing soldiers much greater protection as they crossed no man's land. A wall of shells exploding around 50yds in front of them meant that the enemy had to keep under cover and that the advancing troops could get amongst the Germans without coming under the kind of machine-gun fire they had faced on the Somme. The infantry had become far more efficient also since the catastrophe of 1 July 1916, and now fought in specialised platoons using fire and movement tactics. It certainly worked on Tuesday 31 July for the advance made by the British was over a mile. However, if the British had learned from the Somme, so had the Germans and they placed their faith in the tactics that they had tried to use on the first day of the Battle of Arras in April, notably defence in depth and the counter-attack. As the Germans counter-attacked the weather turned and heavy rain began to fall and for the next ten days little fighting was possible. Indeed it was so bad that it was extremely difficult even supplying the troops who were occupying the positions captured on 31 July. The mud that will always be associated with Passchendaele got worse now as the rains continued to fall, and attacks became more difficult. On 10 August, and then again on 16 August, the BEF attacked, this time at Langemarck but without any real success. Plumer's 2nd Army now replaced Gough's 5th Army as the instrument of the British advance. Immediately Plumer reverted to the tried and tested tactics of Messines and meticulously planned the next stage of the attack.

On 20 September Plumer's troops attacked but, true to his doctrine, his men only advanced as far as was safe, and then waited for the inevitable German counter-attack that was destroyed by Plumer's artillery. During September the weather turned and the sun shone, drying out the battlefield and, on the 26 of the month, Plumer again enjoyed success as further advances were made, Once more the German counter-attacks were destroyed by British artillery and machine-gun fire. At the start of October Plumer attacked again and German casualties were very high when troops who were about to counter-attack were caught in their jump off trenches by the BEF's guns. Yet, just as it seemed that 3rd Ypres would be a resounding success, the rain began to fall again and the remainder of the battle was a dreadful slog for the BEF as conditions deteriorated. The capture of Passchendaele Ridge, it has been argued, became an obsession for Haig, and both Gough and Plumer advised him to call off the attack. Haig persisted though and, after another month of desperate fighting, the Canadians took Passchendaele Ridge and village in early November. The fighting stopped on 10 November. The BEF had around 125,000 troops killed during the campaign and men from Biggleswade were amongst them.

The first news of casualties for the town concerned men who had been killed in the build up to the battle. There were six brothers from the Grummitt family serving in His Majesty's Forces and already one of them, Harry, had been killed at Arras. Another, George, had been so severely wounded by gunshot wounds that he had been invalided out of the army and was to be a cripple for the rest of his life. Now another was to die when Fred, who was serving with the 'Shiny Seventh' Bedfordshires, was killed on 18 July. He had been out at night with a working party repairing barbed wire when they came under shell fire that killed him and four other men. Fred's body was recovered though and he rests today in Railway Dugouts Burial Ground in Ypres.

At almost the same time that Fred Grummitt died another from Biggleswade was killed when Captain Clifton Welsh was mortally wounded at midnight on 17 July. He had volunteered at the outbreak of the war and had joined the Royal Field Artillery where, after training, he had been given an officer's commission. In April 1915 he had found himself on the Western Front, then his battery fought on the Somme and at Arras. By 1917 he was in the Salient and had just been promoted to captain following being mentioned in dispatches. As news of his death reached Biggleswade so did his last letter home that told how pleased he had been when, recently he had met up with his brother who was a flight commander in the Royal Navy Air Service. Clifton Welsh was an observation officer with the RFA and this was certainly a very dangerous job. As such he often found himself ahead of the front line trying to spot enemy artillery and, if successful, sending messages back to his own battery to bring down fire on these enemy guns. However he was killed on 17 July in stranger circumstances when he became a casualty of a German air raid. The very nature of the fighting was now much different to that of 1914 and 1915, and bombing raids and strafing behind the lines were now much more common. A bomb dropped from a German aeroplane killed Clifton Welsh as he was supervising the sorting of supplies at an ammunition dump in preparation for the forthcoming battle. Clifton Welsh was twenty-nine when he was killed and today his grave can be found in Poperinghe New Military Cemetery

On the actual first day of the 3rd Ypres twenty-one-year-old Robert Stocker became the first man from Biggleswade to die, and the second son from that family. His brother Herbert had been killed in action in November 1914 and now John and Rebecca Stocker, of Gladstone Terrace, Sun Street were to receive further more dreadful news with the death of their younger son. Bob Stocker had originally been with the Bedfordshire Regiment but had been accepted into the Machine Gun Corps, and it was with them that he was killed in action. The evolution of tactics following the Somme had seen the growth of the use of the machine gun, with barrages from them being a prominent feature for protecting attacking troops. A machine gun could fire up to 400 rounds per minute and these barrages preceded attacks, forcing the Germans to keep their heads down. Understandably this prompted a deadly response, and both artillery and mortar shells were quickly directed towards the machine gun positions by the Germans. It is not surprising that the Machine Gun Corps acquired the nickname 'the Suicide Club'. It was equally true that both sides were quick to dispatch any machine gunners, and they were rarely allowed to surrender. This deadly response to the machine gun was what accounted for Lance Corporal Bob Stocker. His parents were later to receive a letter from one of Bob Stocker's chums, a Private H. Bottom and he told them that their son 'died nobly doing his duty'. Unlike his brother Herbert though, Bob Stocker has no known grave and his name rests on the Menin Gate. The war had indeed been hard on the Stocker family for as well as losing two sons they were also to lose two sons-in-law. Another son Arthur would be seriously wounded in December and the gunshot wounds to his leg were bound by fellow Biggleswadian Private Herbert Bilcock. A fourth son, Harold, but like Arthur would survive.

The second phase of the battle commenced on 10 August and the Seventh Bedfordshires, 'The Shiny Seventh' were involved. Amongst their number was Fred Cole, a thirty-six-year-old man from Biggleswade who had moved from the town and who before the war was living with his wife in Surrey. As the Seventh Battalion moved up towards the jump off point for the attack Fred Cole was shot in the head by a sniper, as a letter to Fred's wife from a Captain Ferguson told:

Dear Madam,

I am very sorry to have to inform you that your husband, Pte F. Cole was killed instantly by a sniper's bullet, through the head, on the 10th August. He was killed doing his duty nobly, and I hope that this will be some small consolation to you in your great loss … he was buried on the field of battle just west of Glencourse Wood.

Headstone for Private Fred Cole, killed at Passchendaele 1917.

After the war Fred Cole's body was one of those that were relocated to Tyn Cot Cemetery, and his body rests there today, close to the Cross of Sacrifice.

On the same day, and serving with the same battalion twenty-one-year-old Private Tom Housden was also killed in action. Tom Housden had seen almost three years' service on the Western Front and had fought at, and survived 1st Ypres in 1914. He had been wounded on the Somme but after recovery he had transferred to the 'Shiny Seventh'. Their attack on 10 August caught the Germans unprepared and they drove them from Glencourse Wood in the early hours of the morning. They were not able to hold onto their gains though, as supporting troops on their right had not been so successful. As the Germans counter-attacked the Bedfords found themselves in an increasingly dangerous position. The Captain Ferguson who had written to the wife of Fred Cole played a prominent role in resisting this German attack, but the strength and the number of Germans and British Artillery shells falling short of their targets made the position desperate. Tom Housden was a bomber with the 7th Bedfords and he was killed in this frantic fighting to hold onto Glencourse Wood. He again was to be one of those added to the list of whose bodies were lost on the battlefield, and who have no known grave. Tom Housden's name sits on the Menin Gate Memorial in Ypres.

Sixteen days later, well to the south of Ypres, the good fortune that John Newman had experienced so far during his war came to an end. He had been badly wounded on the Somme but had recovered, and had also seen his best friend, Herbert Goss, killed a year earlier. On 26 August he was to join that friend when he was killed outright by shellfire whilst asleep in a trench in the Arras sector. Although the fighting had ceased here trench raids and shelling continued. Private John Newman was amongst the three men from the

4th Bedfordshires to die that day. John Newman had survived trench foot, wounding and shell shock before his luck ran out on the fateful Sunday morning, well away from the heavy fighting to the north.

Equally unlucky had been Gunner George Warner who had only been on the Western Front for a matter of a few days. This nineteen-year-old was serving with the Royal Field Artillery when, on 24 August, he was wounded by shellfire in the face and neck. The seriousness of the wounds was immediately obvious and he was taken to a casualty clearing station but he failed to recover. George's mother wrote to the Army Records Office in the hope that there was a mistake and that, by some chance, her son might be alive. The response confirmed George's death and took from the family their only male, for Mrs Warner was a widow and her other children were George's sisters.

September proved to be a terrible month for those waiting in Biggleswade for news of their loved ones as the delivery of the ominous brown envelopes increased. On 10 September Acting Sergeant George Senior was hit in the head by a German bullet. He had only been back in the front line five days when this happened. George Senior had belonged to the Bedford Territorials before the war and had seen service initially with the 1st Bedfords before transferring to the Royal Berkshire Regiment. On 14 September the Royal Berkshires had been involved in both artillery and machine gun duels with the Germans to the west of Ypres and it was during this that George Senior was hit in the head by a bullet. His comrades took him back to the casualty clearing station and, at first, it was thought that he might recover but gradually he weakened and then passed away. George Senior was aged twenty-two when he died of wounds. Fred and George's younger brother William was also in uniform and he was serving as a stoker in the Royal Navy. In the following year he would have a close brush with death during the Spanish 'flu epidemic. His condition was that bad that his mother was summoned to his bed in Chatham Hospital in Kent, but fortunately he was to pull through.

In just over two weeks' time two more men from the town would be killed as the families of Privates Henry Garner and James Harpin would find out. Both died as a result of the wounds they received in the fighting to take Polygon Wood. Henry Garner was aged twenty. He had joined up in June of 1915, having seen the recruiting march of the 2/5th Bedfords as it passed through Biggleswade. He had been on the Western Front for only six weeks, and had been transferred to the Hertfordshire Regiment from the Bedfordshires. In the attacks on Polygon Wood he had been seriously wounded in the leg and infection set in. At the Casualty Clearing Station he had passed away peacefully and was buried in the soldiers' cemetery at Bailleul which is where his body rests today. Two days later nineteen year old James Harpin succumbed to his wounds. As the Cambridgeshires attacked on 26 September he had been wounded in the abdomen, and had been taken to a casualty clearing station by his friend Private Victor Wakes. The Harpin family then received two letters within a matter of days that took them from the heights of hope to the brink of despair. At first they read that their son had a stomach wound but that it was not serious, that he was cheerful and it was likely this 'blighty one' would get him home. This letter had come from James Harpin's platoon commander who had been told it seems by Victor Wakes, that when he had left

James Harpin his friend had been in quite good form – 'He seemed fairly cheerful when he was taken away'. The second letter dashed all of their hopes. It read:

Dear Mrs. Harpin

I am very grieved to tell you that your son Pte J.W. Harpin was admitted to this hospital very seriously wounded with a gunshot wound penetrating the abdomen. Although everything was done for him he passed peacefully away today at 12.30 o'clock. He was not conscious at the end, and was too ill to realise he was dying or suffer much. I told him I was writing to you, and he said I was to send his love. He was very brave and patient. He will be buried with military honours in the little cemetery here. His name will be on his cross. The graves are well looked after. If you write to the Graves Committee, BEF they will forward to you a photograph of his grave later on. His few personal belongings will be forwarded to you by the Military Authorities, and this usually takes some time.

With sincere sympathy, very truly yours,
J. Greaves, Matron'.

James Harpin had been enthusiastic about the war and had tried to join up on several occasions before he was eventually accepted in May 1916. Reaching France in December of that year he had quickly discovered the reality of war and had been hospitalised with trench foot and septic poisoning. He had then suffered from shell shock before rejoining his regiment for his appointment with destiny at Passchendaele.

As the casualties on the Western Front increased the thought of a 'Blighty One' wound became more attractive to the men in the front lines. Such a wound would take them away from the conflict for some time, if not for good, and a non-fatal wound was not seen as such a bad thing in comparison to the alternative. Albert Cartwright was one who had received this kind of wound when he was shot through the lungs and for a while he was in a critical state, with his parents even going over to France to visit him. In the summer of 1917 he was discharged from the army and returned to Biggleswade. He would play no further part in the battles of the Western Front. Sergeant Ernest Skilliter was another to be wounded in August of 1917 and for him it was the third time. He would wear with pride the three wound stripes on the arm of his uniform to accompany his sergeant's stripes. At Passchendaele he received a wound to his left arm to add to the head wound he had received in 1916 and the slight wound he had suffered in 1914.

In Biggleswade the growing numbers of those who had been killed or wounded struck a chord and in September a service of remembrance was held. The fact that so many were now dying abroad and being buried overseas was very hard for families, and at this service the idea of a war memorial for families to focus their grief was mooted, and a collection taken to try and build one.

As the BEF struggled to make progress in the Salient more soldiers from Biggleswade were killed or wounded. Private Herbert Albone was a thirty-two-year-old who had been in France and Belgium since December of the previous year, and he was one such soldier.

Initially he had served with the 1st Bedfords but then had been transferred to the Machine Gun Corps, and it was with them that he was so seriously wounded in the second week of October. His wounds could not be treated on the battlefield and he was taken back to a casualty clearing station, but even the care he received there was not enough and he passed away on Friday 12 October. Herbert Albone's wife would later receive a letter from the sister-in-charge at the clearing station that gave more details. It read:

> I am writing to let you know that your husband, Private Herbert Albone, 55692 died from wounds, in this hospital yesterday. He was very badly wounded in several places and although everything possible was done for him he was too ill to recover. One of the last things he said was, would I write to you, and he told me to send his love and say he was doing fine. He thought so much about you.
>
> Yours truly, U. M. Smith (Sister).

Herbert Albone did get to be buried in a grave that was not lost and today his body rests in Nine Elms British Cemetery.

News of other soldiers revealed that their wounds, although serious, were not fatal. Private Len Gray had been wounded in the back severely by shell splinters but he would pull through after treatment at a Canadian Field Hospital at Etaples. Len Gray had joined up following the death of his elder brother in 1914, and this former apprentice of the *Chronicle* was another who had enlisted during the Bedfords' recruiting march as it passed through Biggleswade. His parents were relieved that their second son had not met the fate of their first William who had died in 1914. That relief was however to be only temporary and 1918 would bring the family dreadful news.

Others who were wounded in the October fighting in Flanders included Private H. Housden, hospitalised with a gunshot wound to the left forearm and a compound fracture of the radius, and Private J. Oakley who had a severe bullet wound in his right leg. Both would recover following treatment. Wounded to the head was Gunner Frank Carpenter who was with the Canadian Field Artillery and whose parents lived at the Golden Eagle, Stratton Street, whilst Private Fred Milton, whose brother Harry had been killed at Arras, found himself back in Biggleswade after surgery to a leg wound. All would survive the war.

Back in the Ypres Salient the rains were now falling heavily and turning the battlefield into a quagmire. Private Joe Bilcock, who had earlier written home complaining about the cost of beer in France, would tell of the changing nature of the battlefield graphically in a letter that he sent home in October to his wife:

> It is very wet here and has been for some time, and the fields are nothing more than a swamp, and all shell holes full of water, ten times worse than the Somme. I would rather be there. Last night I was stretcher bearer and I was drenched to the skin. It was a twister, dark and wet, and with the thunder and flashes of the guns and the shells, it puts whiskers on you.

This was to be the last letter from Joe Bilcock that would arrive back in Biggleswade and the next news of him would not be so welcome. At first his wife and family were told that he was missing in action on 28 October, but later in the year they received information that they did not wish to hear. Initially it was the Red Cross that wrote to his wife and told her that their enquiries discovered that he had in fact been killed on 28 October. A few weeks later a letter from one of Joe's best friends arrived in Biggleswade that confirmed what the Red Cross had said. Private Farraday wrote – 'I am sorry to say that Joe, your loving husband, was killed by an aerial bomb instantly. He had his pipe in his mouth when he was dead so he must have been smoking at the time of his death. The Red Cross buried him.'

Soldiers often told of finding men, both friend and enemy killed following shell or bomb explosion without a mark on them. It was often the case that these men died from concussion. Joe Bilcock was certainly unlucky for his battalion, the 1st Bedfordshires were due to be relieved later that day by the Devonshire Regiment. Joe Bilcock was one of the last fatalities before they were relieved. Aeroplanes, and their effectiveness, had certainly changed over the first three years of the war. From initially carrying out reconnaissance work they had been developed to become instruments of wounding and death. The flimsy machines that soared above the trenches initially fascinated the soldiers below, especially when dogfights took place, but the allure of watching these aerial duels changed as the role of the aeroplane altered. Bombing and strafing had become a part of aeroplane tactics and turned these aircraft into something altogether more deadly. Although the Red Cross buried him Joe Bilcock's grave was another that was lost as the fighting continued.

October would continue to see the trend of September with further sadness and grief over the growing number of casualties, especially for the Bridge family who lived at No. 14 High Street. This month saw two of their three serving sons killed. On 4 September twenty-four-year-old Tom Bridge had gone missing in action as the 8th Lincolns had attacked at 6 a.m. at Broodseinde, coming under heavy machine-gun fire. This was so fierce that the Lincolns had to retreat and then they were counter-attacked by the Germans. Tom Bridge had been in the BEF on the Western Front for two years when he was officially declared presumed killed. Towards the end of the month the Bridge family received the devastating news that a second son, Horace, a Lance Corporal with the 4th Bedfords had been killed in action. Attacking in support of the Canadian Corps the 4th Bedfords had had to contend with very heavy and boggy ground and had been only able to advance between 150 and 200yds. It had cost them the lives of two officers and fifty-two other ranks killed, amongst who was twenty-two-year-old Horace Bridge.

The casualties for October did not stop here for another young man from Biggleswade was killed in action on 30 October with the 4th Bedfords. Private Victor Milton, who had worked for Alfred Wakes, the baker before he had enlisted in October 1916, died in the same action as Horace Bridge and was only nineteen. On Whit Monday he had had a lucky escape when he had been buried alive during enemy shellfire. He was dug out but, not surprisingly, was deeply traumatised. He had recovered from the ensuing shell shock but had returned to his battalion to be in the front line for the attack at Broodseinde.

When his name was inscribed on the Biggleswade War memorial in 1921 an error was made, and his niece Mrs Dorothy Hutchinson campaigned for many years to rectify this. In April 2008 the error was corrected and the memorial was rededicated in the presence of Mrs Hutchinson.

Wounded badly also in the attack at Broodseinde was twenty-seven-year-old Private Herbert Legate who had been in France and Flanders for just over seventeen months. Although he was taken to a specialist chest clinic his wounds were too bad and he had died on 4 November. Herbert Legate had been back home on leave only a month before he was killed and his wife learned of her husband's injury and death from an Army Chaplain. The final person from Biggleswade to be killed on 30 October was twenty-eight-year-old Private Headley Rowland who was also serving with the 4th Bedfords and although he was initially reported as missing, his wife, who lived off Hitchin Street, would later receive the sad news that her husband had died. His body was never found and he is commemorated at Tyn Cot.

Luckier on 31 October was Private James Milliner who was one of three brothers serving. He had been with the Suffolk Regiment in the attack at Broodseinde and had been wounded, but he had survived. Also reported wounded in the late October fighting, was Private Harry Wagstaff, yet another who was with the 4th Bedfords. This was the third time that this had happened to him and he had recovered from shrapnel wounds to the stomach whilst on the Somme in 1916. Now his father Samuel received news that his son had been wounded again but it would later transpire that he was indeed missing in action. It would almost be a year before that was changed to presumed killed. The *Chronicle* would confirm this in September 1918 when they printed that Harry had been wounded but that he had been killed by shell fire whilst he was being taken to a dressing station to treat the initial wound. Indeed Harry Wagstaff's body was never found and today he is commemorated on the Tyn Cot Memorial that sits across Passchendaele Ridge. So within a year Samuel Wagstaff had lost a second son, Harry, following the earlier death of his elder son George.

While the battle raged in Flanders, men from Biggleswade were also involved in combat in other parts of the world. In Palestine the 5th Battalion of the Bedfordshires had been in action since March in the battle for Gaza. This oft overlooked theatre of fighting was quite remarkable for the majority of the British troops here were territorials or mounted yeomanry. The conditions that they had to fight in were very different from the Western Front with searing heat, swarms of flies, and lack of water. The enemy they faced was equally as dangerous as the Germans. 'Johnny Turk', as the Tommies labelled their adversary here, had proved to be a formidable foe in Gallipoli and the same was true in Palestine, especially the Anatolian Turks. The British Egyptian Expeditionary Force had been trying to advance into Palestine and the fortress that was Gaza stood in their way. Gaza was a fortified coastal city that dominated Southern Palestine and it was the key for the British advance. Without its fall there could be no rewarding progress for the Allies here. The initial battle in March had been without success and Gaza was not taken. In April there was a second attempt to take the stronghold but again this did not succeed even though tanks and gas shells were used to support the attack. Gas proved to be unsuccessful for the heat caused it to disperse without effect, whilst the soft sand of the area caused problems for the engines of the tanks.

In July the 5th Bedfords would be involved heavily with raids on Umbrella Hill that was part of the fortified trench positions in front of Gaza. Indeed those familiar with the Western Front would have recognised what lay before Gaza, for it was exactly the same as the trenches that stretched from the Belgian Coast to Switzerland. Umbrella Hill was a section of the trench line built by the Turks to defend Gaza and there was a front-line trench together with support trenches, communication trenches and dugouts. In front of the Turkish trenches was a formidable belt of barbed wire that was up to 12ft deep and 4ft high. The 5th Bedfords were positioned about a third of a mile away from the Turkish front line here, and in July they received orders to carry out raids. The first of these took place on 17 July and was very daring indeed, with the Bedfords penetrating the Turkish trenches and causing mayhem there. Numerous medals were won for gallantry, most notably nineteen Military Medals, and they included one won by Harold Taylor of Ickwell Green. This twenty-two-year-old would go on to be promoted to Corporal and then Sergeant, and tragically would die of malaria just four days after the Armistice with Turkey was signed on 30 October 1918. In the last days of the fighting in Palestine the Egyptian Expeditionary Force would capture Megiddo in a brilliant feat of arms, but battle deaths of 453 would be greatly outnumbered by death from disease of 2,158.

Ten days after the first raid in July 1917 there was another, and again there was fierce hand-to-hand fighting within the Turkish trenches and eleven more Military Medals were won. Amongst those who were to receive these medals for gallantry was Sergeant Charlie Clifford of Biggleswade. The raid followed a hurricane bombardment of the Turkish trenches and the men went in at 9 p.m. As they advanced they were hit by raking machine-gun fire but they continued and broke into the Turkish trenches where their Mills bombs and bayonets did their deadly work. By 9.35 p.m. the raid was over and the Bedfords were back in their own trenches and amongst them was a wounded Charlie Clifford. The second attack had found much stiffer resistance from the enemy and it later transpired that the raid had gone in at just the time the Turks were changing over their troops, so the Bedfords faced twice as many men as was expected. Charlie Clifford had not been born in Biggleswade but had moved there from Stow-on-the-Wold. Before the war he had been in the Territorials and he had enlisted in 1914. In the following year he had been at Suvla Bay in Gallipoli where he had been wounded but had survived. When the 5th Bedfords moved to Egypt and Palestine in late 1915 he was with them, serving there until he was killed on 5 October, just three months after winning the Military Medal. Charlie Clifford had been in a patrol that had gone forward towards the Turkish lines near Umbrella Hill to get information and to try to draw Turkish troops out, to ambush and possibly capture some. The patrol ran into heavy fire and the commanding officer Lieutenant Dennis and Sergeant Clifford were amongst those who did not return. Initial reports suggested that Charlie Clifford had been wounded and that he had been captured. A letter home from Private Ernest Brown writing to his wife in Biggleswade confirmed that Charlie Clifford had been wounded and captured, but also that he had died in captivity. The letter read:

Sergeant Alfred Carr, killed during the Third Battle for Gaza, 1917.

I am sorry to tell you the sad news of Sergeant Clifford, who was taken prisoner by the Turks. He was wounded and has died from his wounds. Poor Clifford, he was a grand good boy. The best always go first. He was a good sergeant in his section and was first in all things. He has done his bit and done it well.

Charlie Clifford was buried by the Turks and after the fall of Gaza he was given a military funeral there, and this is where his body rests today. Ironically thirteen days after he died his award of the Military Medal was mentioned in the *London Gazette*.

Charlie Clifford was not the only Sergeant from Biggleswade to die in the fighting for Gaza, and when the third attempt to take the stronghold commenced at the end of October, another would be only days away from death. Alfred Carr, at the age of twenty-one, was four years younger than Charlie Clifford, and he too had been a territorial before the outbreak of the war. The Carr family was another where many sons had answered the call and Alfred Carr was one of five brothers who were fighting in France, Salonika and Egypt. Alfred had trained initially as a signaller before he found himself at Gallipoli where he had survived both Suvla Bay and Anzac Cove. When the 5th Bedfords were moved to Egypt he got his first stripe with promotion to Corporal, and then had been made Sergeant shortly before he was killed on 3 November during the Third Battle of Gaza. This time the allies were successful, and Gaza fell after a flanking movement cut off the citadel, and so caused the Turks to have to retreat. The fighting for Gaza had been fierce throughout 1917 and costly. The British had lost around 18,000 men killed, wounded or missing, and for the Turks the figures were also very high, and 25,000 had either died, been wounded or been captured. It was shellfire that did for Alfred Carr and, cruelly for his parents, they were to receive his last letter home just days after they received official notification of his death. Poignantly that last letter read –'Forgive short letter, will write again soon. Au revoir and fondest love to all. Think of me and forget me not.'

Alfred Carr's widow received a letter from her husband's commanding officer towards the end of November that gave details of how Alfred died. It read:

Dear Mrs Carr,

It is with great personal sorrow that I write to sympathise with you in the loss of Sergt Carr, who was killed during the severe fighting on November 3rd. On November 2nd he commanded No.5 platoon in the assault which captured the fortified garden which was the battalion's objective, and keeping his men well in hand, in spite of heavy shelling, took up the correct position for consolidating. During the night the enemy, expecting a further attack, put down a heavy barrage about 2 a.m. on the 3rd. I happened to be with No.5 platoon at the time. Sergt Carr was on the left bay with 10 others. After about two hours of shelling one heavy shell landed right in Sergt Carr's bit and killed all except three who were wounded. The tragedy could not have been helped in any way, as several hundred shells fell in the couple of hours. Death was instantaneous and we buried Sergt. Carr in the morning.

With sincere sympathy.
J. Yarde (Captain)

Captain John Yarde would win the Military Cross in December leading a bayonet charge against the Turks at Yafa Hill and would then go on to win it again (MC bar) in 1918, in the action that would see Private Samuel Needham of the 5th Bedfords awarded the Victoria Cross. Samuel Needham was not a Bedfordshire man, having been born in Grimsby, and he had initially served in France with the Army Service Corps. He had been wounded there and had, after recovery, been sent to the 5th Bedfords in Palestine. It was here that he had won his VC when the patrol he was in was attacked by a much stronger Turkish force. Private Needham's patrol was being driven back when this brave man, with total disregard for his own safety, charged the Turks and drove them back, thus saving the patrol. In another of those terrible tricks of fate he too would survive the fighting only to die of wounds five days after its ending. Captain Yarde, who came from Kempston, near Bedford was killed by shell fire barely six weeks before the war ended.

Confirmation of how Alfred Carr had died came again from Ernest Brown, who was a private in the same company of the Bedfords. Writing home once more to his wife, who lived in Palace Street, he told how 'one of the Turks shells killed Sergt. A. Carr of Biggleswade' and wounded him and several others. He went on to describe how the two wounds in his head were only slight, telling that 'the splinters made three holes in my steel helmet as big as pennies, and if it hadn't been for the helmet I should be a dead man now.' This was the same Ernest Brown who had written regarding Charlie Clifford's death.

Another to die in the fall of Gaza was Leonard Maudlin, a private with the Northamptonshire Regiment, who was killed on 2 November. Amongst those wounded in the fall of Gaza was Private Charles Frost who received a head wound. Charles Frost had been a time-expired reservist at the start of the war, but when the Recruiting March of the Bedfordshires came through the town in 1915 he had re-enlisted. He had found himself sent to fight in the Middle East with the 5th Bedfords and, although he was wounded at Gaza, he would go on to survive the war. Also during the third battle of Gaza Private Ernest Brown from Biggleswade would become the third man from the town to receive the Military Medal. Ernest Brown had enlisted in 1915 and had joined the 5th Bedfords just as they were leaving Gallipoli and were heading to Egypt. He won the Military Medal for bravery and, as with George Gurney and Charlie Clifford reacted with great modesty to the award, as this letter to his wife reveals: 'I don't call it bravery, it was only doing what every good soldier ought to do – his duty. I must close as I am off into action again. Goodbye for now. Ernest.' This humble and courageous man would survive the war and was demobilised in April of 1919 to return to life back in Biggleswade.

As the battle for Passchendaele Ridge continued back on the Western Front so the casualties grew, and more men from Biggleswade were injured and killed. News trickled through that Private Joseph Watts of the 1st Bedfords had gone missing in action on 26 October, and it was later confirmed that he had been killed in the fighting on that day. Joseph Watts had been a volunteer in early 1916 and he had seen action at Ypres during the attack at Messines before that fateful day in late October. Soon the trickle of bad news became a surge and more families in the town had reason to mourn. First it was confirmed that twenty-six-year-old Jonathan Wade had been killed in action. He was one of those who had left Biggleswade for a better life on another continent and he had emigrated to Canada in 1909 at the age of eighteen. He had settled well there and was working as a farmer when war broke out. In July of 1916 he had enlisted in the 2nd Canadian Mounted Rifles and he found himself on the Western Front in April 1917, two months after his training in the UK was completed. In those initial months he had fought at Vimy and had been wounded in the hand, but he was to meet his death on 30 October at Passchendaele. By now the battlefield was a quagmire and the task of wresting the Ridge from the Germans was given to the Canadians. It was during these final assaults that Private Jonathan Wade died and that the sad news of his death would be reported to his father, William who still lived in Biggleswade at No. 22 Stratton Street. It is not surprising that Jonathan Wade's body and grave were lost in the morass that the battlefield had become and he is now commemorated on the Menin Gate in Ypres. Also killed in the Canadians' assault that took Passchendaele Ridge was twenty-year-old Private Jack Smith who died on 6 November whilst in a bombing party that was attacking to gain the ridge. Jack had emigrated to Canada with his father and the rest of the family prior to the war, but one of his sisters had stayed in Biggleswade as she was married. It was to her that news of her brother's death was forwarded.

During November further unwelcome confirmation of soldiers killed reached Biggleswade and saddened even more families. Charles Butcher, a private with the 1st Bedfords had been gassed in 1915 and two years later he was killed on 28 October just before the battalion was relieved. Charles Butcher was a veteran, having been called up as a reservist and then having fought at Mons, the Marne and the Aisne in 1914. In the following year he had been at Neuve Chapelle, and had survived Hill 60 and Festubert. His wife first learned from the Red Cross that he was missing and then the dreaded news came that he had been killed on 28 October. She was told that he had been seen that day near a pill box and shells were falling all around, and it was one of these that did for him. His body was recovered and buried, and it would later be re-interred at Tyn Cot Cemetery where it rests today.

So Passchendaele, 3rd Ypres came to a close and the BEF had advanced around five miles but at a terrible cost, all of Haig's objectives having not been taken and Plumer's astounding success at Messines seeming an age ago. Seventy-seven thousand men from the BEF were killed during the fighting at 3rd Ypres. Yet Douglas Haig was not yet done with 1917 and the focal point for the BEF switched south to Cambrai.

Critics of Haig accuse him of being a technophobe but here at Cambrai he would use tanks en masse for the first time, and an extraordinary initial outcome was the result. Over 300 tanks went in at 6.20 a.m. after a surprise hurricane bombardment that employed around 1,000 guns, and the attack achieved a stunning breakthrough with a five-mile advance. Lessons had been learned from 3rd Ypres and aircraft were a key feature of the assault, and they targeted, bombed and strafed German artillery and troops. The artillery on 20 November employed a technique that was known as predicted firing. This was certainly a great step forward from the Somme, and the gunners were able to make use of aerial observation, increased understanding of trajectories, gunnery training and improved shells. Linked to calculating the positions of German guns via flash spotting and sound ranging, the surprise bombardment on the morning of the attack proved to be especially effective. The change from destructive to neutralising bombardment was a significant development, and was one that would play a crucial role in the year to come. If the effects of this artillery bombardment shocked the Germans, then the impact of an attack of over 300 tanks staggered them. The Germans were aware that some sort of assault might have been in the offing, but the BEF cleverly disguised the moving of the tanks to the forward positions by drowning out the noise of the tank engines via aeroplanes that flew over the front lines as the tanks advanced. Planning for the attack also saw the improved co-ordination of infantry and tanks, and this, allied to the work of the artillery and the Royal Flying Corps, saw the British break the Hindenburg Line at Cambrai. When news of this reached Britain three days later, church bells were rung for the first time in many a year, and it was felt that victory was close. However the higher ground that was Bourlon Wood was not taken and this would have serious repercussions.

The tactical developments that resulted in the extraordinary advance at Cambrai would today be described as 'all arms fighting' and this prompted a savage counter-attack from the German Second Army on 30 November. Here the Germans showed that they had not been idle in developing their own tactics, and the use of 'storm troopers' would feature prominently. This tactic had been two years in the developing and had been honed in fighting on the Eastern Front. It saw the employment of crack troops, who advanced quickly and who would skirt by any serious resistance. This was to be mopped up by other German troops who were assigned to follow up the storm troopers. It would be used with devastating effect in just under four months when the Germans launched their Spring Offensive, the Kaiser's Battle. By the end of the first week of December 1917 the German Second Army had recovered the vast majority of the territory that had been lost on 20 November. Cambrai had seen casualty figures of around 40,000 for both the British and their German foes, but it had also shown both sides a tantalising glimpse of how tactical progress might win the war.

Men from Biggleswade certainly featured in the fighting at Cambrai and once again there were casualties. In early December news arrived in the town that Chas Archdale had been killed on the first day of the fighting at Cambrai. Chas Archdale was a Norfolk man who had married a girl from Caldecote in 1903. He had enlisted as a private at the start of the war but had reached the rank of Captain with the Norfolk Regiment by the time he was sent to France in April 1917. The Norfolks were a part of the 12th Eastern Division who attacked at the furthest right for the BEF and, after taking their objective, they were to form a defensive shield for the rest of the attackers. Chas Archdale was killed as the Norfolks carried out this role. His wife received the news of his death at their home in West Winch, Kings Lynn and the impact that this had upon her and her five sons is hard to imagine.

Seven days later another from Biggleswade was killed in action when twenty-three-year-old Private Harry Spring fell in battle. The Spring Family had already tasted war for Harry's elder brother had fought at Mons, before being medically discharged because of his severe wounds. A younger brother had enlisted under-age and had been sent home from France when it was discovered that he was only seventeen. Harry was a professional soldier joining the Irish Guards in 1910, but had worked as a boot maker in the regiment. In September 1917, with increasing casualties he found himself overseas and thence at Cambrai. The Irish Guards were part of the famous Guards Division, and were given the task of taking the right flank of Bourlon Wood on 27 November. The Irish Guards attacked fiercely but found it difficult to stick together in the wood. However they managed to take their objective through sheer determination and bloody mindedness. In their assault Harry Spring was to lose his life. The first his wife and young son knew of this was a letter received from Harry's commanding officer Captain R. E. Sassoon:

> I regret to announce that Private Spring was killed in action on 27 November. He had been fighting most gallantly in an attack on a wood in which his battalion performed magnificently. I hear he was killed almost instantaneously and his loss is greatly felt by me and his company. He was a man who was always willing to do anything and good natured; he was well liked by everyone out in France. Please accept my sincere sympathy.

On the very next day Harry Spring's death was confirmed with the receipt of the dreaded brown envelope.

The fighting at Bourlon Wood was fierce and that the Germans were able to hold onto a small section of it proved to be crucial. When their counter-attack came on 30 November they shelled the parts of the wood that were in Allied hands constantly, especially with phosgene-gas shells. The British soldiers had to fight for days with their gas masks on which was very uncomfortable for them. They later told how the gas dripped from the trees, hanging there like fog. Many men made the mistake of taking their gas masks off from time to time to demist them and see if the gas had dissipated. Over a period of days this resulted in them breathing in small quantities of gas that had a cumulative effect, causing many men severe problems that would affect them for the rest of their lives should they survive the war.

Fighting at Cambrai came to an end on 7 December but not before another from Biggleswade had made the supreme sacrifice. Fred Kemps was a lance corporal with the London Regiment and he had only been on leave back home in Biggleswade three weeks earlier. His family lived in Hitchin Street and thirty-one-year-old Fred had a brother who had won the military medal whilst serving with the Royal Garrison Artillery earlier in the war. Indeed this brother was at home when news arrived in a snowy Biggleswade that Fred had been killed by a rifle shot on 4 December. Fred had been a Lewis gunner and these were always prime targets for the Germans as this portable light machine gun was much feared and respected by them. As the BEF withdrew from its advanced positions at Cambrai Fred was killed. By 7 December combat at Cambrai had reverted to the daily routine of the Western Front of shelling, sniping and mortar bombing.

The final casualty for Biggleswade occurred on 11 December when Private Harry Cartwright of the Essex Regiment was shot in the chest. He was treated at a casualty clearing station but he died three days later. His father, who lived in Palace Street, received news of his son's death from a matron at the CCS who wrote:

> It is with deep regret I write to tell you that your son Pte. H Cartwright, who was admitted here on the 11th, suffering from a gunshot wound in the chest, died from his injuries at 1 a.m. today, 14th. You may rest assured that we did all in our power for him to try and save his life but his wound was too severe. He was beyond our powers to save. Last evening he knew he was not going to get better and he wanted you to know that he was dying bravely like a soldier, and he sent his love to you.

Harry Cartwright was laid to rest in the military cemetery adjacent to the CCS and today his body still remains there at Rocquigny near Manancourt.

Others were perhaps more fortunate at Cambrai. Corporal Bob Villiers had escaped all injury during his two years on the Western Front. Here he was wounded in the stomach, but he would survive this and the war, as would Corporal George Clayton who had been wounded in the face.

From Palestine came the welcome news that Jerusalem had been captured by General Allenby's troops. The campaign had started at the beginning of October and Jerusalem had finally fallen on 9 December. Killed at the start of November was twenty-six-year-old Private William Smith of the 7th Battalion Essex Regiment. Initially he had been reported as being missing but he was then presumed dead. His body was later recovered and he was buried in Gaza War Cemetery. Also amongst those engaged in the fighting was twenty-year-old Edgar Wallis, one of four brothers serving in the forces. He had been in Palestine but a few weeks when his battalion, the 4th Essex entered the fray and on 4 December he went missing in action. At first it was thought that he had been captured by the Turks and indeed this was the case, but he was badly wounded and he succumbed to those wounds whilst in captivity, dying on the following day, 5 December.

As 1917 drew to a close Biggleswade had experienced its greatest number of sons, fathers and husbands killed yet, and allied to this was the fact that a significant number of others had either been badly wounded or were prisoners of war. These men were not far from the thoughts of the town's residents, and concerts and exhibitions were used to raise funds for both the wounded and the imprisoned.

In December Carol Services were held in the parish church on 23 and 25 December for those who had been blinded in the war with all proceeds going to soldiers and sailors who had lost their sight. Meanwhile at

Private W Housden, POW.

Little Tich.

No. 50 Shortmead Street was the depot for the Prisoners of War Fund. Here, during December, a whole host of trophies from the fighting on both the Western Front and from Gallipoli were on show. German helmets, German Field Service caps, and a Turkish fez that a Private Grayson from Old Warden had collected in both France and Gallipoli could be seen. Joe Bilcock, who had been killed at Passchendaele, and George Street, who had been killed in the advance from the Somme in February, had both given swords, trench daggers and bayonets taken from the Germans. Trench art was also on view, as well as a French bayonet from the Franco-Prussian War. All of the items were for sale and offers for them were welcomed.

Another contribution to the Prisoners of War Fund that was received in late December was though much less welcome, for it came as the last bequest of Little Tich, Charles Carr who was killed in action on Friday 7 December at Ypres. Little Tich had been serving with the 2nd Bedfords since joining the army twelve years earlier. In 1915 he had gone to the front and had survived all that had been thrown at him until that fateful Friday. Little Tich had been part of a rations party that was detailed to take food and water up to the front line. This was a dangerous and thankless task for soldiers to have to carry out. Rations parties went forward during the night as it was felt that their movement would be less likely to be spotted by the enemy. However each night the Germans shelled front-line trenches, the rear areas and the communication trenches, for they knew that this was when supplies were being taken forward. It was rare for a rations party to complete the round trip without suffering casualties, for their journey was a laborious one, having to negotiate muddy trenches in darkness, and having to carry water-filled petrol tins for over a mile. Sometimes such a journey could take hours.

The first news of the death of this very popular man had been when a comrade, Corporal Maidment, wrote to Little Tich's sister telling of how her brother had been killed by shrapnel to the head. The letter read:

Dear Madam

I very much regret to have to write to tell you that 8744 Pte C. Carr was killed in action on the night of Dec 7th. He met his death on the same battlefield we had our first scrap on in 1914. It was instantaneous so he did not suffer any pain. We went up with the rations and had just unloaded from the pack mules when a shell burst right against us and a piece of shell caught him on the head, killing him instantly. I caught it in the neck, but only slight and I am thankful to be alive now. It will be some consolation to you to know that we brought his body back to the transport lines some way behind the front lines, and that he was buried in a cemetery alongside some more of our Battalion and a cross was erected. I send you my deepest sympathy and shall be pleased to let you know any other details.

Corporal Maidment was not the only one to write to Little Tich's sister and further letters quickly arrived. First of all the chaplain of the regiment wrote telling how Little Tich's body had been left after the shell explosion but that his comrades risked themselves to go back to retrieve it and bring it back for burial. Then a letter was delivered from Private James Walker, an old school friend of Little Tich's that told: 'He was greatly respected by all his comrades and has always done his duty well. It was me who fetched him in from where his death occurred on Dec 7th.' A Private Wise of the Bedfords was the next to write and he told how a splinter from the exploding shell had pierced Little Tich's head just above the left eye, entering his brain and killing him on the spot. The last missive came from Little Tich himself, for he had left an envelope with a note inside his pay book with instructions that it should be delivered to Mrs Skilliter, his foster mother. It read: 'In the event of my meeting my death in the field will you kindly write to the address on envelope as this woman (Mrs Skilliter) has been as good as a mother to me. C. Carr, Pte 8744.'

He also left instructions that, on the event of his death, he wished any money found on him to be forwarded to the '*Biggleswade Chronicle*'s British Prisoners of War Fund.' As a result the 3s 2d, and 15 French francs and 95 centimes were sent to Biggleswade. In the columns of the *Chronicle* of 14 December, Little Tich was described as follows: 'He was a tiny little fellow but he had a big heart.' The words did not fall short of the mark. Today Little Tich's grave can be found in Bedford House Cemetery in Ypres.

The *Chronicle* was very active in its support of men from Biggleswade, Sandy and all of the surrounding villages, regularly devoting sections of the newspaper to news of these men, printing photographs of them in captivity and letters from them. In early December they even printed an article concerning Private W. Housden, who had been a prisoner since 1914, and showed a photograph of him before capture and a recent one of him as a prisoner in Munster Camp after three years in captivity. The article simply was headed 'A Contrast' and went on to say how he was changed, and then commented that he would have looked even worse if he had not been in regular receipt of the parcels that the *Chronicle* was sending to POWs. Those parcels must have been a godsend to the POWs, for Britain was waging a campaign that saw the blockade of German ports, and foodstuffs were certainly in short supply in Germany. The German word *ersatz* meaning substitute, was in everyday use in Germany and coffee made from acorns was standard to name but one example. During the winter of 1917 the blockade was hitting hard and Germans called the winter, the 'Turnip Winter' for this was the only foodstuff that was in plentiful supply. The parcels from Biggleswade would have been most welcome if the contents of those sent in December are anything to go by. From their depot at No. 50 Shortmead Street parcels containing 1½lb cheese, margarine, Quaker oats, jam, syrup, butter beans, two tins of paste, suet puddings, salmon, fifty cigarettes, biscuits, bacon, tins of beef, herrings, sugar, tea, dripping, soup and Nestlé's milk were shipped. In the edition of the *Chronicle* of 21 December letters from Privates W. Housden, S. Bilcock and G. Head were published, and they all showed the importance of receiving the parcels. Private Housden though longed for a cake, whilst Private Bilcock asked for a change in biscuits and Private Head was simply delighted to have got his parcel on his birthday. As well as organising the parcels the *Chronicle* also set up 'The Challenge Scheme' whereby local people and firms were encouraged to make regular weekly payments to help provide for the POWs, and lists of these benefactors were printed in the paper with the amounts donated.

For those soldiers who had been discharged from the army because of their injuries there was also help from the community, and a civil programme was set up in late December to try to find them suitable work in the vicinity of Biggleswade.

Many homes in Biggleswade had unexpected but welcome visitors for Christmas when a number of men serving abroad came home on leave, much to the joy of the families of Albert Clark, Frank Aubrey, Arthur Rollins, Jesse Wheatley and Walter Wren. Christmas Day proved to be ideal, for the sun shone, however snow fell quite heavily on Boxing Day. By the end of the third year of fighting the war was starting to have another effect upon the people of the town, for rationing was now in evidence. Germany had resumed unrestricted submarine warfare in early 1917 and, indirectly this had led to the USA's entry into the conflict. Germany had realised that victory on the Western Front was now unlikely, and that the best option was to try to starve Britain out of the war by preventing both foodstuffs and raw materials getting through. By December this policy was hitting hard and potato was being used in baking bread, whilst margarine, butter, tea and sugar were all rationed.

On the last day but one of 1917 disaster struck hundreds of miles away from Biggleswade when the troopship SS *Aragon* was torpedoed as it waited to enter Alexandria Harbour. As the ship started to sink the destroyer HMS *Attack* steamed to the rescue, but the same fate awaited her as another torpedo from U-Boat UC-34 struck her, and almost blew her in two. Over 600 lives were lost, and amongst them was twenty-nine-year-old Sapper Horace Green of the Royal Engineers. His body was never found and he was presumed drowned at sea. Horace Green had an Aunt Lizzie and cousins living in Biggleswade, and the depth of their sorrow can be seen in that three and a half years later one of the wreaths laid at the inauguration of the Biggleswade War Memorial was from them for him.

As the year ended the conflict showed no sign of conclusion, and some had noted a change in mood of some of the men serving, and for the first time their optimism was noticeably absent. Quite what 1918 would bring would be anyone's guess. It was true that American troops were now arriving in numbers but they were raw and untested in battle, and would need time for their fighting skills to be honed. On the Eastern Front the October revolution had seen Russia's withdrawal from the war, and the ominous release of the majority of Germany's battle-hardened troops from that front. As far as the BEF was concerned, Haig was coming under growing pressure from David Lloyd George following Passchendaele and Cambrai, and the Prime Minister would have replaced him if a suitable candidate could have been found. As for the composition of the BEF, increasingly it was being made up of young conscripts who would have to cut their teeth in the New Year.

FIVE

1918

From Defeat to Victory

The start of the New Year in Biggleswade saw more families rejoice in welcoming home their men folk who were on leave. Walter Marsh and Joseph Wren both spent a restful time recuperating in the town, and were able to tell of their war so far. In Walter Marsh's case this was quite a story for he had already served on three fronts, having seen action as a driver in Mesopotamia, Salonica and Egypt, and had been wounded once. If the families of Walter Marsh and Joseph Wren had reason to smile then the same could not be said for Mr and Mrs William Haynes. They had already lost two of their sons in 1916 and 1917 respectively, and 1918 was to start worryingly for them when they received news that the third of their four serving sons had been posted as missing towards the end of 1917. Apprehension though was soon to turn to relief when they discovered that their son Fred, a Lance Corporal in the same regiment, the Middlesex, as his two killed brothers, was in fact a prisoner of war. Fred Haynes and Herbert Haynes, who after contracting and recovering from trench foot in 1917 was posted to Ireland, though would both survive the war.

If some solace was experienced by William and Susan Haynes then the same cannot be said for the friends and the relatives of Private Albert Clark of the 2nd Bedfordshire Battalion, who was killed by shellfire on Saturday 5 January at Ypres. Albert had only been back on leave in Biggleswade six days earlier and had spent Christmas in the town. He had enlisted in 1914 but had later been discharged as medically unfit owing to leg trouble. However as the need for men grew, in 1916 he offered himself again and was accepted, which speaks volumes for the effect of the increasing number of casualties from the war. On the Somme he had been badly wounded by a shell that dropped into the dugout he was in, and which killed several of his comrades. He had been invalided back to 'Blighty' but had returned to the front, and had been in action throughout 1917 with the 2nd Bedfords. In the spring of 1917 he had written home saying that he thought the end of the war was in sight. The letter read:

> I think if we keep on like this we shall not have another winter in the trenches. I was sorry my old work chum, Alec Ambrose got killed and also my chum at enlistment, Corporal

Roberts, who was trained with me. The Biggleswade boys in our battalion want to be remembered to you all. We are all 'tres bon'.

On 5 January 1918 he was with his company in the front line at Polderhoek when a German shell fell, killing him and four of his comrades. Although both of Albert Clark's parents were dead he had a brother who was serving in East Africa and it took time for news of his Albert's death to reach the Dark Continent.

Also wounded in January with the Bedfords was Private Walter Howe who had joined under the Derby Scheme. He had been wounded in his side but he would recover, and survive the war much to the relief of his mother who lived in the High Street. Sapper William Field was another who would require medical treatment in January. He had been climbing a telegraph pole in France to carry our repairs, when a German gas shell exploded close by, and he was blinded. This was the second time that he had been wounded, for in 1915 his hands and head had been badly burned by a German bomb. Now in 1918 his blinding had necessitated treatment at a specialist hospital in Aberdeen and he responded, for after a few days, although his eyes were still sore, he could see. Writing home he could not praise enough the care he had received in Scotland.

Another wounded man, Private Harry Day, was discharged from the army at the start of 1918. Harry's career in the army had started with the wars in South Africa and, when hostilities started in 1914, he was amongst the first to be sent abroad, serving with the 2nd Bedfords. He had been with his close friend, Fred Rowlett, when he was killed at 1st Ypres, and indeed Harry, himself was wounded then. From there, after recovery he was drafted to the Balkans and in the retreat from Serbia he was seriously injured falling down the side of a mountain. Recently he had hurt his hand so badly on barbed wire that he had been hospitalised for a considerable time. Now he was discharged fully and would take no further part in the fighting.

Casualties were not only limited to the Western Front and Biggleswade would see one of its own in January. The threat of German air raids was taken seriously and Gotha bombers had attacked London just forty miles away. Therefore there was no street lighting in Biggleswade and the hours of darkness could prove to be dangerous as Mrs Taylor, who lived in Norfolk Place, discovered. She was found unconscious in the road and it was suspected that she had been knocked down by a vehicle of some kind. She was helped home by PC Rawlins and two soldiers billeted in the town, and although she recovered from the injuries to her head and back, she could not remember how she had got them. More welcome was the fact that, at auction, a finely worked crest of the Bedfordshire Regiment made by a Private White, who had been invalided out of the army when he lost his right hand fighting in France, had made a good price. He had used his remaining limb to create the crest and it was sold for £6 and 13s which was given to the *Chronicle* British Prisoners of War Fund. More tragically January would see the death of someone who had fought through the Western Front but who succumbed to those horrors and died at the Three Counties Asylum on 16 January. He was Private Robert Clark of the 7th Battalion of the Bedfords and today his grave can be located in Biggleswade Cemetery.

As usual during January and February fighting on the Western Front remained limited to trench raids and daily shelling. However things would certainly change in March, and change significantly, in that this time the BEF would be on the defensive rather than the offensive. On Friday 1 March Private Percy Clark became the third man with that surname to die in 1918 when he went missing in action. It was often the case that raiding parties lost men who were captured and Percy Clark, who was serving with the North Staffordshire Regiment, fell into this category. The Red Cross in Geneva would later confirm that his name appeared on a list of dead soldiers that the Germans published in Berlin on 24 April. Percy Clark was thirty-four and had only been at the front for a few weeks when he was killed. Meanwhile though some lucky soldiers found themselves on leave back in 'Blighty' and home in Biggleswade, including Canadian Frank Carpenter, Sapper Bert Farr, Hugh Woodward and Frank Garner. For them and those serving on the Western Front this would be the calm before the storm that would break on 21 March.

By 1918 the Germany that Britain had declared war on four years earlier was much changed and was now much more similar to the military dictatorship associated with the Second World War. Power within Germany now rested with General Erich Ludendorff, and the military controlled both civil and military life. The harsh terms of the treaty of Brest Litovsk that Germany imposed upon a beaten Russia showed that this Germany was intent upon creating a sizeable empire in the east, and Ludendorff was now the real master, with the Kaiser becoming simply a figurehead. Ludendorff now could call upon hundreds of thousands of battle-hardened veterans from the Eastern Front, and he would now easily outnumber the combined French and British armies on the Western Front. The key, as he saw it was to break these original foes before the full impact of America's intervention could be realised. Millions of American Doughboys were reaching Europe but, as yet, they were not ready to enter the conflict fully, and Ludendorff now prepared to risk all by breaking the British and French, and securing a favourable peace before the Americans could make an impact. What perhaps he felt was the key card to play was the development of tactics that he believed would bring mobility to the war, and would drive a decisive wedge between the British and their French allies. If he could break the allies' line where the two armies met, then he was convinced that the British would be forced to retreat northwards towards the Channel and that the French would see surrender as their only option as they fell back towards Paris.

The tactics that he would employ on 21 March had been honed in Russia and Romania, and they centred upon the use of storm troopers. These were men who were chosen especially for their aggression and they had been trained to move quickly, independently and to achieve maximum infiltration. Whenever they met serious resistance they were to skirt around it and progress, leaving the resistance to be mopped up by supporting troops who followed on. Ludendorff also instructed his gunners to use the same kind of short, hurricane bombardments that the British and French were employing. Gas shells were to be a critical a part of this artillery tactic, but there would be no use made of tanks, for the Germans did not seem to rate the impact of these machines. The place for the attack was to be St Quentin, and the troops that were to bear the brunt of the German offensive were the BEF of Gough's 5th Army.

So what of the BEF in early 1918? Well, it had been used to taking the offensive for the past three years, and there was a lack of experience or familiarity with how to employ defensive tactics. The BEF that faced the fury of the attack on 21 March was also seriously depleted and had just had to extend the front that it covered, taking over a considerable section from the French. Actual numbers of men were also reduced, for five divisions had been sent to support the Italians, and the 5th Army at St Quentin was clearly under strength. Soldiers later described how they had company strength to cover an area that previously would have been the responsibility of a battalion (see Appendix 5). There was also the question of familiarity with the concept of elastic defence. By this the battlefield was divided into zones, notably a forward zone and a battle zone. The forward zone saw a series of redoubts connected by trench lines, but these were not supposed to be held indefinitely, but rather to inflict damage on the advancing enemy, and then the troops were to pull back to the battle zone where the real resistance was to commence. It would be something of an understatement to say that the BEF at St Quentin did not fully comprehend this, for many of the 5th Army fought to the bitter end on 21 March or until surrender.

At 4.40 a.m. of 21 March the Germans attacked when almost 6,500 guns opened up, supported by around 3,500 trench mortars. Allied to the shock of this bombardment was the fact that it was very foggy, and visibility for the defenders was poor, resulting in the storm troopers being able to overrun or, if necessary, slip by the redoubts. The fog also prevented British artillery from being able to range in on the advancing German soldiers as they entered the battle zone. German artillery additionally played havoc by shelling the British rear areas, and this caused serious problems for communication, and artillery response.

In the face of this onslaught it is not surprising that the 5th Army fell back. By the end of the day Ludendorff was exhilarant. His troops had advanced significantly, taking almost 100 square miles of the British front, and had broken the static warfare of the last four years. In doing so Ludendorff's troops killed around 7,500, wounded over 10,000, and captured almost 20,000 British soldiers. Noteworthy though was the fact that the Germans had suffered around 40,000 casualties themselves, and most of these came from this elite storm-trooper group. Equally significant was the fact that, although the British had been pushed back, and severely stretched, they had not broken, and, to the north of Gough's 5th Army, Byng's 3rd Army was holding firm at Arras. For the next few weeks the battle raged and Germans continued to progress, eventually seeing an advance of around forty miles, crossing the old Somme battlefields and nearing Amiens. However Amiens did not fall and this was the crucial to British resistance. On 11 April, during what seemed to be the BEF's and Haig's darkest hour, the Commander-in-Chief issued a special Order of the Day that was almost Churchillian in its message and style. It read: 'There is no course open to us but to fight it out. Every position must be held to the last man: there must be no retirement. With our backs to the wall and believing in the justice of our cause each one of us must fight on to the end.'

During April, May, June and July Ludendorff changed the focus of his attack in a desperate attempt to make the crucial break that would divide the French and the British but gradually the initiative was shifting. On 14 April the Allies took a staggering decision. Up until now both the British and the French had insisted upon each country maintaining control of their own armies. Now it was agreed that Foch should be made General in Chief of the Allied Armies. Immediately the effects of this were seen as the Generalissimo rotated troops from the front line, giving the besieged British soldiers relief, and also moving French troops to take over sections of the front under attack. It was equally significant that some degree of indiscipline was starting to occur within the ranks of the advancing German troops. They had been told that the Allies were suffering as much as they were, in terms of supplies, and yet, as they advanced they found Allied supply dumps full of food and drink. Unsurprisingly they looted these and the impetus of their attacks suffered. The territory gained also brought into focus the problem of supply for the Germans and having to defend a longer line. The Allies, having taken and absorbed the blow were now ready for the counter-attack and this came in on 8 August, and would see the start of the 100 Days that would bring the war to an end.

However, returning to 21 March and the launch of the Kaiser's Battle, the 2nd Bedfords were one of the battalions that were right in the centre of the German attack, and, bearing in mind the casualty figures above, it is not surprising that they lost considerable numbers. Amongst those who faced the fury of the German assault was Sergeant George Gurney of the Bedfords as they stood to in the Battle Zone trenches and Stevens Redoubt. The regimental diary tells of how the 2nd Bedfords could see the advance of the Germans as they passed through the forward zone and then how they fought a ferocious struggle to try to hold back large numbers of the enemy. Sergeant Gurney was in A Company and they came under attack from the Germans immediately they broke through the Forward Zone. George Gurney and his men were shelled heavily and then the Germans advanced in large numbers, and they started to surround both A and B Companies. The men fought valiantly but eventually had no alternative but to withdraw, with only a few of them getting back. George Gurney was not among them, for he had been killed during this desperate fighting.

For four years George Gurney had survived the horrors of the Western Front, having risen to the rank of Sergeant and having been awarded the Military Medal for gallantry on the Somme. He was a serving soldier when war broke out but returned with the 2nd Bedfords from South Africa, and had fought in all of those early battles that secured Ypres from the Germans. During the fighting in October 1914 he had been badly wounded and was away from the action, recovering until he returned in time for the Somme. On the first day of that battle he was wounded in winning the Military Medal and was helped out of danger by a fellow Biggleswadian and medal winner Private Fred Senior, DCM. By 1917 he had been promoted to Sergeant and had become an integral part of A Company. On 20 September he was mentioned in dispatches for his part in a successful trench raiding party on the Ypres-Comines Canal. By 1918 he was back in France at St Quentin and about to face an onslaught every bit as dangerous as the one he faced at Ypres, when the Prussian Guards were repelled. His obituary in the *Chronicle* described him as 'one whom the men trusted and would willingly follow anywhere and on any mission.'

The letter that his mother received from the chaplain of the 2nd Bedfords told of his death, expressed sympathy and added simply but poignantly 'Sergt. Gurney died just like a brave soldier.' His body was never recovered.

There was no let up in the fierce fighting and as the Germans moved further forward so the BEF's casualties grew. On 23 March, further to the north of St Quentin, the Royal West Surrey Regiment, the Queens, found themselves under attack and, although the advance of the Germans was much better resisted here, the BEF did suffer losses, amongst whom was another from Biggleswade. Omar Housden was twenty-eight and had enlisted in 1915. He had seen service on both the Western Front and the Italian Front and so far he had come through unscathed. That was to change drastically for this former footman to the Governor of the Tower of London on Saturday 23 March. Initially Private Housden was reported as missing and his parents became very worried when they failed to hear from him. That concern grew and then their worse fears were confirmed when they learned from the Records Office of the Regiment at Hounslow that their son had indeed been killed in action, resisting the German advance. Another man from Biggleswade was caught up in this German breakthrough. Private William Champkins was also serving with the Queens, and he was captured as the Germans moved forward. His family were relieved that he had not been killed but relief turned to despair just six months later when he died in captivity on 28 September.

It is no surprise however that details of what was happening to members of the BEF were sketchy, for the German advance was rapid when considered in the light of the stalemate of the previous three and a half years. Men lost contact with their battalions as they retreated and it was difficult to keep tabs on them. For worried relatives these were difficult times and the *Chronicle*'s Prisoner of War Fund received many enquiries for information about missing men as their relatives searched for news.

The parents of Private Percy Harradine were one such family and they were most anxious when they received a letter from the chaplain of the Royal West Kent Regiment telling them that their son was missing in action. Percy Harradine had even written to his parents on the very day that the Germans had launched their offensive, Operation Michael, and his parents' concern increased when they then received another letter that officially told them he was missing. It would not be until July that their fears were allayed when they received a card from their son telling them that he was a prisoner of war in Germany. This former printer at the *Chronicle* had been captured as the Germans pressed on, and, although he had suffered a slight bout of dysentery after being captured, he was alive. He wrote on 28 April to say that he hoped that his capture was known to them, but the card took over two months to reach Biggleswade. Also captured by the Germans during these first few days of Operation Michael were Privates Alec Taylor of the Machine Gun Corps, Samuel Smith of the Middlesex Regiment and Walter Wagstaff.

Others who fell during these dreadful first few days of Operation Michael, as the Germans called this first assault, included Private Claude Airey of the 1st Battalion of the Royal Fusiliers. This brave man came from a military family, for his father was a captain in the Royal Veterinary Corps, and having enlisted in 1914 he had seen a great deal of action, having been badly wounded prior to the Kaiser's Battle. On 22 March he was reported missing, and later it would be confirmed that he had died on that day. Three days later Private Aubrey Webb would be added to the growing list of the fallen when he was killed as the 2nd Bedfords were falling back at Golancourt, coming under attack by massed infantry and being hit by heavy shellfire. Aubrey Webb had served for over two years and survived being wounded in 1917 before he fell at Golancourt. No bodies were ever found, and Claude Airey's and Aubrey Webb's names sit on the same Pozieres Memorial as George Gurney.

April would see the German attack continue and six more men from Biggleswade killed. By the start of the month the British retreat had reached the old Somme battlefields, close to Albert. On 4 April twenty-seven-year-old Private George Cole who was serving with the 4th Battalion of the Royal Welsh Fusiliers was wounded as the offensive continued. Those wounds would prove to be fatal for he died two days later. On the same day, 6 April, the Germans attacked in force with supporting artillery and the 4th Bedfords were in the thick of the fighting but they held their ground. On the following day they were relieved by a Royal Navy battalion, The Hood, but not before Private Jack Waller had been killed in action together with seven others from the 4th Bedfords. Jack Waller's death is especially sad for this young man had only arrived in France on 12 March and had merely served for three weeks at the front. Jack Waller was just nineteen when he was killed and both his family and workmates at Pearl Insurance mourned the death of this popular young man. Around the same time Private Fred Thorn of 6th Northants was reported missing. Back in Biggleswade his wife received the disturbing news that this was the case when a letter from his commanding officer arrived. It read – 'From what I can ascertain I think it is possible he was taken prisoner so I hope you will hear news to that effect soon.' The fact that his commanding officer could not be more definite tells much about how the nature of the fighting had changed and, now that there was much more movement, it was more difficult to discover the fate of soldiers. Fred Thorn had actually been killed on 5 April and his body was never to be found. April had not been kind to Fred's wife for her brother Private A. Farr of the Cambridgeshire Regiment had been captured and he would remain a prisoner until the war ended.

On 7 April George Sidney Fairbanks was killed over 100 miles to the north in a German attack at Ypres that pre-empted their major assault in the area later in the month. Private Fairbanks was no stranger to intensive fighting, and had fought and been wounded on the first day of the Somme. When he was being treated there it was discovered that he was too young to be at the front, being only seventeen, and he was returned to Britain. By 1918 he was nineteen and eligible for service abroad and he did not shirk that duty. He was back with the Highland Light Infantry as they were in the front line at Ypres and this time fortune did not smile upon him for he was killed in a German attack.

As April progressed the German offensive continued to make inroads and cause further casualties. On 27 April Private Ernest Watts of the 2nd Battalion of the Coldstream Guards was killed by shellfire. His mother was to find this out when a Lieutenant Cross wrote telling the sad news. His letter read:

> Private Watts was killed by a shell which landed actually in the trench. The same shell killed his officer, Mr. St Ledger, and two men and wounded four others. I can truthfully say he suffered no pain, not a second, for death was instantaneous. In the company and the battalion your son was much respected and liked for his good hard working nature, and we all miss him very much ... I am unfortunately not at liberty to state where your son is buried, but he was laid to rest in a little village, and the service was said by the Battalion Chaplain. In a few

months time all being well I will write you a line giving you the name of the place. If there is anything at all I could let you know about your son I will be only too pleased if you ask me. I really do feel for you in your great loss.

Ernest Watts was twenty-six and had only been in France for about a month. His elder brother Arthur had died during the first year of the war, and now the death of a second son did little for the health of their ailing mother, Louisa.

On 19 April the German offensive switched attention to Flanders and within days the BEF were forced to shorten their line and in doing so had to give up Passchendaele Ridge that they had fought so hard to capture just months earlier. To the south of Ypres on 5 April, with the crack Alpine Corps to the fore, the Germans attacked at Mount Kemmel and they captured it from the French. Four days later they once again set upon the Allies, this time striking against the British and French between Ypres and Bailleul. It was here that Corporal Victor Gale died at his post according to his commanding officer who wrote to Victor's mother in Dunton. This twenty-year-old was serving with the 49th Company of the Machine Gun Corps and had been in the army for just two years, recently having been promoted to corporal. Victor Gale's body was never found and his name rests on the back wall at Tyn Cot with over 30,000 others who shared the same fate.

As the month drew to a close further distressing news reached Biggleswade that Gunner William Lincoln of the Royal Horse Artillery had died in captivity in Germany on 20 April. William Lincoln had been taken by the Germans during their counter-attack at Cambrai in November of the previous year. He had moved around POW camps and had had spells at Dulman Camp and then Freidericksfeld Camp. It was whilst at the latter he bumped into fellow Biggleswadians and he at least had the company of men he knew in his last few months. On 20 April he died from heart problems and was buried at what has now become Conde sur L'Escat Communal Cemetery that contains the graves of ninety Commonwealth servicemen who died in German hands in 1917 and 1918. William Lincoln was not the first in his family to die in captivity, for his cousin John had earlier died as a prisoner of the Turks in 1916.

Early in May reports reached Biggleswade of missing men who had been taken captive during these first six weeks of the Kaiser's Battle. They included Sergeant Major Harper of the Hussars, who at some stage in the previous weeks had been posted as wounded, gassed or simply missing. In early May it came to light that he was in captivity. At the same time another man with the name of Percy Clarke, but this time with an 'e' at the end, was reported as being missing. He had been with the 1st Bedfords when they had arrived in France from Italy at the beginning of April and quickly found themselves facing the German onslaught. Percy Clarke was captured after a very short career as a soldier and he would spend the rest of his war as a prisoner, as would Private Jack Coote of the Machine Gun Corps. He was captured in March, but it would not be until June that his distressed parents would find this out. They had had to endure three months of worry and anxiety until news reached their home in Drove Road that their son was alive.

Other information arriving in Biggleswade revealed a number of men having been wounded in March and April. They included Private Chris Partlett of the Highland Light

Infantry, who had been wounded in the back by shellfire and Private Ernest Ibbs who was with the Australians. Private Tom Charter, who had been wounded in the leg earlier in the war, suffered again when he was injured in May. His Surrey Regiment had been under attack when he was hit by a piece of shrapnel in what sounds a gruesome incident. The metal struck him on the nose and came out at the bottom of his jaw, only missing his eye by about an inch. Writing home to his wife he told how he had been placed in the same ambulance as a Private A.J.York, who was also from Biggleswade.

The Grummitt family who lived in Sun Street had all of their six sons serving and the war had hit them hard. Two sons, Fred and Harry had already died, whilst two others had been seriously wounded, one being maimed for life, and then further bad tidings came in May that another of their sons, Maurice had been hospitalised after being struck by shrapnel in the leg, the buttock and the arm.

Although the spring of 1918 was a harrowing time for many families in Biggleswade, for some it was a time to feel pride as a number of men were awarded medals for bravery in resisting the German thrust. Squadron Commander W.L. Welsh was the first, for action against the enemy over Dunkirk, where his aircraft was brought down, and he had to spend the whole night in the water until he was picked up by boat. Nine months earlier his brother, serving with the Royal Field Artillery, had been killed at Ypres. Following Squadron Commander Welsh's award of the Distinguished Service Cross came news that Lieutenant Cecil Soundy had received the Military Cross for bravery in the field. The list of medal winners grew with the award of a Military Medal to Corporal Girling of the Royal Army Medical Corps for his work at Passchendaele where even though he himself was wounded, he treated injured men on the battlefield. Then a further Military Medal came when Sergeant Robert Jollands of Drove Road was awarded his for courage whilst serving with the Railway Corps of the Royal Engineers in France. The last medal awarded for gallantry in the opening phase of the Kaiser's battle came in May when Driver Herbert Thompson won the Military Medal, together with five other drivers in an extraordinary example of dedication and daring. As the Germans were advancing a section of the Royal Field Artillery found itself under attack and for a while it looked as if their guns would be captured by the enemy. Driver Thompson and his comrades were having none of this and they galloped to the rescue, bringing back both the guns and two wounded gunners as shells exploded all around them. Herbert Thompson was wounded himself in saving the guns and would later send home to his father the piece of shrapnel that was extracted from his neck. News of another Military Medal winner was less welcome in Biggleswade for Private Reg Jones of the Machine Gun Corps was posted as missing. He was the grandson of the former stationmaster of the town and had won his Military Medal when only seventeen, for bringing in wounded men under heavy shell and rifle fire.

At the start of May, Mr and Mrs Gray of Sun Street had received their second brown envelope of the war, and their loss was shattering. Both sons had been killed, William in 1914 and now Len. The family were said to have been heartbroken by this devastating news. Len Gray had enlisted when he was seventeen and, when he reached nineteen, he was sent to France with the 1st Bedfords. He had been wounded in 1917 and had also seen action in Italy, before the Battalion returned to the Western Front in April 1918.

He had been at the front for just a month when he was killed by a trench mortar bomb together with his officer Lieutenant Frederick Ray, on 16 May. They were the only two men in the Battalion who were killed on that day, just as they were about to be relieved.

Eleven days later another man from Biggleswade was killed. Private Fred Page was serving with the 3rd Battalion of the Worcestershire Regiment on the Aisne when they were attacked. Initially he was posted as missing but that was later changed to 'presumed killed' and this indeed did prove to be accurate when his body was recovered afterwards

27 May proved to be a day that the Lovett family of Sun Street would never forget, for on this day their third son was killed. Henry Lovett was a private with the 2nd Battalion of the Northamptonshire Regiment and at first he was posted as being missing. However his comrades, who were fighting alongside of him on that Monday, were to say that he could not possibly have survived. Their words proved to be prophetic for his body was never found and today he is simply commemorated on the Soissons Memorial on the Aisne in France. The irony is that the 2nd Northants were amongst the 5 British Divisions that had been in the firing line, as far as the German advance during spring was concerned, and they had been moved away from the danger areas to the Aisne, where it had been quieter, to rest and recuperate. On 27 May Ludendorff switched his attack to that very area and the artillery bombardment that preceded the attack was horrendous. The advance virtually destroyed five British and seven French Divisions and penetrated twelve miles. The war was so cruel to the Lovett family and no other family in the town lost so many sons.

At the start of June two men from the town were killed in very contrasting circumstances. Firstly Mr and Mrs Samuel Northwood received information about both of their boys who were serving in France. The first news was more welcome than the second. Charles Northwood was a Sergeant with the Royal Engineers and he had fought in the Boer War. In 1914 he had re-enlisted and had broken his leg. Four years later he had been injured again when his horse fell on him but the relief that one of their sons had only broken fingers and a thumb was tempered by very grim news indeed of their other son Arthur. He was thirty-six and a gunner who was serving in the Royal Garrison Artillery with a trench mortar battery in the Arras sector. He was hit by a rifle shot on 4 June. Nothing could be done for him and he was buried in Arras. Today his grave can be found at the main Commonwealth War Graves Cemetery in the town, and his headstone has the poignant inscription from his wife, 'Remembrance Love, Jenny'.

On the following day Lieutenant William Elliott of the newly formed RAF was test flying an aeroplane off the coast of Scotland when his plane came down, and he drowned. Initially his body was not found, but a week later it was washed ashore and was brought back to Boxworth where his family had moved. His obituary said how sad it was that he should have met his death while flying over home waters, having previously served with distinction in France twice. He was buried in Boxworth Cemetery. Neither British or French pilots were issued with parachutes during the Great War as it was felt that this might encourage them to abandon their aeroplanes before this was really necessary. Whether a parachute might have saved Lieutenant Elliott will never be known, but on the Western Front the sight of aviators falling to their deaths was a tragic sight. Each day men in the trenches would view with wonder the dogfights between the Germans and the Allies high above their subterranean world. Sometimes they even got to fire upon enemy aircraft that were low enough, and both Vickers and Lewis machine guns were used for this. Indeed Manfred Von Richthofen was brought down by such early anti-aircraft fire in April 1918 over the Somme, close to Heilly.

Towards the end of the month of June another death that was not directly associated with the fighting would be confirmed when Harry and Fanny Baxter of Potton found out that their sixteen-year-old son Leslie had died in hospital in Plymouth. Leslie Baxter was Boy, second class on HMS *Impregnable*, a training vessel moored at Plymouth. Spanish Influenza would kill more people in 1918 and 1919 than were killed throughout the Great War, and it was now starting to wreak havoc in both mainland Europe and Britain. Unusually for flu, it hit the young and those up to forty, hardest. Leslie Baxter fell victim to it and died on Saturday 29 June.

By July Ludendorff's gamble was almost played out and the Allies were getting ready for the counter-attack. Spanish flu was hitting German soldiers, as were food shortages, and the strength of the German army was waning. Added to this was the fact that the American Army was now starting to play a fuller role, and in late June they had won their first battle in clearing Belleau Wood. Their casualties were high, with losses of 11,000, for they attacked with the same kind of bravado, tactical naivety and enthusiasm that had marked the Citizen Armies on the first day of the Somme. On 4 July a taste of what would come was shown when the Australians attacked at Hamel using 'all arms tactics' that saw infantry, aircraft, tanks and artillery all coordinated. It was a resounding success that would be repeated with devastating effect in just over a month at Amiens.

As the fighting in France continued so did the casualties and on 5 July another man from Biggleswade was killed. Gunner William Ewart Lampey was a twenty-nine-year-old, who was well known and respected in the town, being recognised as one of the best bass singers that the choir of the Wesleyan Church had seen. He played both cricket and hockey for Biggleswade, and had been a prime mover in the establishment of the Wesley Guild Tennis Club. In 1917 he had married whilst home on leave and had then gone back to the Western Front. In July of 1918 he was serving as a gunner with the Howitzer Brigade of the Royal Marine Artillery in Ypres when he was killed following German shelling. His death was mourned by many back home, not least his young widow, Eunice. Equally sad tidings also reached the Wallis family when they received official confirmation that their son Edgar, who was with the 4th Battalion of the Essex Regiment, had died of his wounds as the British were taking Jerusalem. At first it had been reported that he was missing and wounded and for six months his family lived in hope that he had become a prisoner. This was the case for the Turks had captured him, but he was badly wounded and he succumbed to those wounds on 5 December 1917.

At the same time that news of Edgar Wallis's and Gunner Lampey's deaths was reaching Biggleswade, so also did further information of how Lieutenant Cecil Soundy had won his Military Cross. The official version of his award read as follows:

As intelligence officer to a dismounted brigade during six days' operation he made a daring reconnaissance on one occasion and brought back timely warning that the right flank of the brigade was in danger of being enveloped, thus enabling the brigade to withdraw successfully. He showed splendid skill and resource throughout the operation.

Cecil Soundy had started his wartime military career with the Yeomanry and had then gone on to serve with the 5th Bedfords, before transferring to the Scottish Horse and then the Royal Dragoons.

8 August 1918 would see the beginning of the end of the Great War when the Allies launched their counter-attack. On this day, the BEF, together with the Canadian and Australian Corps initiated the offensive that would last exactly 100 days and would see Germany forced to sue for peace. In these 100 days the BEF achieved a series of stunning victories that showed how tactically adept they had become in employing artillery, infantry, aircraft and tanks together – the so called 'all arms attack.'

The offensive began at Amiens on 8 August, and the effect upon the Germans can be gauged by the fact that Ludendorff described this day in his memoirs as 'the black day of the German Army in the history of this war.' On this day General Rawlinson, who had led the 4th Army on the Somme in 1916, led it again here and sent in ten Dominion divisions and four British divisions, together with one American division, supported by both cavalry and over 400 tanks against Ludendorff's 2nd Army. The planning had been meticulous and the counter battery work on that day was exemplary, for virtually every German gun emplacement was nullified by the Allied gunners. British artillery had evolved strongly following the trials of the Somme, and by 1918 it was proving to be a tool that could go on to win the war. As well as improved shells with graze fuses that exploded on impact, technological advances had also occurred in counter battery work, especially in how to locate, target and destroy enemy guns. Most notable here were flash spotting and sound ranging, and both of these techniques were employed during the 100 Days to very good effect. Flash spotting required artillery observers to get an accurate cross-reference of muzzle flashes from German guns from at least three different positions. This was then plotted and an accurate placing of the enemy's artillery could be made. Added to this was the development known as sound ranging, whereby a number of microphones were employed to detect the positions of enemy artillery. Together, these two techniques gave Allied artillery a definite edge, especially with regard to the cover offered to troops. Attacking Allied troops were now not subjected to the kind of deadly German shelling that had been experienced on 1 July 1916 as they advanced across no-man's-land. Equally significant were the evolution of the creeping barrage and the box barrage. These both offered increased protection in the crossing of no-man's-land and the consolidating of captured enemy trenches. The creeping barrage saw soldiers advance behind a wall of exploding shells. This forced the Germans to stay in their dugouts until the BEF were almost upon them. It was usual for the creeping barrage to be made up of a third shrapnel, a third high explosive and a third smoke, and when it worked it worked very well indeed. The successful employment of the creeping barrage meant that there was no repetition of the slaughter on the Somme from German machine guns that were set up before the Tommies had crossed no-man's-land. If the attack was a success then a box barrage was laid down and this protected against German counter-attacks. A box barrage enclosed the tired troops behind a protective screen of exploding shells that the counter-attacking Germans could not penetrate. Box barrages were also used as a tool during assaults by the BEF to isolate sections of the enemy front line, and to prevent any German reinforcements from reaching the area under attack.

The build up to the attack at Amiens had seen Rawlinson cleverly disguise the point of attack, and the Germans were certainly deceived. By 1918 the German army was decidedly wary when the Canadian Corps were around, and the reputation of this Dominion Corps was excellent. They would play a leading part at Amiens, and Rawlinson went to extraordinary lengths to ensure that the Germans did not know that they were there. He had let it be seen and known that the Canadians were in Flanders, but then secretly the majority of the Corps had been moved south in sealed trains, leaving two battalions behind in Flanders to maintain the subterfuge. When the attack went in at 4.20 a.m. on 8 August these 'shock troops' as the Canadians have been described, were to the fore as were the Australians. They were very ably supported by the BEF, but the Canadians were much fresher as they had generally been spared from the German onslaught of earlier in the year. Attacking after a surprise hurricane bombardment from over 200 guns, the British, Canadians and Australians were helped by a dense morning mist. They overran much of the German line with advances of up to eight miles being achieved, and significantly they suffered only 9,000 casualties. In comparison the Germans lost around 27,000 men, of whom 12,000 had been killed whilst the others were now prisoners. Added to this the Germans lost around 400 of their artillery guns that day, and it can be seen that Ludendorff's words were not an exaggeration.

The British had indeed learned lessons over the last two years and the troops that went in on that Thursday morning employed the much more sophisticated tactics described above than those used on 1July 1916. Creeping barrages and box barrages were now standard use, whilst the development of flash spotting and sound ranging had taken counter battery work to an entirely different level. Machine gun barrages were another very useful addition to their armoury. In addition to that the emphasis was now on the platoon and each man knew his job, whether he be a Lewis gunner, a bomber or a rifle grenadier. They worked as a team and, together with more efficient tanks and aircraft that now were employed to attack enemy ground troops as well as just observing, it proved to be a winning combination. What is equally noteworthy is the fact that achievable targets were being set by those in charge. The Great War was primarily an artillery war and the protection given from one's own guns was vital for advancing infantry. In order to maintain that protection the guns had to be moved forward with the advance. Therefore, although the advance at Amiens was very deep it did not go so far as to be out of the reach of the British guns. Another key tactical improvement saw the BEF shift the focal point of attack if they ran into serious resistance and the use of a series of rolling attacks with limited bite and hold tactics to move forward. When the Germans offered stiff resistance after the initial Amiens attack, the focus of the fighting was switched northwards with Byng's Third Army leading the charge between Arras and the Somme. This tactic prevented the Germans from moving support troops around and they did not know when the next blow would come. During August the emphasis moved from Amiens to Arras and then back down to Albert, before finally hitting the Germans on the Scarpe.

Along the whole of the Western Front the German Armies were falling back and in Flanders the trend continued. Towards the end of September they had been driven back to the Hindenburg Line but not without cost, for the British Third and Fourth Armies were suffering casualties on a day-to-day basis that were worse than for the Somme campaign of two years earlier. By the time that the Hindenburg line was reached about 190,000 men from Third and Fourth Armies had been killed or wounded. The Germans retreated in an organised fashion and their machine guns exacted a terrible toll on the advancing British. By this period the very make up of the BEF had changed considerably, with large numbers of conscripted young men with limited experience of fighting finding themselves at the front. The ages of many of those from Biggleswade who died in those last 100 Days confirms this, with the majority killed being aged nineteen to twenty-three.

On 29 September the British 4th Army took on its most difficult challenge when it stormed the Hindenburg Line in an extraordinary feat of arms. Prior to the attack there had been a four-day bombardment that saw almost ¼ million shells fall on German positions that were daunting to say the least. Part of the Hindenburg Line that was assaulted saw the BEF having to get across a wide strip of water, the St Quentin Canal and then ascend steep banks that were up to 60ft high. That the Hindenburg Line was taken speaks volumes for the attacking troops, and especially for the 46th Division that had been so cruelly cut down on the 1st July 1916 on the Somme. This Territorial Division showed formidable determination and no lack of invention in crossing the canal and taking their objectives. Using improvised boats and floating piers they got across with the men using life jackets secured from Cross Channel ferries, and they then scaled the high steep banks before capturing the German trenches here, taking over 4,000 prisoners. This breach in the Hindenburg Line was followed by further ruptures, and by early October the Line had been broken. How the fall of the Hindenburg Line impacted upon German morale is not hard to judge, for if the Allies could break this supposedly impregnable defence then what would stop them?

Next to fall was Cambrai, followed by serious inroads being made in Flanders. Everywhere the Germans were in full retreat and Ludendorff was coming under increasing pressure, and by October the only solution was to call for an armistice. After negotiations the guns fell silent on the eleventh hour of the eleventh day of the eleventh month.

So what of those men from Biggleswade who fought in these last 100 Days? On the first day of the offensive at Amiens two fell. Private George Housden was with the Royal West Surrey Regiment, the Queens, who were in the northern wing of the offensive and on that Thursday he was killed instantaneously by shellfire. Georgie Housden was typical of many of those conscripted young men killed in the last 100 Days of the war for he had only turned nineteen in the spring of 1918. He had not been long in France, and prior to his conscription he had worked at the *Chronicle* and then at the University Club in Pall Mall in London. On the same day another nineteen-year-old, Private Fred Scott of the 10th Essex was reported missing. Fred Scott was also a conscript but he had served for longer on the Western Front, and was part of a Lewis Gun team. These men were feared by the Germans for this light, portable machine gun significantly increased the firepower of attacking platoons, and there were stories of wounded Lewis gunners being dispatched if they were captured. Fred Scott's parents did not receive confirmation of the death of this Biggleswade Brewery worker for almost two months.

At the same time that news of the deaths of Georgie Housden and Fred Scott was reaching Biggleswade equally sad tidings arrived in the town concerning a former employee of the Capital and Counties Bank. Harold Reaney had been a very popular man during his time in the town and had won himself a reputation as both a sportsman and a singer. At the start of the war he had joined the Bankers Battalion of the Royal Fusiliers, had seen some hard fighting in 1915 and had been promoted to lieutenant. In 1916 he had fought on the Somme and had won the Military Cross in the capture of Beaumont Hamel in November of that year, but was seriously wounded in doing so. By 1918 he was deemed to be fit enough to return to the fighting but with the Bedfordshire Regiment. After all he had been through fate dealt him a deadly blow in late July when he fell from the platform of Elephant and Castle Underground station and he was killed aged just thirty-four.

As August progressed more and more men from Biggleswade were involved and some of them paid the ultimate price. On 22 August Bert Tasker was reported as having been killed in action as the BEF advanced. Letters from the chaplain and the battalion major of the Kings Royal Rifles were confirmed when Bert Tasker's mother received an official telegram telling of her son's death. This twenty-four-year-old had joined up in 1915 with the Post Office Rifles and he had fought throughout the Somme battles but was wounded there. He was then invited to try for a commission and, after successful completion of the training, he was appointed to the Kings Royal Rifles where he saw a fair amount of action in the spring and late summer of 1918. Major J.J. Shepherd, his battalion commander told Bert's mother what a respected officer he was, and how much his men mourned him. Both Bert's father and brother, who were serving in Egypt and with the navy respectively, would be more fortunate and both of them would survive.

On 24 August Rifleman Jack Chandler of the London Regiment became the fourth man from Biggleswade to be killed in that month. Once again the initial reports were unclear and it was hoped that he had fallen captive of the Germans. For two anxious months his parents clung to that hope that this was the case but in October they received news of his death from the regimental chaplain. He told Mr and Mrs Mark Chandler that their son had been killed in action. At first, he told them, it had been reported by fellow members of his platoon that Jack had been wounded. Afterwards it came to light that he had succumbed to those wounds on the battlefield before he could be taken back to a field hospital. His body was buried near a place named Moislaine but the exact spot was lost and his grave was never relocated. Jack Chandler was yet another nineteen-year-old, and he also had served as an apprentice on the *Chronicle*. Today he is commemorated on the Vis-en-Artois Memorial.

The last casualties for the month of August saw Private Francis Mann of the 7th Battalion of the Northamptonshire Regiment wounded in the head, shoulder and leg. Francis Mann was an only son and again was just nineteen. His condition was so bad that he was transported back to Britain to King George's Hospital, but his wounds were too serious and he lost his battle to survive almost two months later on 24 October. His body was brought back to Biggleswade and was buried in the town's cemetery.

On 28 October Lieutenant Colonel Edward Twelftree Saint of the 1st Battalion of the Cambridgeshire regiment was badly wounded and died the very next day. He had been in France since 1915, had won the Distinguished Service Order and had been mentioned in dispatches. Edward Saint had grown up in Biggleswade before his family moved to Cambridge.

August also saw news of a stranger sort of casualty reach Biggleswade when it was learned that the vicar of the town had been injured on the Western Front. The Reverend G. Carter Rolfe had been serving in France for about a year when, on 25 August, he was sheltering in a house just behind the front line when it came under shellfire. Carter Rolfe had been assigned to the 51st Highland Division and the collapse of the house had caused him to suffer a broken collar bone and three broken ribs. After the war he would recount how this Territorial Division had won itself a fearsome reputation during the war, and that the Germans called them, because of their kilts, the 'ladies from hell.' In December 1918 Carter Rolfe would call for the building of a war memorial in Biggleswade to honour the fallen.

As September started the BEF battled away in driving the Germans back towards the Hindenburg Line. Back in Biggleswade a service was held at the parish church for those from the town who had fallen. The list that was read out on 4 September ran to 158 names. At the same time forty men residing in the area received news of their applications to be exempt from being conscripted. They came from Biggleswade, Potton, Shefford, Arlesey, Stotfold, Ickwell Green, Langford and Gamlingay, and the majority shared the fact that they were in their late forties or even fifty. Their fates had been decided at the Biggleswade Rural Tribunal that had met in late August in the Masonic Hall and their ages reflect the increasing pressure that was being felt in providing men for the BEF. Those whose applications were refused quickly found themselves being prepared for the Western Front, not for the front line but rather to take over the work of men behind the lines. These men could then be released to move up the line, and thus see action.

On the Western Front the fighting now was close to the old Somme battlefields of 1916 and Private William George Wells of the London Regiment was badly wounded. He was taken back to the Casualty Clearing Station at Daours, but his wounds were to kill him. William Wells was twenty-eight and, having enlisted early in the war, he had fought originally with the Bedfordshire Regiment, seeing much service on the Western Front. The wound stripe on his uniform he wore with pride and he had also suffered from trench foot. After recovering he had returned to the front with the London Regiment in 1918, and it was whilst serving with them that he was killed.

As the month progressed the BEF continued to push the Germans further back and on 18 September Private Edwin Sidney Sims of the 6th Northants was severely wounded in the shoulder as the battalion advanced before Peronne. Three days later twenty-one-year-old Sidney Sims succumbed to this wound and the only son of Mr and Mrs Arthur Sims died. Sidney Sims had been called to the colours in April 1917 and had been at the front since August of that year. In November 1917 he had returned to Britain suffering from trench foot and was treated up in Bradford. At one stage it had looked as if he would have to have his toes amputated, but the skill of the doctors prevented that and he was able to enjoy leave back in Biggleswade that coincided with the August Bank Holiday. By 21 September he was back with his regiment and was just a month away from the fatal wound that would take his life. In October his grieving parents received a letter from Miss E. Schofield who nursed him through his last days. Her letter read:

Dear Mrs Sims,

Your son was admitted here on Sept. 21st at 11.50 a.m. from a wound in the shoulder. He passed away free from pain. I know this will be a great shock to you but a little comfort I hope for you to know that everything possible was done for him. Also to know that he was thinking of you all, and especially sent his love to his mother. He said 'I know they will fret for me.' Oh, he was so patient and thought of how you would all be worrying about him. 'Give my love to all, especially mother,' was the last thing he said. He will be buried by our chaplain in the military cemetery near here.

And so he was, resting there today in Doingt Communal Cemetery Extension on the Eastern outskirts of Peronne.

Eight days later the second son of John Henry and Rose Smith died when Ernest, serving with the 8th Battalion, the Winnipeg Rifles, Manitoba Regiment of the Canadian Infantry was killed in action. Ernest was twenty-three, had served and survived on the Western Front for over two years and died as the Canadians advanced towards Cambrai.

By October the Allied advance was in full swing and this month would see even higher casualty figures for the BEF with 121,046 men being killed or wounded. Not surprisingly these figures were mirrored in the casualties for Biggleswade and ten men from the town died in this month but not just on the Western Front.

On 2 October the second son of Frederick and Annie Millard was killed in action as the BEF attacked at Ypres. For over a month his parents had not heard from Bertie and they were obviously fearful, especially as they were still coming to terms with the fact that their elder son, Arthur had been wounded in late August. He would spend the last two and a half months of the fighting recovering in hospital and survived the war. The younger Bertie Millard had arrived in France in April, and was serving with the 11th Battalion of the Queens, Royal West Surrey Regiment. Once more here was a nineteen year old conscript who would lose his life. Frederick Millard was to hear more details of how Bertie had died when the Lieutenant Colonel of the Regiment wrote:

Dear Mr Millard,

It is with the greatest regret that I have to inform you of the death of No. G70082 Pte Millard B.G. in action on 2 October, 1918, attached to Light Trench Mortar Battery. The success obtained by the Battalion on this day was entirely due to the gallantry and devotion to their country's cause displayed by No. G70082 Pte Millard and his comrades. The present evacuation of Belgian territory was largely due to the attack carried out on that day. Nothing finer could have been imagined than the loyal and gallant spirit in which all ranks attacked. Please accept our sincerest sympathies in your loss,

W.C. Owen, Lieut.-Col, Commanding.

Percy Starnes had seen more of life for he was thirty-three, and was on the point of getting married. He was expected back in Biggleswade during the first two weeks of October for the ceremony to take place. That was not to be, for tragedy befell Percy Starnes on 3 October when he was thrown from his horse at a Royal Army Service Remount Depot near Abbeville. He died from his injuries the following day. His parents Fred and Amelia went from preparing for their son's wedding to Miss Hancock, to having to come to terms with his accidental death. After they were told of his demise they tried to arrange for his body to be returned to Biggleswade, but by the time their request reached Abbeville their son had been buried. They received a number of letters from Percy's commanding officer, the chaplain of the regiment and one from his friend, Private F. Phillips, who wrote:

> You will no doubt be surprised to hear from me but I felt that it was my duty to write to you as I was an old chum of your son. I thought you would like to know that he had a proper funeral; a few of the boys followed to the cemetery and put two wreaths on his grave. The wreaths had been subscribed for by the men of the unit who liked and respected your son very much, and he is greatly missed among them. It seems a great pity that he should come out here and miss all harm from the enemy and yet fall through an accident with a horse. Should you wish to have a flower from the wreath let me know and I will send you one. Please accept my sincere sympathy in your sad loss.
>
> Yours faithfully, F. Phillips

As the month progressed more and more families in the town were to experience similar losses. Walter Cocks was the next parent to grieve when he was told that his son Charles, who was twenty-five and serving with the 10th Battalion of the Queens, had been killed in action at Ypres on Monday 7 October. A week later, on 14 October the BEF struck here again in the north and the fighting moved towards the old battlefields of 1915 and Aubers Ridge. It was here that Private Leonard Clayton was killed as the 15th Battalion of the Suffolk Regiment attacked. Leonard's mother heard of her twenty-five-year-old son's death when official notification reached her at her home at No. 25 The Baulk. Leonard Clayton was buried close to where he fell and rests today in Aubers Ridge British Cemetery. Then on 18 October further bleak tidings were received when Private Ernest Bilcock died of his wounds at Ypres. He had only been back home in Biggleswade during August and yet just two months later he was killed as the BEF pressed the Germans here in the Salient. Ernest Bilcock had served on both the Western Front and in Italy. When he died he was with the Machine Gun Corps, and it was his battalion major who wrote with details of his death. Ernest Bilcock's friends were concerned as they had not heard from him for some time and they contacted the prisoner of war fund who got in touch with his battalion. A Major Hartley was able to provide the information that confirmed Ernest had died. He wrote:

> Pte Bilcock and many of his comrades were wounded by a shell striking the house where they were billeted. He was badly wounded and was rescued by his comrades. The house was filled with gas and several were gassed while engaged in the work of rescue. His comrades did all they could for him, but Pte Bilcock died shortly after admittance to hospital. I knew Pte Bilcock when he and I served in another Company. I might say that I never wish to serve with a better man. He was brave under fire and was always willing to volunteer for any of the hundreds of petty little things which have to be done. I should be obliged if you would convey to Mrs. Bilcock my most sincere sympathy in her great sorrow.

On 23 October three men from Biggleswade were killed, two of them with the same surname. Private Alfred Walker was with the 2nd Bedfords as they set about the Germans close to Le Cateau, where just over four years earlier the BEF had fought such a critical rear-guard action. The fighting was fierce and the Bedfords suffered 231 casualties, forty-five of whom were confirmed as being dead. Nineteen-year-old Alfred Walker was amongst them. The war diary of the battalion confirms how ferocious the fighting had been and tells how great a loss was inflicted on the enemy, whose dead were numerous all over the battlefield. The captures amounted to 100 prisoners, three guns, three trench mortars, two anti-tank rifles and upwards of sixty machine guns.

Further south, Private Horace Walker was in action with the 6th Battalion of the Northants Regiment as they attacked close to Cambrai. Horace had been in France for only six weeks when he met his death. His parents heard of the demise of their son when Lieutenant Stanley Keep wrote to them in November: 'I am very sorry to tell you your son died in action on 23 October. He was killed immediately by shell fire. He was always bright and willing, and did his duty well.' Horace Walker was a deeply religious man and he wrote home shortly before he died believing that he would not return from the fighting. He also left in Biggleswade a letter to be given to his fiancée, Miss Swain, in the event of his death. The letter reveals his strong religious faith, and contained many references to the Almighty. He ended the letter: 'I trust you will not look too much on the dark side, but that you will put your trust in Him Who can conquer all things. Try and cheer mother up. I loved thee well and could love you no more, but God thought it best we should meet no more. God be with you till we meet again.'

Slightly further to the south the 10th Battalion of the Essex Regiment were engaged on the Aisne and it was here that Private Fred Waters would at first be posted as missing but that would later change, and not for the better. Fred had been in the army for a year and nine months, and had been on the Western Front for seven months, during which time he had been wounded once. On the 23 October he was wounded again but this time very seriously. At first his parents were told by telegram that he was wounded yet alive. A week later their hopes were dashed when they received a letter from the chaplain of the regiment that read:

Dear Mr and Mrs Waters

I deeply regret to have to tell you your son Pte F. Waters, Essex regiment passed away here on the 23rd at 6 p.m. He was admitted on the same day and passed away without regaining consciousness. He was suffering from wounds being in the head. It may comfort you to know that everything possible was done for him. He was laid to rest in the military cemetery at Primont. His effects will reach you from the War Office in due course. With deep sympathy, yours very truly,

Cyril V. Campler-Cogan,
Service Chaplain.

Beyond the Western Front the campaign on the Italian Front was nearing its end and the Austrian Army was in retreat, and another tragedy was about to be played out. Corporal Fred Stone of the 14th Battalion, Army Cyclist Corps, Machine Gun Section was thirty-six when, in pursuit of the fleeing Austrians, he was killed on 30 October, the very last day of the fighting on this front.

October's other casualties for Biggleswade saw the following men wounded, but at least they would live to see the war's end. Corporal Joseph Deamer of the Royal Engineers was gassed and hospitalised, but the action that had seen this also saw him awarded the Military Medal for bravery in the field. Trooper George Osborn of the Hussars had had a lucky escape, for the bullet that wounded him passed clean through his body hitting him in the back and exiting through his chest. Albert Edgeley was another to survive. This corporal with the Hertfordshire Regiment had been wounded in the neck, shoulder and back and his wounds were serious enough for him to be brought back to Whipp's Cross Hospital on the outskirts of London. Tom Charter of the East Surreys was a private who found himself back home in Biggleswade, and whilst there he showed a very charitable side to his nature when he gave to the Secretary of the Prisoners of War Fund souvenirs from the fighting on the Western Front. They included an Iron Cross ribbon and a horn snuff box taken from the Germans. Fred Head of the Essex Regiment was another injured in the intense fighting. He suffered a facial wound and was removed from the front to a base hospital. Corporal H.A. Ward was also wounded when he was hit in the right arm and the left leg. He was to recover in hospital in Blackpool. Other men, though not wounded, saw their war come to a close when they were captured during the 100 Days. Private Jack Coote and Sapper A. Sells would both spend the remaining weeks of the war in captivity.

So, after over four years of conflict, the last eleven days of fighting were to be played out before the guns fell silent. Strangely, the BEF would find itself at Mons, where it had all started four years earlier, as the war was brought to a close. These last eleven days were not without incident for the men from Biggleswade and, sadly some of them were to be added to the long list of the fallen. Francis Wagg was a private with Rifle Brigade and he had caught the Spanish 'flu. This debilitated him so much that he was hospitalised in Falmouth. At first it looked as if he would pull through, but his condition weakened and he then caught pneumonia which finished him on 3 November. The senior chaplain for the Falmouth, B.J. O'Rorke area wrote to Francis Wagg's father to tell him of the death of his son. He wrote:

Dear Mr Wagg,

I was deeply grieved that your son succumbed to his severe attack of sickness in hospital. I saw a good deal of him there and was beginning to know and understand him. It came as a shock to me to hear that he was seriously ill, for he seemed cheery and talkative when he first came to hospital. I saw him three times on Sunday – morning, afternoon and evening; but unfortunately I was not present when he passed away. During my visits he was only half-conscious and could not say very much. I prayed with him and he thanked me and seemed to appreciate it. Even when I last saw him a couple of hours before he died there seemed to be hope that he would pull through. I feel deeply for you and yours in this very sad blow, and I pray that God will give you grace to bear it bravely.

On the same day, 3 November, Private James Kitchiner died of bronchitis and pneumonia over in France. He had initially fought with the 2nd Battalion of the Royal Fusiliers, but after injury he had been reassigned to the Labour Corps, and it was whilst he was serving with them that he died. The effects of the 'flu epidemic were also being felt in Biggleswade and a number of schools were closed at the start of this month. The obituary pages of the *Chronicle* showed that the 'flu was very virulent indeed with churches and the Picture Palace being closed to soldiers on leave. Any soldiers who came down with the infection were quickly taken to the military hospital in Potton Road, close to the Infectious Diseases Hospital.

In France, Belgium and at home the final tragedies were about to be played out. Firstly Private Walter Lincoln, who had been invalided out of the army after being wounded and gassed, was to give in to these cumulative effects and die in Biggleswade. His brother John had died in 1916 as a prisoner of the Turks, and his cousin William had died under similar circumstances as a prisoner of the Germans. Then Corporal Fred Garner was wounded as the BEF advanced, just days before the armistice. This was a cruel end for a man who had fought right through from the first year of the conflict. He asked the Minister of the 1st Bedfords to write to his wife Alice to let her know that he expected to be brought home to a hospital in England shortly. Sadly though, ten days after the signing of the ceasefire he would succumb to the chest and thigh wounds and die.

On Monday 11 November news of the end to the fighting reached Biggleswade at 8.00 a.m. It was revealed when Colonel French, who commanded the local signal depot, had intercepted a message broadcast from the Eiffel Tower. That transmission told of how Germany had signed the Armistice at 5 a.m., and that it had been agreed the fighting would stop six hours later at 11.00 a.m.

On the Western Front the fighting continued in some areas right up to that 11 a.m. deadline and incredibly there were almost 11,000 casualties for the two sides, with just under 3,000 dead. Artillery crews continued to fire shells until 11 a.m., even though the ceasefire was known, simply because it was easier to get rid of the shells this way, as opposed to having to haul them back to supply depots. Some commanders remained in a belligerent mood and men were sent forward again until the last minute, with the last recorded casualty being Private Henry Gunther of the American Expeditionary Force, who was killed by machine-gun fire just one minute before the guns fell silent. He and his fellow soldiers had not been told that the armistice was about to take effect, and he charged forward towards the German lines, bayonet at the ready, despite the fact that the Germans tried to warn him of the impending ceasefire.

In Biggleswade the news of the intercepted message transmitted from the Eiffel Tower spread quickly throughout the town and flags were hung out, church bells were rung and then the fire bell was rung for several minutes. This caused many to rush to the fire station to see what was wrong. As a crowd started to grow in the market square the 'All clear' signal was given, and a thanksgiving service was hastily arranged to take place in the parish church. On a dull and wet day in Biggleswade, the National Anthem boomed out from the church. The Great War was over.

Epilogue

If Biggleswade felt that it was done with the Great War then the Great War was not finished with the town. It would continue to exact its toll throughout the rest of 1918 and 1919, and sadly, more men would die.

One day after the Armistice, Private Freddie Albone died from pneumonia brought on by the Spanish 'flu. He had been taken ill at Holme near Peterborough at the start of the month, and the influenza had progressed alarmingly and caused fatal consequences. Freddie Albone was twenty-three and had fought with the 2nd Bedfords early in the war. This had taken its toll and, after he was deemed to be unfit for fighting at the front, he was transferred to the Labour Corps. Many soldiers found themselves in similar situations, being deemed unfit for action but well enough for labouring. He was survived by a wife and a father who was still serving with the Bedfordshire Regiment. Then at the start of December John (Jack) Reynolds was visiting his parents at their home in Sun Street when he was taken ill with the flu. Jack Reynolds was twenty-four and had been invalided out of the army in 1916 as a result of a severe wound to the muscle of his arm. He had tried many times to enlist before being accepted by the Bedfordshire Regiment. His injured arm had been treated for over a year in hospital but he was left with a limb that was practically useless, and he was discharged. Following this he had gone to live in Huntingdon with his wife, trying to live off his army pension and what work he could do. A week after his visit to see his parents he passed away. So in just over a year and a half Mr and Mrs Reynolds had lost two sons, the first, nineteen-year-old Fred being killed in action at Arras, and now John to the 'flu.

His death was followed by that of Driver John Munns of the Royal Horse Artillery who died on 8 December in France, again as a result of pneumonia brought on by the 'flu. John Munns had survived almost four years of the conflict only for the 'flu to take him after its conclusion. His wife had travelled to France when she was told of his illness, and was with him when he died.

The start of 1919 saw further deaths and on 7 February Private Fred Basterfield, who had worked as the porter at the Biggleswade workhouse before joining up, died of 'flu at Hal, near Brussels. Private Ted Maudlin of the Labour Corps became another to die from pneumonia on 25 February two years after his brother Leonard had died at

Gaza; on 27 February 2nd Lieutenant Norman Brown of the 4th Royal Fusiliers died in Aldershot of pneumonia and was brought back to Biggleswade to be buried in the town's cemetery. In March further unwelcome news reached Biggleswade with the death of Corporal Fred Woodcraft of the Bedfords Yeomanry who was with the British Army of occupation at Cologne. Here was another who had served and had seen action right from 1915, only for the Spanish 'flu to take the life of this corporal of the 19th Hussars. At the start of April Private Alfred Patrick of the Army Service Corps died just three days after returning from Salonika, and then Jack Franklin, who had been a lieutenant with the Royal Army Service Corps died following an accident at a nursing home. He was buried in Biggleswade Cemetery. Sergeant Wallace Albone of the Machine Gun Corps then died on 18 May after returning from Palestine. Finally twenty-one-year-old Private Ernest Radford of the 5th Battalion of the Bedfordshire Regiment died on 26 June just ten days after returning from Egypt.

In Germany, with the end of hostilities many prisoners of war had simply found themselves without guards, and they had to make their own way back home. Gradually these men returned to the UK. In Biggleswade some arrived home to unexpected news. Reg Boness, a sergeant with the Bedfords who had been captured during the German Spring Offensive, arrived home to find that his wife had given birth to twins whilst he had been in captivity. All of the men who came home said how important the parcels from the *Chronicle*'s War Fund had been. In December the *Chronicle* closed subscriptions to the fund.

Also during December of 1918 a ceremony took place in the Market Square to honour men from the Royal Engineers Signal Section, who were billeted in the town at the London Road depot. Military Medals were presented to a number of NCOs and Privates, and they included one for Sergeant Edwin Samuel Wadman who had won not only the Military Medal but also the Distinguished Conduct Medal. Sergeant Wadman had won his medals, as the presenting officer, General Godfrey Faussett told:

> … for conspicuous gallantry and devotion to duty. He was in charge of a party laying a cable to a forward position under heavy fire, and completed the work, taking charge when his officer was killed. He showed great skill and courage in handling his party and it was largely due to him that the cable was completed in time for the attack.

The work of the Signallers in the Great War is often overlooked but these brave men had the unenviable task of trying to maintain communications by the laying of telephone cables through, and across, no-man's-land before and during attacks; an exacting, dangerous and demanding job.

Back on the Western Front, the grim task of locating the graves of the soldiers who had died began. Initially many of those men had been buried in civilian cemeteries in Belgium and France as the fighting started in 1914, but as the number being killed grew, so did the need to bury them close to where they fell. Shell holes became the final resting place for many, whilst others were buried close to the casualty clearing stations where the surgeons had not been able to save them. With the end of hostilities the War Graves Commission began its work. The decision to bury soldiers where they had fallen was a logical one, for the mechanics of bringing home so many bodies was beyond possibility. However the bodies were scattered across hundreds of cemeteries; some large, others quite small. The War Graves Commission brought order to the situation and the consolidation or construction of the cemeteries that we know today began in 1919. Initially soldiers waiting to be demobbed carried out the gruesome work of exhuming and reburying the bodies, but later the Chinese Labour Corps took on much of the undertaking. It was not an easy chore, for the battlefields contained much dangerous material, including unexploded shells and grenades. Together with the Spanish 'flu this exacted a very high toll of casualties and nine per cent of these Chinese workers died or were killed, a figure that is on a par with the overall casualty figures for the BEF during the four and a half years of conflict.

As the bodies were either reburied or brought to communal cemeteries the difficulty of identification became apparent. Soldiers in the Great War did wear dog tags but they were made from leather and they had rotted in the ground. This partially explains the high number of graves that bear the inscription 'A soldier of the Great War, known unto God'.

Many of those men from Biggleswade, whose graves were lost as the fighting continued, quite likely occupy such an inscribed grave. Those whose graves could not be identified were added to the huge monuments that were built at Thiepval, Menin Gate, Tyn Cot, Arras, Pozieres and Cambrai to name but six.

In 1920 Edgar Wood, the secretary of the Town War Memorial Committee was able to publish the definitive list of those from or associated with Biggleswade who had died during the four years of fighting. A year later the amended version was to form the basis of those whose names would appear on the town's war memorial. The 1920 list, as it appeared in the local press, is below. It contained 199 names and reads, in the style of the war memorial as follows:

1914–15

Gunner Horace Bryant, L Battery, Royal Horse Artillery, killed in action
Private Arthur Butterworth, Kings Royal Rifles, died of wounds
Private William Gray, 1st Bedfords, killed in action
Private George Thomason, 2nd Bedfords, killed while giving water to a wounded comrade
Private Ernest Emery, 1st Wiltshire regiment, killed in trenches
Private George Dean, 3rd Bedfords attached to 1st Bedfords, died of wounds at Douai while a prisoner of war
Private Fred Rowlett, 3rd Bedfords attached to 2nd Bedfords, killed by shrapnel at Ypres
Corporal Herbert Stocker, 2nd Bedfords missing since 1914 now presumed killed
Private Walter Storton, 3rd Bedfords, attached 1st Bedfords, killed in action at Neuve Chapelle
Lance Corporal Sidney Carr, Yorkshire Light Infantry, died of wounds
Private Arthur Endersby, 1st Bedfords, killed by shell fire
Private George Tear, missing since 1914 now presumed killed
Private George Smith, missing since 1914 now presumed killed

EPILOGUE

1915–1916

Private Dick Bosworth, reported wounded and missing in August 1915, now presumed killed

Private F.B. Potton, West Kent Regiment, killed in action

Private Edmund Stratton, 7th Bedfords, killed when preparing to attack enemy in great advance

Private Steve Runham, Brigade Trench Mortar Battery, killed by shell fire in front line trench

Private Chas Pepper, Essex Regiment, died of wounds

Private Herbert Goss, 8th Bedfords, killed while out with trenching party

Private Clifford Huckle, RAMC, killed in action

Private Arthur Boness, 1st Bedfords, killed in action

Private George Boness, Beds Regiment, posted as missing in July, unofficially reported killed Jan 1917

Lance Corporal Joseph Loveridge, Yorks and Lancs Regiment, killed in action

Private Leslie Whitbread, Manchester Regiment, died in hospital ship home ward bound from Gallipoli

Private William Gauge, 2nd Bedfords, killed in action

Private Leonard Chambers, Middlesex Regiment, killed in action

Sergeant Harold Morgan, Canadian Expeditionary Force, killed in action

Private Bert Morgan, Canadian Expeditionary Force, killed in action

1916–1917

Captain Herbert Purser, Royal Marine Artillery, died from fever in German East Africa

Captain Clifton Cyril Welsh, Royal Field Artillery, killed in France by aeroplane bomb while superintending the sorting of supplies at an ammunition dump

Private William Warner, Notts and Derby Regiment, died from gunshot wound to head

Private Robert Plumbridge, Machine Gun Corps, posted as missing on 16 Sept, now presumed killed on that date

Private Archie Boness, Beds Regiment, killed in action

Lance Corporal Albert Haynes, Middlesex Regiment, reported as missing, now presumed killed

Corporal Walter Haynes, London Rifle Brigade, killed while asleep in trench

Private Fred Land, died from gunshot wound in the back

Private George Jackson, Beds Regiment, killed on the Somme while serving with the Tanks

Private Cecil Batten, Kings Royal Rifles, reported missing on the Somme, now presumed killed

Private Alec Lovett, Canadian RAMC, killed by a shell

Private Robert Lovett, Beds Regiment, posted as missing and then reported as killed

Private Fred Wells, Suffolk Regiment, died from wounds

Private William Smith, Hampshire Regiment, posted as missing and then reported as killed

Private Laurie Brown, died while training with the Canadian Expeditionary Force

Private Francis Harry Taylor, Middlesex Regiment, died from wounds

Private Harry Huckle, Beds Regiment, killed in action
Private Maurice Woodward, killed while on way to dressing station after being wounded
Private Sydney Circuit, Middlesex Regiment, killed in France
Private John Lincoln, Norfolk Regiment, died while a prisoner of war in Turkey,
Private Frank Kefford, Beds Regiment, wounded while with a bombing party, presumed buried by the enemy
Private Harry Rowlett, Beds Regiment, killed in action
Private Fred Skilliter, Essex Regiment, killed in action
Rifleman George Wagstaff, Post Office Rifles, died after operation in London
Private Henry Wall, Australian Expeditionary Force, reported missing now presumed killed
Private Arthur Rainbow, East Kent Regiment, reported missing now thought to have died in Germany
Private Arthur Dellar, Beds Regiment, posted missing then reported killed
Private Alexander Drysdale, Beds Regiment, wounded in action, died in London
Private Walter Walker, Northants Regiment, died from wounds
Private Horace Smith, Middlesex Regiment, killed in action
Private George Street, Machine Gunner, Northants Regiment, killed in action
Private Edmund Sells, Royal West Surreys, posted missing then reported killed
Private Arthur Garner, Australian Expeditionary Force, killed in action
Corporal Fred Roberts, Beds Regiment, died of wounds
Corporal Dick Alvey, Machine Gun Section, London Regiment, killed in action
Private Alec Ambrose, Beds Regiment, killed in action
Private George Dickens, Essex Regiment, killed in action
Private Walter Gatward, Beds Regiment, killed in action
Private Harry Milton, Essex Regiment, died of wounds
Private Percy Cole, Hon Artillery Company, killed in action
Private Alfred Brunt, Beds Regiment, killed in action
Private Robert Brown, Beds Regiment, killed in action
Private Jack Gauge, Beds Regiment, killed in action
Corporal Harry Garner, Beds Regiment, posted missing then reported killed
Private Absolum Smith, Essex Regiment, died of wounds
Gunner Percy Bonfield, Royal Field Artillery, killed in action
Private Percy Brown, Northants Regiment, killed in action,
Private Harry Simms, Beds Regiment, killed in action
Private Harry Grummitt, Beds Regiment, died from gas poisoning,
Private Fred Grummitt, Beds Regiment, killed in action
Sergeant Harry Figg, Canadian Imperial Force, died from wounds
Private Bob See, Australian Imperial force, died from wounds
Private Sydney Bygraves, Royal West Surreys, died from wounds
Private Ernest Woodward, Middlesex Regiment, killed in action
Bombardier William King, RFA, killed in action
Lance Corporal Robert Stocker, Machine Gun Corps, killed in action
Private George Cole, Beds Regiment, killed by sniper
Private Tom Housden, Beds Regiment, killed in action
Private John Newman, Beds Regiment, killed by shell fire whilst asleep

1917–1918

Lieutenant William Elliott, RAF, drowned off Scotland whilst on test flight
Sergeant George Senior, Royal Berks, died of wounds
Gunner George Warner, RFA, died from wounds
Private James Harpin, Middlesex Regiment, died from wounds
Private Henry Garner, Herts Regiment, died from wounds
Private Tom Bridge, Lincoln Regiment, reported missing then killed
Lance Corporal Horace Bridge, Beds Regiment, killed in action
Sergeant Charlie Clifford, 5th Bedfords, killed in a night raid
Corporal Herbert Legate, Beds Regiment, died of wounds
Private Victor Milton, Beds Regiment, killed in action
Private Jonathan Wade, Canadian Mounted Rifles, killed in action
Private Headley Rowland, Beds Regiment, posted missing then reported killed
Sergeant Alfred Garr, 5th Bedfords, killed in action
Private Leonard Maudlin, Essex Regiment, killed in action
Private Joseph Watts, Beds Regiment, posted missing then reported killed
Private Charles Butcher, Beds Regiment, killed in action
Private Joseph Bilcock, Beds Regiment, killed by an aeroplane bomb
Private Herbert Albone, Machine Gun Corps, killed in action
Private Harry Cartwright, Essex Regiment, died from wounds
Private Jack Smith, Canadian Infantry, killed in action
Private Chas Carr, Beds Regiment, killed by shell fire
Private Chris Runham, Beds Regiment, killed in action
Lance Corporal Fred Kemps, London Regiment, killed by a rifle shot
Private Harry Spring, Irish Guards, killed in action
Private John Lincoln, Royal Marine Light Infantry, posted missing then reported killed
Private Edgar Wallis, Essex Regiment, posted missing then reported dying in captivity
Sapper Horace Green, Royal Engineers, drowned following torpedoing of ship
Private Albert Clark, Beds Regiment, killed by shell fire
Private Fred Reynolds, died at Three Counties Asylum
Private Jack Waller, Beds Regiment, killed in action
Private George Cole, Royal Welsh Fusiliers, killed in action
Private Aubrey Webb, Beds Regiment, killed in action
Sergeant George Gurney, Beds Regiment, killed in action
Private Omar Housden, Royal West Surrey Regiment, killed in action
Private Ernest Watts, Coldstream Guards, killed by shell fire
Private Len Gray, Beds Regiment, killed by trench mortar bomb
Gunner Arthur Northwood, Royal Garrison Artillery, killed by a rifle shot
Private Percy Clark, North Staffs Regiment, posted missing then reported dying in captivity
Boy Leslie Baxter, Royal Navy, died from pneumonia in Plymouth
Gunner William Lampey, Royal Horse Artillery, posted missing then reported dying in captivity
Private William Smith, Essex Regiment, posted missing then reported killed
Gunner William Lincoln, Royal Horse Artillery, posted missing then reported dying in captivity

EPILOGUE

KNOWN ADDRESSES OF FAMILIES OF MEN KILLED

Back Street   2
- George Boness
- Tom Housden
- Harry Simms
- Alfred Walker
- William Warner

Bank's Road
- Alfred Carr

The Baulk   1
- Jack Chandler
- Leonard Clayton
- Percy Cole
- Frederick Garner
- James Harpin
- Ernest Smith
- Jack Smith

Bensons Row   20
- Harry Milton
- Ernest Watts
- James Watts
- Horace Walker

Bridge Street
- John Lincoln

Brooklands Cottages
- George Thomason

Cemetery Street   3
- Alec Ambrose
- Bill Gauge
- Edgar Wallis
- George Wagstaff
- Harry Wagstaff

Church Street
- Bert Tasker

Cowfairlands   4
- Herbert Albone
- Charles Cocks
- William Smith
- Harry Spring

- George Warner

Drove Road   5
- George Sidney Fairbanks
- William King
- Sidney Simms
- Henry Wall

Fairfield Road   6
- Fred Grummitt
- Harry Grummitt
- William Lampey

Gladstone Terrace, Sun Street
- Bob Stocker
- Herbert Stocker

Golden Pheasant Pub**
- Omar Housden

Havelock Road   7
- Bertie Millard

High Street   8
- Horace Bridge
- Tom Bridge
- Omar Housden

Hitchin Street   9
- Arthur Boness
- Dick Bosworth
- George Dickens
- Harry Figg
- Herbert Goss
- Walter Haynes
- Fred Kemps
- Fred Land
- Victor Milton
- John Newman
- Arthur Rainbow
- Bob See
- Edmund Sells
- Horace Smith

- Fred Waters

Holme View Cottagges   10
- Sidney Carr

Ivel Terrace
- Bob Plumbridge

Langford Road
- Sidney Carr

Lawrence Road   11
- Wallace George Albone
- Percy Clark
- Reg Peddar

Lindsell Crescent
- Albert Haynes

London Road   12
- Arthur Boness

Mead House
- Francis Wagg

Newtown   13
- George Dean
- Arthur Endersby
- Arthur Garner
- George Housden
- James Kitchiner
- William Smith
- William Wells

Palace Street
- Harry Cartwright

Rose Lane   14
- Fred Scott
- Harry Simms
- Fred Skilliter

St John's Street   15
- Alfred 'Punch' Brunt
- Ernest Emery
- Chris Runham
- Steve Runham

- Walter Walker
- Fred Wells

Shortmead Street   16
- Archie Boness
- Horace Bridge
- Tom Bridge
- Herbert Legate
- Francis Taylor
- George Tear
- Harry Rowlett

Station Road   17
- Hubert Purser

Stratton Park Cottages   8
- Horace Bryant

Sun Street   19
- Percy Brown
- Albert Clark
- Harry Garner
- Jack Gauge
- Len Gray
- William Gray
- George Jackson
- Alexander Lovett
- Henry Lovett
- Robert Lovett
- Leonard Maudlin
- Ted Maudlin
- Arthur Northwood
- Fred Reynolds
- Jack Reynolds
- Fred Rowlett
- William Swepstone

Two Brewers Pub*
- Francis Mann

Victoria Place
- George Senior

York Terrace
- William Lincoln

Biggleswade Streets in 1910 (source Biggleswade Historical Society)

Back Street	Drove Road	Palace Street	St John's Street
Bank's Road	Fairfield	Potton Road	Station Road
Baulk	Havelock Road	Railway Bank	Stratton Street
Cemetery Street	High Street	Rose Lane	Sun Street
Chapel Fields	Hitchin Street	Saffron Road	Windsor Terrace
Church Street	London Road	Shortmead Street	
Claremont Terrace	Market Square	St Andrew's Place	
Cowfair Lands	Mill Lane	St Andrew's Street	

York Terrace was off Sun Street next to the Sun Inn,
* Two Brewers Pub - No 14 Hitchin Street, now occupied by Gunns Bakers - Licensee 1912-1918 Francis Mann.
** Golden Pheasant Pub No 71 High Street opposite the old Town Hall
Licensee 1906–1937 John Housden, also an engine driver.
Victoria Place – Back Street, the lane to the west of the railway that connects with the lane that runs north of the Town Hall.
Town Fields – This was the area bounded by the railway, Potton Road, Banks Road and Lawrence Road. It included Havelock Road and what was to become Lindsell Crescent.
Brooklands Cottages – On Gypsy Lane, With Brooklands Farm off to the west and in the parish of Old Warden.

1918–1919

Lieutenant Bert Tasker, KRR, killed in action
Lieutenant Norman Algernon Brown, Royal Fusiliers, died from pneumonia
Lieutenant Jack Franklin, ASC, died after accident in nursing home
Private George Housden, Middlesex Regiment, killed in action
Private Claude Airey, Royal Fusiliers, posted missing then reported killed
Private Sidney Fairbanks, Highland Light Infantry, killed in action
Private Fred Page, Worcs Regiment, posted missing then reported killed
Private Fred Thorn, Northants Regiment, posted missing then reported killed
Private Harry Wagstaff, Beds Regiment, posted missing then reported killed
Private William Wells, Beds Regiment, died from wounds
Private Fred Scott, Essex Regiment, killed in action
Private Edwin Sims, Northants Regiment, died from wounds
Rifleman Jack Chandler, London Regiment, died from wounds
Private Percy Starnes, ASC, killed in accident
Private Francis Mann, Northants Regiment, died of wounds,
Private Walter Lincoln, Beds Reg died Biggleswade
Private Ernest Bilcock, Machine Gun Corps, killed in action
Private Charles Cocks, Royal West Surreys Regiment, killed in action
Private Francis Wagg, Rifle Brigade, died from pneumonia
Private Alfred Walker, Beds Regiment, killed in action
Private Fred Waters, Essex Regiment, died from wounds
Private Bertie Millard, Trench Mortar Battery, killed in action
Private James Kitchener, Labour Corps, died from pneumonia
Corporal Fred Stone, Army Cyclist Corps, killed in action
Private Ernest Smith, Winnipeg Rifles, killed in action
Private Leonard Clayton, Suffolk Yeomanry, killed in action
Private Freddie Albone, Labour Corps, died from pneumonia
Private Horace Walker, Northants Regiment, killed in action
Corporal Fred Garner, Beds Regiment, died from wounds
Driver John Munns, Royal Horse Artillery, died from pneumonia
Private Jack Reynolds, Beds Regiment, died Biggleswade
Private William Champkins, Royal West Surreys Regiment, posted missing then reported dying in captivity
Private Henry Lovett, Northants Regiment, posted as missing then presumed killed
Private E.J. Maudlin, Labour Corps, died from pneumonia
Private Fred Basterfield, Royal Engineers, died from pneumonia
Corporal Fred Woodcraft, 19th Hussars, died from pneumonia
Private Alfred Patrick, ASC, died soon after returning to Biggleswade
Private Ernest Radford, Beds Regiment, died soon after returning to Biggleswade

On Sunday 24 April 1921 the people of Biggleswade gathered for the unveiling of the town's war memorial. Thousands gathered in the High Street at 3 p.m. to pay their respects, including ex-servicemen and the relatives of the men whose names

EPILOGUE

were carved in the Cornish granite of the memorial. They had much to consider and reflect upon.

In 1914 ten men who died were commemorated on the War Memorial. In 1915 a further nine men died, whilst 1916, the year of the Battle of the Somme, saw a significant increase to thirty-six. That figure soared to sixty-seven in 1917, the year of Passchendaele, Arras, Gaza and Cambrai. For 1918 another forty-three from the town lost their lives and then another ten died after the armistice of 1918 in accidents in Germany or of influenza.

Those men commemorated on the memorial ranged in age from sixteen to forty-two. The youngest was Leslie Baxter whilst the oldest was Private George Jackson. They included three brothers from the Lovett family who lived in Sun Street – Alexander and Robert who died in 1916, and Henry who died two years later in 1918. All three had no known grave and are commemorated on memorials at Vimy, Soissons and Thiepval. Other families had suffered similar loss and grief as can be seen with the deaths of Leonard and William Gray, again of Sun Street, Albert and Walter Haynes of Hitchin Street, Frederick and John Reynolds, yet again of Sun Street, Chris and Steve Runham from St John's Street, and Bert and Harold Morgan who had both emigrated to Canada from Biggleswade but who had returned in response to Kitchener's call to arms.

Two men commemorated on the memorial had won the Military Medal – Charlie Clifford and George Gurney.

Forty-eight per cent of them were buried in France, Belgium, Palestine, Syria and Turkey, whilst forty-three per cent have no known grave and are commemorated on memorials on the Somme, in Ypres, at Arras, Loos, and throughout the Western Front. One was buried in Canada, Albert Brown who died while taking part in a training exercise in 1916. A further thirteen were buried locally. One, Frederick Garner, as noted earlier had served right through, writing home frequently in encouraging terms only to be wounded in the final 100 Days of the war when the BEF achieved that series of stunning victories that history often forgets. It was tragic that 199 men from Biggleswade did not return from the conflict – this was just the tip of the iceberg and countless villages and towns saw the same kind of losses. Throughout England and Wales only forty-one parishes saw all of their men folk return alive. These communities have no war memorials and they have become known as 'Thankful Villages'.

On that Sunday in April 1921 thousands stood to honour the dead, and the memorial was festooned with wreaths. As the ceremony progressed the time came for the unveiling of the memorial. Mr Samuel Whitbread, the Lord Lieutenant of Bedfordshire was the dignitary who would do this. As he spoke he emphasised that although this was a war memorial, it was something other than that. 'None of us want a memorial to remember the war' he said, but rather a focus for the people of Biggleswade to remember those young men from the area who had made the ultimate sacrifice for King and Country. He concluded:

> Let us therefore look upon these names, not with sadness but with pride and respect, and let us see that their example and their record shall be carried on from generation to generation and shall never fade as long as this, our country, shall endure … May their example and their spirit never fade for many years to come.

The War Memorial gave the people of the town a focus for their grief. Today it remains important that we remember the generation that is commemorated on war memorials that can be found in virtually every city, town and village throughout Britain; there are about 36,000 and, sadly, they have almost become unnoticed as we pass them by every day, without stopping to look at the names upon them. Those whose names are carved into the stone were as real as we are today. They had wives, girlfriends, children, and family and were husbands, fiancés, brothers, nephews, cousins and uncles to their families. They made the ultimate sacrifice as a regular, a reservist, a territorial, one of Kitchener's volunteers or, from 1916, as a conscript, and they participated in a struggle to defend the rights of small nations in the face of militarism. It is something of a great shame that their sacrifice still continues to be viewed today by some as futility, for they certainly would not have seen their efforts as such. They were of a generation that firmly believed that they were doing the 'right thing' in coming to the defence of Belgium in 1914. They were men who did not enjoy the freedom to travel in the way that we do today, and it is true that for many the war was a chance to experience new lands and cultures. Yet this initial defence of Belgium and the ensuing four and a half years of fighting saw them experience unimaginable horrors, and their sacrifice deserves to be remembered.

Those commemorated on the memorial were a part of the great tragedy that was the First World War. It would be another tragedy if their sacrifice was to be forgotten.

The *Biggleswade Chronicle* carried a detailed report in its next edition, 29 April 1921, and these words stood out, 'They were not unknown warriors, they were our own flesh and blood.'

The dedication of the Biggleswade War Memorial, April 1921.

Appendices

APPENDIX 1

British Casualties on the Western Front, Month by Month (source – Official British figures)

1914
August	14,409
September	15,189
October	30,192
November	24,785
December	11,079

1915
January	6,542
February	9,195
March	24,483
April	31,264
May	65,730
June	22,563
July	16,315
August	14,587
September	59,615
October	25,909
November	9,263
December	11,117

1916
January	10,975
February	13,014
March	18,949
April	22,409
May	24,661
June	39,959
July	196,081
August	75,249
September	115,056
October	66,852
November	48,238
December	13,803

1917
January	15,289
February	26,140
March	25,788
April	120,070
May	76,040
June	75,123
July	84,695
August	81,080
September	81,249
October	119,808
November	73,888
December	38,620

1918
January	13,042
February	9,809
March	173,721
April	143,168
May	69,049
June	32,436
July	32,562
August	122,272
September	114,831
October	121,046
November	20,925

APPENDIX 2

Total British and Empire Casualties During the Great War:

Killed	946,023
Wounded	2,121,906
Missing	108,346

APPENDIX 3

Biggleswade Roll of Honour 22 April 1915 as it Appeared in the *Biggleswade Chronicle*:

For September 1914 the roll numbered 194; by 1 January 1915 it was up to 251; by 16 January it was at 274 and by 22 April the Roll numbered 342.

Albone, John, National Reserve
Albone, F.J., Bedfordshire Regiment
Albone, A., New Army
Albone, J., Bedfordshire Regiment (Service Battalion)
Albone, Chas, 5th Beds Territorials
Alvey, R.G., Beds. Regiment (Service Battalion)
Allen, L., Yorkshire Territorial Infantry
Albone, H., Beds Regiment (medically unfit)
Armstrong, W.J., Duke of Bedford's Regiment
Ashwell, T., 5th Beds Territorials
Ashwell, J., Rifle Brigade
Ashwell, H., 1st Herts Territorials
Ashwell, W., 1st Herts Territorials
Ashwell, G., Royal Engineers
Ashwell, F., 3rd Bedfords.
Aubrey, F., Northern Signal Co., RE
Beaumont, Frank, Royal Engineers
Bones, H., Army Service Corps
Butterworth, A., King's Royal Rifles (died from wounds)
Ballard, E., Royal Garrison Artillery
Bilcock, Sam, 1st Bedfords, (prisoner of war)
Bilcock, Joseph, Duke of Bedford's Regiment
Barrett, Frank, RAMC
Bosworth, R., Scottish Borderers (wounded in action)
Burnett, C.K. Lieutenant Corporal 18th Hussars
Barley, W., Yorks Light Infantry (medically disqualified)
Bowles, A.C., Beds Yeomanry
Buck, E., 1st Royal Dragoons
Buck, G., 1st Royal Dragoons
Bygraves, A., 2nd Bedfords
Brown, Chas, 2nd Bedfords (twice wounded in action)
Brown, R., 3rd Bedfords
Brown, A., 3rd Bedfords
Brown, E., Beds Yeomanry
Brookbanks, Robt., Beds Yeomanry (medically disqualified)
Brookbanks, Leslie, Beds Yeomanry (medically disqualified)
Brookbanks, Gordon, Beds Yeomanry
Butcher, C., 1st Bedfords
Batten, Cecil, Rifle Brigade
Bridge, H., 6th Battn., Beds Regiment
Bridge, G.E., East Surrey Regiment
Blore, P.H. Lieutenant, Sherwood Foresters
Baskerville, J., Beds Yeomanry
Buttress, H., Royal Garrison Artillery
Bonfield, Samuel, *Mercury* Training Ship
Bryant, H., L Battery, RHA (killed in action)
Bailey, S., Royal Artillery
Bailey, A., Beds Regiment
Brown, Harry, Beds Regiment
Boness, Geo., Duke of Bedford's Regiment
Boness, A.J., Duke of Bedford's Regiment
Bryant, R., Duke of Bedford's Regiment
Brown, S., Rifle Brigade
Brice, F., 5th Beds Territorials
Burton, Cyril, Royal Navy
Clark, Fred, Royal Artillery
Cocks, W.C., Army Service Corps
Charter, T., East Surrey Regiment
Cottam, F., National Reserve
Clark, R., Beds Regiment
Chambers, Arthur, Northern Signal Co. RE
Coote, J., Duke of Bedford's Regiment
Coote, A., Duke of Bedford's Regiment
Chambers, J.C., RAMC, attached to Indian Army
Cole, J., Duke of Bedford's Regiment
Clark, A., Beds Regiment (medically disqualified)
Croft, H., 5th Beds Territorials
Cox, J., Northern Signal Co. RE
Clifford, E.G., 5th Beds Territorials

APPENDICES

Creighton, F., 3rd Bedfords
Cartwright, A., 5th Beds Territorials
Chambers, J., Royal Navy
Chaundler, P.R., Lieutenant, 5h Beds Territorials
Chaundler, O.S., Lieutenant, 5th Beds Territorials
Chaundler, C., Rhodesian Rifles
Cocks, C., Beds Yeomanry
Clark, G., Beds Yeomanry
Camp, B., Dragoon Guards
Carr, Chas, 2nd Bedfords, (suffered from frostbitten feet, now recovered)
Carr, Arthur, Royal Artillery
Croot, F., RAMC
Carr, A. 5th Beds Territorials
Chivers, Frank, Motor Transport ASC
Chivers, Stanley, Royal Marine Artillery
Clark, W., National Reserve
Chambers, R., 17th Lancers
Cooper, Geo., Northern Signal Co., RE
Course, P., Western Signal Co., RE
Dundon, J., Royal Horse Artillery
Dickens, G., 1st Bedfords, (twice wounded now in England sick)
Dean, G., 2nd Bedfords, (died of wounds in Germany whilst a prisoner of war)
Day, H., 3rd Bedfords (wounded whilst serving with 2nd Bedfords, now recovered)
Day, C., 1st Bedfords (prisoner of war)
Dennis, J., 3rd Bedfords (attached to 2nd Battn)
Dennis, W., Beds Yeomanry (medically disqualified)
Day, F., Royal Artillery
Derham, R.P. Beds Yeomanry
Derham, Percy, Beds Yeomanry
Debney, A., Beds Yeomanry
Durham, J., Beds Yeomanry
Day, Jack, 3rd Bedfords
Daisley, S., Beds Regiment
Dodimead, H., Royal Engineers
Davies, W.J., Beds Yeomanry
Davey, A.G., Suffolk Yeomanry
Daulby, K., Beds Yeomanry
Day, Walter, Motor Transport Services
Emery, F., 5th Beds (died shortly after being medically disqualified)
Emery, J., Bedfords Regiment, (medically disqualified)
Emery, Ernest, 1st Wiltshire Regiment (killed in the trenches)
Endersby, H., 3rd Bedfords
Endersby, W., National Reserve
Endersby, Sam, Beds Yeomanry
Endersby, Sam, Jnr., Royal Horse Artillery
Eden, H., Beds Yeomanry
Elliott, J.H., Beds Yeomanry
Elliott, E., Beds Yeomanry
Eales, A., Royal Artillery
Endersby, A.J., 1st Bedfords
Endersby, A.B, RARC
Franklin, W.J., 1st Bedfords (badly wounded in a charge after capturing a prisoner)
Filler, A., Army Veterinary Corps
Franklin, H., Royal Artillery
Franklin, L.C., Beds Yeomanry
Finding, E., 5th Beds Territorials
Finding, A., 5th Beds Territorials
Fox, W., 5th Beds Territorials
Foxley, A., 3rd Bedfords
Ferguson, C.W., Beds Yeomanry
Ferguson, Tom, Beds Yeomanry
Farr, H., former Recruiter
Fuller, G.F., Australian Expeditionary Force
Field, Bert, Australian Army
Field, W., Western Signal Co., RE
Francis, H. Duke of Bedford's Regiment
Figg, Albert E., Canadian Army
Figg, Harry, Canadian Army
Fig, Ernest A., Canadian Army
Green, J., Army Service Corps
Gray, W., 1st Bedfords (killed in action)
Goodwin, W.J., 1st Bedfords (wounded whilst Reconnoitring, now recovered)
Goodwin, G.H., 5th Beds Territorials
Garner, E., Beds Yeomanry
Gurney, G., 2nd Bedfords (wounded in action, now recovered)
Gurney, P.J., Beds Yeomanry
Gurney, F.J., Beds Yeomanry
Gauge, W. 2nd Bedfords
Gauge, S., 3rd Bedfords
Goss, H., Beds Regiment
Garner, H., 5th Beds Territorials
Gee, Frank, Beds Regiment
Grummitt, A., Beds Regiment

Goodship, G., 2nd Bedfords (missing since October)
Garner, Frank D., Pioneer Highlanders
Gray, Henry, 1st Bedfords (wounded in thigh at Hill 60)
Gray, George, 2nd Bedfords
Harper, Alfred, 11th Hussars (wounded at Messines, now recovered)
Hatton, C., 3rd Bedfords (medically disqualified)
Harper, Herbert, Royal Field Artillery
Hester, A., 5th Seaforths
Hallybone, A., 2nd Bedfords (wounded, now recovered)
Humphreys, T., RAMC
Hawkes, A.J., New Army
Hutchinson, G.W. Beds Yeomanry
Housden, Sam, Beds Regiment (medically disqualified)
Hopkins, J., East Anglian RE
Housden, W., 3rd Suffolks (prisoner of war)
Housden, T., 2nd Bedfords (wounded)
Hill, F.C. Beds Yeomanry
Hare, Fred, Beds Yeomanry
Haddow, E., Middlesex Regiment
Haddow, A., Territorial Artillery
Harlow, V., 2nd Grenadier Guards (badly wounded in action)
Haynes, F., 7th Middlesex
Haynes, W., 7th Middlesex
Haynes, A., 7th Middlesex
Haynes, Frank, Army Service Corps
Head, Chas, Duke of Bedford's Regiment
Ibbs, J., Suffolk Regiment
Jones, R., 11th Gordon Highlanders
Jollands, R., RE Railway Corps
Jackson, T., Beds Yeomanry
James, C.R. Lieutenant, 5th Bedfords Territorials
Jordan, W.H, Beds Yeomanry (medically disqualified)
Jones, W., 5th Beds Territorials
Jones, Albert, 7th Beds Regiment
Jones, F., Duke of Bedford'ss Regiment
Jeeves, Jack, 3rd Bedfords
Jackson, Geo., Duke of Bedford's Regiment
Keene, H.G., 5th Beds Territorials
Kefford, A., Northern Signals Co. RE

Keeling, A., Beds Yeomanry (medically unfit)
Kitchener, H., Northern Signals Co. RE
Kitchener, A., Army Veterinary Corps
Knott, G., 3rd Coldstream Guards (invalided home with frostbitten feet)
Kitchener, Chas, Beds Regiment
Kemp, C., Suffolk Regiment
Lee, H., Beds Regiment (Service Battn.)
Lovett, A., 3rd Bedfords, (thrice wounded whilst serving with 2nd Bedfords, home on leave)
Lincoln, C., 3rd Bedfords
Leach, C., Beds Yeomanry (medically disqualified)
Lee, C., Beds Regiment (Service Battalion)
Lincoln, J., Norfolk Regiment
Loveridge, E., 3rd Bedfords (wounded in action and frostbitten feet, on sick leave)
Loveridge, J., Yorks and Lancs Regiment (invalided from the front with frostbitten feet)
Lindsell, C.T., National Reserve
Leonard, E., 2nd Royal Sussex (invalided home with rheumatism, now recovered)
Larkinson, D., New Army
Lincoln, A., Western Signal Co. RE
Lincoln, F. Northern Signals Co. RE
Marsom, L., Beds Yeomanry
Marsom, Fred, Beds Yeomanry
Morgan, H.T. Canadian Army
Matthews, F.W. Royal Flying Corps
Mahoney, A., 2nd Bedfords
Minney, G.W. Cycle Section, Essex
Milton, A., 5th Beds Territorials
Munns, A., Northern Signals Co. RE
Munns, G.H., Beds Regiment (Service Battalion)
Maskell, W., Beds Regiment (Service Battalion)
Milliner, H. 4th Bedfords
Marsh, W., Western Signal Co. RE
Marsh, E., New Army
Newman, J., Beds Regiment (Service Battalion)
Northwood, H.T. Royal Field Artillery
Northwood, A. Royal Garrison Artillery
Northwood, C. Royal Garrison Artillery
Norman, R., 4th Bedfords

Odell, H.C., Beds Yeomanry (medically disqualified)
Pates, W., Northern Signals Co. RE
Pope, E.R., Beds Yeomanry (medically disqualified)
Pope, Ernest, RAMC
Purser, H., Captain. Royal Marine Artillery
Pressland, H., Army Service Corps (since disqualified)
Patrick, J., 5th Lancers
Phillips, D. 5th Beds Territorials
Pyett, Reg, Beds Regiment (Service Battalion)
Pell, A., Northants Regiment
Perryman, H., 3rd Bedfords
Rowlett, F., 3rd Bedfords, (killed in action whilst serving with 2nd Battalion)
Rowlett, T., 18th Hussars (discharged under age)
Runham, C., 2nd Bedfords
Runham, S., Beds Regiment (Service Battalion)
Radford, F., 5th Beds Territorials
Radford, E., 5th Beds Territorials
Roberts, J. Beds Regiment (Service Battalion)
Roberts, F. Beds Regiment (Service Battalion)
Rollins, C., 1st Bedfords (invalided home)
Rook, C., Duke of Bedford's Regiment
Rowlett, E., Railway Corps, RE
Randall, E., Duke of Bedford's Regiment
Smith, G., 1st Beds (wounded and missing since October)
Stocker, H., 2nd Bedfords (wounded and missing since October)
Smith, George, Royal Garrison Artillery
Smith, Jonah, 5th Bedfords Territorials
Shankland, C.T., East Anglian RE
Senior, F., 1st Beds
Senior, G., 5th Bedfords Territorials
Sale, John, 2nd Life Guards
Styles, G., Beds Yeomanry
Storton, Walter 3rd Bedfords (killed in action at Neuve Chapelle)
Street, J., 3rd Bedfords
Street, W., 4th Bedfords
Saunders, R.G., East Anglian Engineers
Stratton, E., Beds Regiment (Service Battalion)
Simms, H., Beds Regiment (Service Battalion)
Soundy, H.C., Lieut. 5th Bedfords Territorials
Skilliter, C., Bechuanaland Rifles
Skilleter E., Lancs and Yorks, Regiment
Summers, F., Royal Artillery
Stocker, A.J., Beds Regiment (Service Battalion)
Swepstone, W., Beds Regiment (Service Battalion)
Smith, H.B., Beds Yeomanry
Smith, E., East Anglian RE
Smith, W., Beds Regiment (medically unfit)
Skuse, A. 5th Beds Territorials
Spong, R.M., Beds Yeomanry
Stacey, W., New Army
Sells, Robert, Royal Field Artillery
Tear, Geo., (missing since October)
Tear, J., RE Railway Corps
Tarry, J., Railway Corps RE
Tarry, E., 5th Beds Territorials
Thomas, G.D., Beds Yeomanry (medically disqualified)
Taylor, A.M., Beds Yeomanry
Turland, H., Grenadier Guards
Tuthill, W., Norfolk Regiment
Thomason, G., 2nd Bedfords (killed in action)
Tasker, W.E. Remount Dept. ASC
Taylor, F.H., 7th Middlesex
Villiers, H.G. 18th Hussars
Welsh, W.L., Sub-Lieut., Royal Navy Air Service
Welsh, C.C. Royal Artillery
Woods, A., Northern Signal Co. RE
Wood, M.T., 5th Beds Territorials
Waller, W., RAMC
Wrigley, A., Royal Artillery (wounded in action)
Wade, John, Canadian Army
Wheatley, O., Captain, Canadian Army
Woodcroft, Bert, Beds Yeomanry
Woodcroft, Fred, Bedfords Yeomanry
Wilson, F., Beds Regiment (Service Battalion)
Webb, W.E., 5th Beds Territorials
Webb, A., 1st Bedfords
Walker, F., Beds Regiment (medically disqualified)
Wilshaw, A.E., Army Veterinary Corps
Wheatley, R.S., West African Naval Force
Wheatley, Bertram, Signal Co., North Midland Brigade
Wheatley, A.C., London Territorials
Waldock, F., 1st Herts Territorials

Wells, W., Beds Regiment (Service Battalion)
Wells, F., Beds Regiment (Service Battalion)
Wells, H., Beds Regiment (Service Battalion)
Wells, F., Royal Navy
Wells, W., Beds Yeomanry
Wells, W.G., Duke of Bedford's Regiment
Wagstaff, H., 3rd Bedfords
Walker, Jas., 2nd Bedfords
Wagstaff, Geo., Post Office Rifles
Walker, Cecil, 1st Bedfords
Weedon, A., Royal Field Artillery
Wakes, D., Beds Yeomanry
Whitehurst, F.W., Beds Regiment (Service Battalion)
White, C., Bed Yeomanry

White, R., Beds Yeomanry (under age)
Wheatley, W.B., 3rd Bedfords
Wheatley, J.C., Duke of Bedford's Regiment
Waterfield, F., National Reserve
Waters, W.E., Royal Fusiliers
Wilkins, E.H., Beds Regiment
Warner, W., Duke of Bedford's Regiment
Wren, S., Duke of Bedford's Regiment
Wootton, R., Canadian Army
West, A.J., Hussars
Wright, Chas, 1st Bedfords (wounded in action)
Yarrell, J., Inst., Duke of Bedford's Regiment
Yerrill, Jerry, Duke of Bedford's Regiment
Young, Geo., Army Service Corps
York, A., Beds Regiment (Service Battalion)

APPENDIX 4

The Learning Curve of the BEF from the Somme 1916 to the 100 Days in 1918, showing how the BEF evolved tactics that would win the war.

1916	1917/1918
Lifting Barrage Pre-timed lifting of the artillery barrage on enemy lines. The problem here was the difficulty that infantry had in keeping up with the lifts and, as a result, finding themselves exposed to enemy machine-gun fire and artillery.	*Creeping Barrage and Counter Battery work* The aim was for infantry to follow closely a wall of shells that would give them protection from the enemy. Supporting troops would be used to mop up any surviving enemy soldiers. Although this tactic required troops to be as close as 50yds to the barrage, it was much preferred by soldiers to the alterative, of having to advance unprotected over no-man's-land. Counter battery work saw enemy artillery either destroyed or made ineffectual by improved British gunnery. Sound ranging and flash spotting techniques were very important developments here.

Destructive shelling For the Somme the seven-day barrage that took place before the attack was designed to obliterate the German trench lines and, more importantly, the troops occupying them. It failed as the Germans were underground in shellproof bunkers.	*Neutralising shelling* The emphasis now was to make sure that German troops were dazed and confused by high-explosive shells and that British troops could get in amongst them before they could recover. Counter battery work meant that the German artillery were either destroyed or rendered incapable of pouring down shells on advancing British troops.
Advance in waves The troops that attacked on the first day of the Somme were largely inexperienced. General Rawlinson felt that they would not be able to employ the traditional tactics of fire and movement. They were therefore ordered to form up in no-man's-land and advance in lines at walking pace. Not all did this. Those who were successful on the first day did not do this – they ran and got into the German lines before the enemy could emerge from deep dugouts.	*Fire and movement* This represented the restoration of the traditional tactics employed by the British Army. Quite simply it meant that there was a return to the use of smaller groups of soldiers, platoons, with one group advancing whilst being covered by another group. The development of and increase in Lewis guns and 'bombers' (grenade throwers) was highly significant here. Each platoon now had specialist troops who worked together as a team.
Daylight attacks Again this is a question of experience and initially there was a doubt over the ability of the New Armies to carry out such an attack. On 1 July 1916 the British had wanted to attack at dawn but the French insisted that the attack take place at 7.30 a.m. so that the advances of the troops could be seen and that artillery could see what they had to support.	*Night attacks* The attack on 14 July 1916 saw the use of tactics previously believed to be beyond the capacity of the New Armies but it proved to be a total success. White tape was used to show troops where they were to attack and they were into the German lines before they had a chance to respond. Night attacks then became an established part of BEF tactics.
Prolonged bombardment For the attack on 1 July there had been a seven-day bombardment with the aim of destroying the opposing troops. Deep dugouts negated this and the cessation of the bombardment, together with the exploding of mines was a sure signal that the attack was about to begin.	*Hurricane bombardment* This saw the change from extended to short bombardment of the German positions. The aim was to cause confusion and to daze the enemy rather than to obliterate him. In the 100 Days the British even attacked on occasions without any preliminary bombardment to add to the element of surprise.

Shells Although the volume of shells fired before the attack on 1 July was the greatest seen in the war up to that date, there were problems. There were not enough high-explosive shells – these would have had a much greater chance of destroying the German dugouts. Also there were too many shrapnel shells used – these were not appropriate and were designed to be used against attacking infantry, not defending troops ensconced in deep dugouts. Many of the shells used were duds. These were manufactured in the UK by novice ammunition workers, and others were imported from the USA. A third of all the shells fired up to the first day's attack were duds	*Improved shells, detonation on impact* The advances in artillery following the Somme battle were essential for all future engagements. First the powder used to fill the high-explosive shells used from July onwards: this was improved, as was the number of high-explosive shells available for the initial bombardment for any attack. By 1917 the concussion caused by these shells was so severe that it caused a dire effect on the nervous system – shell shock. Fuses also improved considerably – The 106 graze fuse ensured that the shell detonated on impact with the ground before it had dug itself into the earth. Thus barbed wire could be cut more effectively.
Expectation of walking to success Troops had been told that the Germans could not have survived the artillery bombardment and that their role was one of occupying destroyed German trench lines. They therefore were burdened by up to 60lbs of extra weight in carrying over tools for consolidation.	*Rehearsed attacks* This featured strongly during 1917 and 1918 and saw considerable success, most notably at Vimy Ridge and Messines in 1917. It had been tried at the Somme but much improvement occurred afterwards
Reliance on troops The first day of the Somme is a prime example of the over reliance on infantry to accomplish their targets. It should be noted that the actual strength of divisions in the 100 Days of 1918 was much below that for the Somme, but improved tactics more than compensated for this.	*Use of tanks, aircraft and machine guns* During the Somme tanks were first employed and they were used significantly at Cambrai in 1917 and then during the 100 Days. German aircraft were usually superior to Allied planes but the efficiency of, notably, British industry saw greater production of Allied aircraft. This gave the Allies air superiority for much of the last two years of the war. Machine-gun development was a crucial ingredient of Allied success and this can be seen in the increase in the number of Lewis guns per battalion and the development of machine gun barrages. The heavy machine gun, the Vickers, was used for this. This combination of tanks, aircraft, infantry and machine guns is known as 'All Arms' battle tactics and co-ordination, and was a key feature of the 100 Days. It became a war-winning formula.

APPENDIX 5

British Army Composition/Strength

Armies:
There were five British Armies that fought on the Western Front. Each army had a strength between 250,000 and 500,000 men.

Corps/Divisions:
These armies were divided up into Corps and then divisions. A corps contained between 75,000 and 140,000 men whilst a division's strength was about 20,000 men.

Brigades:
This was the next stage down and a brigade numbered around 4,500 soldiers.

Battalions:
There were four battalions per brigade and each battalion had a strength of about 1,000 men. When a battalion went into action it was usual for about 200 men to be kept in reserve. If the battalion experienced high casualty figures then this reserve was the basis around which the battalion could be brought back up to strength.

Companies:
There would be four companies for each battalion, numbering around 230 men per company. A captain was usually in command of a company.

Platoon:
There were four of these per company and they were commanded by lieutenants. There were usually around fifty men in a platoon.

Sections:
There were four for each platoon and they were led by a corporal or a lance corporal. Each section numbered around ten men.

APPENDIX 6

The Bedfordshire Regiment in the Great War

During the Great War the following battalions served:

1st Battalion	a regular battalion that served mainly on the Western Front
2nd Battalion	a regular battalion that served entirely on the Western Front
3rd Battalion	a reserve battalion that did not see service overseas on the Western Front, although men from the battalion did augment the 1st and 2nd Battalions
4th Battalion	a reserve battalion that did see service overseas on the Western Front
5th Battalion	a territorial battalion that saw service in Gallipoli, Egypt and Palestine
6th Battalion	a Service battalion, one of Kitchener's New Army that served entirely on the Western Front
7th Battalion	a Service battalion, one of Kitchener's New Army that served entirely on the Western Front
8th Battalion	a Service battalion, one of Kitchener's New Army that served entirely on the Western Front

Index

Christmas Truce 1914: 33, 34
Liberal Fete: 12
Mobilisation: 13, 14
Peterborough riots: 15
The War Book: 14
Spy Scares: 14-15
Recruitment: 16, 17, 38, 39, 49, 90

Battles:
Mons: 19, 20, 21
1st Ypres: 27-33
Neuve Chapelle: 44, 45
2nd Ypres: 46-48
Loos: 54-55
Gallipoli: 51-54
Somme: 61-76
Arras: 82-87, 91-92
Messines Ridge: 93-96
Passchendaele: 96-105, 108-109
Cambrai: 109-112
Kaiser's Battle: 118-126
Amiens: 127-129

Soldiers/Sailors/Airmen that died:
Claude Airey: 121
Freddie Albone: 138
Gilbert Way Albone: 68
Herbert Albone: 102-103
Wallace George Albone: 139
Dick Alvey: 83
Alec Ambrose: 83
Chas Archdale: 110
Fred Basterfield: 138
Edward Batten: 71

Leslie Baxter: 126
Ernest Bilcock: 133-134
Joe Bilcock: 91, 103-104
George Bland: 47
Archie Boness: 71
Arthur Boness: 67
George Boness: 67, 68
Percy Bonfield: 91-92
Dick Bosworth: 52-53
Horace Bridge: 66, 104
Thomas Bridge: 104
Albert (Laurie) Brown: 57
Norman Brown: 139
Percy Brown: 86
Robert Brown: 48, 84
Alfred 'Punch' Brunt: 84
Horace Bryant: 23
Charles Butcher: 55, 109
Arthur Butterworth: 24
Sydney Bygraves: 94
Alfred Carr: 107-108
Charles Carr – 'Little Tich': 40, 113-114
Sydney Carr: 48
Harry Cartwright: 112
Len Chambers: 63
William Champkins: 121
Jack Chandler: 130
Sidney Circuit: 74
Albert Clark: 65, 94-95, 116-117
Percy Clark: 118
Robert Clark: 117
Leonard Clayton: 133
Charlie Clifford MM: 106-107
Charles Cocks: 133
Fred Cole: 100

INDEX

George Cole: 122
Percy Cole: 85
George Dean: 43
Arthur Dellar: 67
George Dickens: 44, 50, 80
George Dilley: 84
Alex Drysdale: 78
William Elliott: 125
Ernest Emery: 42-43
Arthur Endersby: 48
George Sidney Fairbanks: 64, 122
Harry Figg 40, 93
Jack Franklin: 139
Victor Gale: 123
Arthur Garner: 79
Fred Garner: 136
Harry Garner: 88
Henry Garner: 101
Walter Gatward: 59
Jack Gauge: 84
William Gauge: 51, 54
George Goodship: 29
Herbert Goss: 76-77
Len Gray: 31, 103, 124-125
William Gray: 31
Harry Grummitt: 92
Horace Green: 115
Fred Grummitt: 98
George Gurney MM: 65, 74, 120
James Harpin: 101-102
Albert Haynes: 39, 72
Walter Haynes: 39, 96
George Housden: 129
Omar Housden: 121
Tom Housden: 31, 100
Cliff Huckle: 68
Harry Huckle: 73
George Jackson: 69-70
Fred Kemps: 111
Frank Kefford: 77
William King: 96
James Kitchiner: 136
William Lampey: 126
Fred Land: 73
Herbert Legate: 105
(Alfred) John Lincoln: 91
John Lincoln: 77
Walter F Lincoln: 136
William Lincoln: 123
Joe Loveridge: 57

Alex Lovett: 71
Henry Lovett: 125
Robert Lovett: 71
Francis Mann: 130-131
Ted Maudlin: 138-139
Leonard Maudlin: 108
Bertie Millard: 132-133
Harry Milton: 83
Victor Milton: 52, 104-105
Bert Morgan: 46
Harold Morgan: 60
John Munns: 138
Samuel Needham VC: 108
John Newman: 86, 100-101
Arthur Northwood: 90-91, 125
Frederick Page: 125
Alfred Patrick: 139
Reg Peddar: 74
Chas Pepper: 63
Bob Plumbridge: 71
Ernest Pope: 73
F. B. Potton: 5
Herbert Purser: 81
Ernest Radford: 139
Arthur Rainbow: 74
Harold Reaney: 130
Fred Reynolds: 91
John Reynolds: 138
Fred Roberts: 83
Headley Rowland: 105
Fred Rowlett: 29, 30
Harry Rowlett: 74
Chris Runham: 69, 86
Steve Runham: 68, 69
Fred Scott: 129-120
Bob See: 95-96
Edmund Sells: 74-75
George Senior: 79, 101
Frank Sharp: 66
Harry Simms: 91
Edwin Sims: 131-132
Fred Skilliter: 75
Absolum Smith: 87-88
Ernest Smith: 132
George Smith: 32
Horace Smith: 78
Jack Smith: 109
William Smith: 112
William James Smith: 72
Harry Spring: 111

Percy Starnes: 133
Herbert Stocker: 35
Robert Stocker: 99
Fred Stone: 135
Walter Storton: 35
Edmund Stratton: 63
George Street: 79
William Swepstone: 71
Bert Tasker: 57, 130
Francis Taylor: 73
Walter Ralph Davidson Taylor: 21-22
George Tear: 32
George Thomason: 33
Fred Thorn: 77
Jonathan Wade: 86, 109
Francis Wagg: 135-136
George Wagstaff: 77
Harry Wagstaff: 72, 85, 105
Edgar Waite: 73
Alfred Walker: 134
Horace Walker: 134
Walter Walker: 80
Henry Wall: 75-76
Jack (Reginald John) Waller: 122
Edgar Wallis: 112, 126
George Warner: 101
William Warner: 69
Fred Waters: 134-135
Arthur Watts: 24
Ernest Watts: 122-123
Joseph Watts: 109
Aubrey Webb: 121-122
Fred Wells: 72
William George Wells: 131
Cyril Welsh: 98-99
Leslie Whitbread: 53
Fred Woodcraft: 139
Ernest Woodward: 96
Maurice Woodward: 71

Soldiers survived:
Tom Adlam VC: 72
Charlie Albone: 94
Fred Ashwell: 39
Arthur Blanshard DCM: 57

Sam Bilcock: 43-44
Herbert Boness: 78, 85
Ernest Brown MM: 88, 106-107, 108
Sidney Brown: 69
George Buck: 31, 32
Albert Bygraves: 41
Albert Cartwright: 102
Jack Cartwright: 72, 73
Tom Charter: 124, 134
Sidney Daisley: 54, 55
Chas Day: 51
Fred Day: 51
Harry Day: 29, 51, 117
John Dennis: 30
Alfred Endersby: 58-59
William Field: 117
William Franklin: 49, 50
Stanley Gauge: 56
Frank Garner: 93
Maurice Grummitt: 124
Arthur Hallybone: 29
Arthur Harper: 30-31
Fred Haynes: 39
Walter Howe: 117
William Franklin: 49-50
Percy Harradine: 121
Charles Jefferies: 48
George Knott: 40
Eli Loveridge: 51, 59, 66
Alf Lovett: 54, 65
Alfred Mahoney: 48
Albert Milton: 32
Percy Mosley: 27
Charles Northwood: 90
Fred Pressland: 78
Fred Senior DCM: 48, 50, 51, 65, 80
Ernest Skilliter: 102
Austin Skuse: 52
James Smith: 87
Cecil Soundy MC: 124, 126-127
Herbert Thompson MM: 124
Edwin Wadman MM: 139
Edward Warner VC: 48
Arthur Webb DCM: 56-57
Jerry Yerrill: 66